Acts of
Recovery

Jeffrey Hart

Acts of Recovery

Essays on Culture and Politics

AVE MARIA UNIVERSITY

Published for Dartmouth College by
University Press of New England
Hanover and London

To Jacques Barzun,
who has expanded the definition of the term
"great teacher"

© 1989 by Trustees of Dartmouth College

Printed in the United States of America

∞

Library of Congress Cataloging-in-Publication Data
Hart, Jeffrey.
Acts of recovery : essays on culture and politics / Jeffrey Hart.
p.   cm.
"In honor of Lionel Trilling"—Pref.
ISBN 0–87451–504–1
I. Trilling, Lionel, 1905–1975.   II. Title.
AC8.H3682   1989
081—dc20   89–40230
CIP

5   4   3   2   1

Contents

---

v

Contents

Preface
In Honor of Lionel Trilling

Lionel Trilling's very important book of essays appeared in 1950, a fact that acquires increasing significance in retrospect. *The Liberal Imagination* was and is a great book. It concedes not an inch of stature to William Hazlitt's *Spirit of the Age* (1825) or Edmund Wilson's *Axel's Castle* (1931). And the year 1950, when *The Liberal Imagination* was published, marked a decisive shift in thought and feeling.

It is curious, in retrospect—curious only in that we did not see it fully at the time—how *political* Trilling's essays actually were. They made literature important in a distinctive way, but the political design was indicated in Trilling's title: the "liberal imagination." The word "liberal" is adjectival and the word "imagination" substantive, and therefore stronger; thus one knows that "liberal" is under criticism. *Imagination* is more important. And this is the thesis of the book. All its essays reverberate within that title's formulation.

And now one has to deal with a statement Trilling made on the first page of the preface to that volume, a statement so often quoted that it is somewhat otiose to re-cite it, though necessary here. It is, at least on the surface, a tremendously assured statement, though the rest of Trilling's book tends to subvert it. His first page confidently asserts:

In the United States at this time [in retrospect, one reflects on "at this time"] liberalism is not only the dominant but even the sole intellectual tradition. For it is the plain fact that nowadays [remember the "nowadays"] there are no conservative or reactionary ideas in general circulation.

In this momentous book, Trilling was clearly concerned with the liberal ideas that were in "general circulation" and constituted "the whole intellectual tradition." "Nowadays," he was clearly worried.

He was worried because the liberalism of which he wrote was at once a cultural, literary, and political phenomenon and was utterly dominant, yet deeply vulnerable. Trilling memorably understood that ideas consort importantly with feelings and that the quality of ideas has much to do with the quality of feelings. That vital ideas are not formulaic pellets he may have discovered independently of William James, but it is a consequential idea in itself. And Trilling understood that liberal ideas, the liberal ideas "in general circulation," had turned themselves into pellets. They had become coarse formulae immune to history, human experience, and complex thought.

This sensitive and Hamlet-like Columbia professor was writing in the wake, politically, of a supposedly triumphant New Deal and Fair Deal. But I think he knew that he was writing in the wake of two world wars fought under gleaming liberal auspices— and probably justly, I think—but with highly ambiguous consequences. A knight of often sorrowful countenance and sensitive intelligence, he knew that there were deep deficiencies in such liberal avatars as Vernon Parrington, Sherwood Anderson, Theodore Dreiser, and Alfred Kinsey. They each had what he considered to be a reductive tendency.

In 1950, Trilling wanted to save liberalism, from within, from its reductivism and apparently irresistible tug to the left. He liked to say that Edmund Burke had been well positioned as a Whig, a man of conservative tendency in a Whig party of liberal tendency. As opposed to the liberalism in "general circulation" in 1950, Trilling appealed to a certain body of literature and thought: to nuance, contradiction, and tragic circumstance; to Henry James, Montaigne, Freud, to the great modernists like Joyce and Proust (though he treated the modernists with increasing reserve and ambiguity), and also to Shakespeare and the Western tradition. He thought that liberalism could be renovated and enlarged, de-pelletized, through such exemplars.

His relationship to Freud was curious and, as almost always in his thinking, ambivalent. It is my sense that, arguably at least, he gradually abandoned his view that Freud had really been a scientist and came to regard him as essentially a Sophoclean thinker, a man of tragic courage.

At about the same time that Lionel Trilling was trying to save the "liberal imagination" from what he perceived as its quite possibly terminal decay, trying to save it with intensive-care infusions from major thinkers and writers who were by no means liberal, a much less impressive thinker, Louis Hartz of Harvard—a historian of ideas entirely unlike the sensitive Columbia Hamlet—published the almost canonical *The Liberal Tradition in America* (1955). This book was a High Mass of liberal certitude, utterly devoid of doubt. Hartz's book, a work of decent scholarship, today seems a distant period piece.

But Trilling's doubts and fears have certainly been validated in virtually every area of our public, literary, and personal lives. His own philosophical vulnerability, his confident—and reductive—"naturalism," the Columbia naturalism of John Dewey, is also not very secure these days, undercut, not least of all, by the post-positivist Wittgenstein. The 1950 liberal political confidence in New Deal bureaucratic management has lost virtually all authority. The progressivist background of Trilling's confidence and fears—the latter based upon a refinement of emotion—has been replaced in our universities by a great coarsening of emotion and a decline of intellectual courage.*

But at the same time, in the broader intellectual community and certainly in the area of public policy, there is a sense of widening skepticism as well as possibility and recovery—an adventurous skepticism and a deep respect for history and experience. The names of Irving Knistol, Charles Murray, Richard Neuhaus, and Michael Novak are synecdochical here and could be added to extensively.

The essays that follow have appeared in a variety of journals. They represent an attempt to push beyond Trilling's hesitations and doubts and to explore the possibility that there really is a wider and deeper tradition than what Trilling believed in 1950 to be our "sole intellectual tradition."

This book has a design. It begins with America and with literature; it moves to Europe—"My end is my beginning," as both Mary Stuart and, after her, T. S. Eliot said. It goes on to some fairly intense literary explorations and then to theology. As Lord Acton said, all

---

*Trilling had some darker intimations, however, about the liberal mind that did not make their way, explicitly at least, into *The Liberal Imagination.* In a 1948 essay entitled "The State of Our Culture: Expostulation and Reply," he wrote: "Stalinism becomes endemic in the American middle class as soon as that class begins to think; it is a cultural Stalinism, independent of any political belief: the cultural ideas of the ADA will not, I venture to say, be found materially different from those of the PAC." PAC stands for the Stalinoid Political Action Committee of the AFL-CIO, circa 1948. By "Stalinism" Trilling meant the crudity of their cultural ideas. During the sixties, the liberal poise Trilling exemplified almost entirely collapsed before crude cultural ideas.

disagreements are ultimately theological, a point confirmed in the rival poetics of Frost and Eliot, and elsewhere.

The assumption throughout the essays is that the study of literature is central to our discourse and that the habits of mind generated by the study and discussion of literature can be applied to a wide range of subject matter. We hold literature in common in a sense that we do not, for example, hold the study of sociology in common, and the literary mind may therefore have the capacity to move the work of the sociologist into our common discourse and relate it to a variety of other things. Which is to say that conversation about literature is a vital human activity, central to civilization as we know it. That assertion, though it strikes me as self-evident, is now under various kinds of attack; but let me for now celebrate the ideal.

From the position that a conversation about literature is a mode of knowing and also central to our civilization—a conversation between essayist and reader, professor and student, or among educated peers—it is possible to identify a particular tradition of literary criticism that has raised that conversation to a kind of perfection. This is not the only tradition of literary criticism, but it seems to me to be the most central and vital one. It begins in English with Samuel Johnson, and it has its roots, often, in journalism, a fact that in itself attests to its public and social character, and to its political character in the broadest sense of the word. With regard to its presumed audience, it is inclusive and available, though never condescending. It avoids all tendency to the exclusive and the esoteric.

As I said, it starts with Johnson. Of course, commentaries on literature existed in English before Johnson, but for the most part they were different in kind from his. They might be elegant workshop notes, as when Dryden discusses rhyme in the theater or the nature of heroic poetry, and there were Addison's polished clichés, meant to provide small talk for the drawing room. In criticism before Johnson, there was a good deal of rehashing of classical commonplaces in an effort to shore up the cultural status of literature. And there was much sheer pedantry, to the immense annoyance of Alexander Pope.

But with Johnson, the discussion of literature in English became in a new way at once public and serious, part of the mental and emotional circuitry of civilization, and this is one of the important developments in our cultural history. Nor is the importance or preeminence of Johnson in any way qualified by the fact that much lesser writers, roughly contemporaneous with him, were attempting the same thing.

It is sometimes said that Johnson's criticism—and, indeed, his writing on a whole range of subjects—rests upon "common sense," an expression that seems inadequate to his intellectual power. Inadequate, unless that term is properly understood. Johnson appealed to the intelligence, or "sense," that we all have in common as human beings. To be sure, such common intelligence is unevenly distributed, but we do possess it ontologically, and Johnson appeals to this common intelligence at its highest level. That is his "method." His was not a specialized appeal, and he did not use a specialized vocabulary. He wrote, for the most part, in periodicals, and in other forms addressed to a general audience, and he conceived of himself, always, as speaking for a shared civilization.

In 1777, Johnson was commissioned by London booksellers (publishers) to contribute brief introductions to a series of volumes devoted to the works of the British poets. Increasingly caught up in this project (notice its popular and journalistic nature), Johnson wrote much more than had been intended and produced the essays we now know as *The Lives of the Poets,* a mixture of biography, careful critical description, and evaluation. The whole is even greater than the excellence of its parts: Johnson relates the works to the poets themselves and his judgments to civilization as he understood it.

Some years ago, when teaching a graduate seminar at Columbia University, I hoped to get the afternoon's discussion rolling with a supposedly controversial assertion. "It seems to me," I said, "that *The Lives of the Poets* is the greatest work of literary criticism in English." I expected a fierce debate among these doctoral candidates. Eliot? Coleridge? Leavis? To my embarrassment as a seminar leader, there was no debate. Having just absorbed *The Lives of the Poets,* the graduate students instead spent their time analyzing and celebrating its strengths. And chief among these was the pervasive sense in this great work, as elsewhere in his writing, that Johnson's mind was essentially shaped by literature on a wide range of subjects: on politics, morality, religion, history, psychology, and manners. He lived intensely, though amidst controversy, the life of his time.

I do not mean, of course, to place excessive weight upon the enthusiastic judgment of a group of graduate students seated around a seminar table. My point is that their judgment of *The Lives of the Poets* is an accurate one but, more important, that Johnson inaugurated—in his overall approach—the central tradition of criticism in English.

It is scarcely surprising, therefore, that Johnson himself gave memorable and even definitive expression to the core of his intellectual position. In a few sentences about to be quoted here, he stated assumptions from which we can move not only to his methods as a literary critic but to his approach to virtually all important matters. Literature was for him ultimately an experience we have in common. Johnson was eccentric in appraisal of a number of literary works: "Lycidas," *Lear, Gulliver's Travels,* and so forth. Yet he also believed that there was a powerful collective judgment at work extending over a considerable period, a collective judgment that corrected the vagaries of individual judgment. In three sentences, Johnson affirms the public, the social character of literature, literature as a shared experience and as helping to constitute a living culture. The moment comes in his *Preface* to Shakespeare, early in the essay, when he is addressing the question of whether or not Shakespeare is indeed a great writer, the peer of the ancient classics, and the issue of how we can possibly settle that question. We know it, says Johnson, empirically and collectively:

To works, however, of which the excellence is not absolute and definitive, but gradual and comparative; to works not raised upon principles demonstrative and scientifick, but appealing wholly to observation and experience, no other test can be applied than length or duration and continuance of esteem. What mankind have long possessed they have often examined and compared; and if they persist to value the possession, it is because frequent comparisons have confirmed opinion in its favor.

The truth was a matter of public consensus, stronger by far than the opinions of his own powerful mind, confident to the point of arrogance though that mind was.

The tradition I am attempting to define begins with Johnson and extends to the present by way of William Hazlitt, Matthew Arnold, G. K. Chesteron, T. S. Eliot, Edmund Wilson, and Lionel Trilling. Obviously I do not intend this list to be all-inclusive. Other names can easily be added. It is meant to define literary criticism as a mode of public discourse that can focus upon a particular work but that can also expand its view to encompass the widest variety of subjects and bring them into the common conversation. The governing assumption is that we share works of literature, meet through them—

though sometimes on a basis of antagonism—and are enlarged by them, and that literature provides a perspective that is distinct from, but that can encompass, science, economics, politics, psychology, theology, and other kinds of essential knowledge.

The critics I have just mentioned as constituting a tradition do not, indeed, always agree with one another. Johnson's opinion of Voltaire and Rousseau is well known, as is his opinion of Hume's atheism, but Hazlitt, also part of the great civilized conversation, was an atheist and admired not only the French Revolution but also Napoleon. Not surprisingly, he disliked Johnson. But Hazlitt's perspective and range were Johnsonian. His lectures and essays— on the English Romantic poets, on the comic writers, on Shakespeare, and on Elizabethan drama—place literature at the center of his intellectual enterprise. In perhaps his most impressive book, *The Spirit of the Age,* he ranged far and wide over the principal figures of his time and the intellectual and political tendencies they represented: Bentham, Godwin, Coleridge, Byron, Wordsworth, Malthus, Jeffrey, Cobbett, Hunt. His imagination was literary and inclusive.

I would rank Trilling's *The Liberal Imagination* with Hazlitt's *The Spirit of the Age* in critical accomplishment; indeed, they are the same kind of book. So too is G. K. Chesterton's *The Victorian Age in Literature,* to which Trilling himself introduced me, and Edmund Wilson's *Axel's Castle.*

The critic is simply the best reader of a poem or work of prose that native intelligence and education can combine to produce. His activity as a critic is not different in kind from that of other readers; it is continuous with it. The critic is merely more skillful and better informed. The education the critic brings to bear includes history, biography, philosophy, the visual and plastic arts, as well as music, and as much of the various specialized disciplines—anthropology, psychoanalysis, sociology, and the exact sciences—as can be usefully absorbed. The critic brings all of this to bear in a style that is at once personal and public, an authentic voice and one that can actually be listened to. The critic lives as intensely as possible the life of his times, taking if necessary the predictable risks in making individual judgments, in all areas. The critic's writings deal, therefore, not solely with literature but with a wide range of subjects, the whole necessarily unified by the critic's own judgment and informed point of view. The critic enjoys the spectacle of human life, whatever judgments he finally passes upon one or another aspect of it. The critic is closely acquainted not only with the range of English literature and the literature of other languages, but with the classics of his Western civilization. But for all of this, his work remains essentially sociable and accessible and therefore likely to be rooted in journalism, a sign not only of its accessibility but of its involvement in both the larger and the commoner concerns of the world.

To paraphrase Johnson's Imlac, no doubt to be a critic so conceived is impossible. But it is not impossible to make asymptotic progress toward that ideal, as all critics mentioned in this Preface have done. They, indeed, have moved rather far along the asymptotic curve.

The appearance and growing influence of another sort of criticism in the academy, however, represents a different and contrary intention altogether, and it has been good neither for the academy nor for the culture at large. It has virtually nothing to do with journalism or public discourse and by its very nature could not, because it tends to be esoteric and exclusive. It does not address itself to a common intelligence or to a shared civilization, but to the specialist and the initiate. It exhibits a powerful hostility, strange to say, toward both the individual work of literature and to the very idea of literature, positing circumstances under which, for example, Shakespeare is no more "privileged" than a television commercial or statistical survey. Under these auspices, literary criticism exhibits an aspiration to become philosophy, linguistics, psychology, a quantitative and exact science, an ideology, and a private esoteric vision.

Johnson was right, not only about the worth of Shakespeare but in his method of determining it: a persisting consensus. And literature is no illusion, fated to dissolve with the culture that nourished it. The epics of Homer, the *Divine Comedy* of Dante, and the plays of Shakespeare are irreducible fact. We read them, but they also read us, testing us on their heights. Literature is the principal vehicle for transmitting the ideas and feelings that constitute our shared and public culture. With a minimum of intellectual and moral courage on our part, it will persist, interpreted and re-interpreted, in other times and other places.

"Out of It 'ere Night"
The WASP Gentleman as Cultural Ideal

On the morning of September 20, 1643, Lucius Cary, Viscount
Falkland, died at age thirty-three in cavalry action before the town
of Newbury. A scholar and poet, an intimate of Ben Jonson, Thomas
Hobbes, John Selden, Clarendon, and Davenant, he embodied in
many ways the ideal of his period. His was not an absolutely first-
rate mind, like those of Hobbes or Selden. They were, to put it one
way, too surpassingly intelligent to be representative of anything.
But Falkland did embody an ideal. He was an English gentleman as
his era understood that idea. He was a man of great moderation, and
in the House of Commons he often stood with the reformers. He
distrusted the power and arrogance of men like Bishop Laud. He
had a broad definition of the Church of England and held to reason
and religious toleration. But he grew increasingly frightened by men
like Cromwell, Hampden, and Pym. When revolution and civil war
loomed, Falkland stood with the king as court advisor and cavalry
officer.

His superlative personal qualities grew in his own eyes increasingly irrelevant to the history that unfolded before him. The air of
England reeked of cannon smoke, and her soil was drenched in
blood. The king was duplicitous and a victim of bad advice. The
long afternoons of discourse at Great Tew, the family estate in
Oxfordshire, might as well have been on another planet. Falkland's
philosophical and platonic friend, Lady Sophia Murray, was impris-
oned in London as a spy and traitor, involved by Falkland himself in
a feckless plot. She died of consumption on the same day—legend
says the same hour—that Falkland in effect committed suicide on
the field of battle.

For months Falkland had been sunk in melancholy and had become uncharacteristically careless about his dress. On the morning

This article first appeared in *The New Criterion* and is reprinted with permission.

before the battle, however, he called for fresh linen, took communion, declared that he would "be out of it 'ere night," and took his place on the right wing of the King's line of cavalry.

The King's infantry were finding it impossible to force their way past a hedgerow manned by Essex's Parliamentary musketeers. The only way through was a narrow opening in the hedge, a bottleneck of slaughtered royalists. Suddenly Falkland and his horse sprang forward and plunged toward the gap. Before he reached it, he was mortally wounded in the stomach. A few minutes later, the rest of the King's cavalry plunged through the gap, widening it, and routing Essex's musketmen. Falkland was buried in a small church at Great Tew.

Falkland exemplified one phase of the idea of the English gentleman, an idea that has remote classical and Christian roots, discernable in Chaucer's "verray parfit gentil knicht" and later in such Renaissance works as Castiglione's *The Courtier* and its English counterpart, Sir Thomas Elyot's *The Governour,* and of course in the legend of Sir Philip Sydney. The idea undergoes a chilling formulation in Lord Chesterfield's conduct-manual letters to his illegitimate son and becomes broadened and more widely accessible in the *Spectator* essays of Addison and Steele. Gradually the idea takes on a distinctively English character, different from anything on the Continent.

In the late eighteenth century, the idea importantly incorporates the idea of sports: riding to hounds, cricket, boxing, rugby. Dr. Thomas Arnold reformed the school at Rugby in order to produce Christian gentlemen; his son, Matthew Arnold, celebrated the idea in a little-known masterpiece of an essay entitled "An Eton Boy" about Arthur Clynton Baskerville Mynors, who died during the campaign against the Zulus. "We see him," writes Arnold, "full of natural affection, and not ashamed of manifesting it; bred in habits of religion, and not ashamed of retaining them; without a speck of affectation, without a shadow of pretention, unsullied, brave, true, kind, respectful, grateful, uncensorious, uncomplaining; in the time to act, cheerfully active; in the time to suffer, cheerfully enduring." The British scholar Philip Mason, in *The English Gentleman: The Rise and Fall of an Ideal* (1982), provides a very rich account of the development of the ideal.

ii

I believe it can be argued that the idea of the gentleman, modified in its American context but certainly derived from the British model and not directly from the Continent, and involving matters of style and conduct comparable to the British model, has been since the eighteenth century the only viable and persisting social ideal in American culture. Nothing has filled the gap left by its relatively recent disappearance—certainly not the Cowboy or the redskinized Natty Bumpo figure from Cooper. The evisceration of the idea of the gentleman as normative is the central subject of, for example, Tom Wolfe's *The Bonfire of the Vanities,* and the idea may even lurk behind the arguments of Allan Bloom's *The Closing of the American Mind.*

Now the idea of the gentleman came under intolerable strain for Viscount Falkland during the seventeenth-century civil war, and the mechanized slaughter of World War I brought comparable strains to bear upon it. In this connection, numerous representative figures might be adduced. Scott Fitzgerald's gentlemen *manqué* represent a tribute to the ideal, though they are usually tragic figures, undone through illusion or otherwise weak character. Faulkner's gentlemen are no match for the Snopses and modernity. Hemingway sought to fashion a new, perhaps partially redskinized, ideal.

The representative figure to set beside Falkland might be the equally doomed American legendary figure Hobey Baker, who met a Falkland-like fate in 1918. Baker has been a figure of enduring interest. Fitzgerald was fascinated by him. John Davies' *The Legend of Hobey Baker* (1966), with an introduction by the Fitzgerald scholar Arthur Mizener, provides an accurate account of him, with numerous photographs. And most recently we have had a fine novel about Baker by Mark Goodman entitled *Hurrah For the Next Man Who Dies* (1985). Mr. Goodman is aware of all the scholars can tell us about Baker, but he uses the genre of the novel to push, quite responsibly in my view, into areas where the historian cannot tread. This *beau ideal* of American society in the period before the Great War did, in Mr. Goodman's view, kill himself as Falkland did, unable to deal with a world in which his very excellence was becoming marginal.

iii

The title of this novel is thoroughly appropriate—about which more in a moment—though it is also obscure. Except to the initiate, *Hurrah For the Next Man Who Dies* certainly sounds perverse and, except to the initiate, does not provide a clue to what the novel is about. And yet you know from the first paragraph that the prose here is full of what the eighteenth century called "energy," by which was meant inventive combinations of words within the sentence, always within the boundaries of usage, of course, but exhibiting the sheer pleasure of using the language.

Structurally this novel owes much to *Gatsby*, even as *Gatsby* owes everything, structurally, to Conrad. We have a recognizably normal narrator like Carraway or Marlow gradually bringing us into the vicinity of a baroque tragic hero, Gatsby and Kurtz. Normality is what we stuff graveyards with and forget about. The tragic hero is unforgettable, though he usually dies young.

Mark Goodman's normal narrator is one Jeb Runcible, a young Southerner who goes north to Princeton, plays football, and goes to war. The baroque tragic hero is Hobey Baker.

Most readers today will know little or nothing about Hobart Amory Hare Baker (1892–1918), but he was an extraordinary phenomenon, and Mr. Goodman, while interpreting them, sticks close to the historical facts. Those who have written about Baker do not shrink from comparing him with Sir Philip Sydney or Yeats' Irish airman, Major Robert Gregory.

Baker may have been the greatest college athlete ever to appear on an American playing field. He was the only athlete ever to be elected to both the football and the hockey hall of fame. Though he played football in that distant pre-war era, when the game was almost entirely defensive and the ball larger and rounder than it is today, when a touchdown counted for five points and scarcely anyone threw forward passes, Baker held the Princeton scoring record of 180 points until 1964 when Cosmo Iacavazzi, who carried the ball on almost every play, surpassed it in his final game.

But Baker was more than a superb athlete. He was the epitome of what pre–World War I, upper-class America ardently desired: a mainline Philadelphia aristocrat. A product of St. Paul's School, he had perfect manners, was a member of the choir, partook in Christmas caroling, and was a good if not brilliant student. He also looked like a young man in one of Charles Dana Gibson's drawings.

College football in the Ivy League when Baker played was a very different matter from what it is today. Our principal source of nonfictional knowledge about Baker is *The Legend of Hobey Baker* (1966) by Professor John Davies. Here is the milieu within which Baker became a "legend."

Within the colleges, of course, football was a sort of civic religion. At Princeton the week before a Harvard or Yale game the tension was palpable, the professors unable to get the attention or even the attendance of the students. The coaches would bring back old-time stars to romp around the field demonstrating old stunts and exhorting the team to victory; there were mass meetings and torchlight parades. . . . In the fall of 1912 Governor Woodrow Wilson went down to practice three times, including the day of his election as President of the United States.

Even at his peak, as a national hero of the upper-middle and upper class, Baker loathed publicity. He saw the "game" as larger than any individual. When he was deliberately fouled in football or hockey, the deed reduced him to tears, not because he had been hurt but because the game had been tainted. More than once he carried an unconscious opponent off the field in his arms, and after a game, hammered and bloody, he always went into the opposing team's locker room to congratulate them on a fine game. The sports writer John R. Tunis remembers Baker as "a kind of panther."

His coordination and footwork were so wonderful that he could take chances and do things that others wouldn't dare do. . . . He would dropkick, tackle and run with a kind of feline intelligence. . . . The whole atmosphere was electric when he was playing. Everyone would just stand up when he got the puck or caught a punt. Never wore a headguard in football and I remember that great shock of blond hair—Hobey standing waiting all alone. (Quoted in *Davies*)

Never wore a headguard in football. In the old photographs, Baker is the only man on the field without one. He was what his era desired, but he was also a cultural throwback, an Edwardian gentleman who had internalized the entire ethos, though in his world of 1914, the manners and morals of the 1920s were already gestating in the back seats of thousands of Henry Ford's new motor cars.

Mark Goodman's novel is divided into two books, peace and war, and what one sees, among other things, in the first book is that there was a very different and much denser texture to college life then than—as I can testify from very recent experience—there is today. It was certainly a texture with its unfortunate and even absurd characteristics, but nevertheless, there was something *there*—style, expectation, tradition, a code of manners (no one wanted to be a "mucker"), a conception of the heroic, a standard of intelligence, even *dating:* chrysanthemums at the railroad station, fur coats and cashmere sweaters, the old songs. Goodman captures this world with a sure eye and ear, and he has learned from Fitzgerald how to weave in those songs. On our present college campuses, all of this has been homogenized into a kind of stylistic glop.

iv

But there is a mystery clinging to Hobey Baker, and it has to do with his last years and the manner of his death at twenty-six in 1918. It is to this mystery that Mr. Goodman addresses himself: he knows all the facts and speaks with authority, and he tries as a novelist to come as close as he can to the heart of the mystery. The plain fact of the matter is that Baker did not have to die. Indeed, there was no excuse for it.

The bare facts are elegantly presented by Professor Davies. After graduating from Princeton in 1914, Baker was bored with his Wall Street job at the Morgan Bank and bored with Manhattan social life. He sought some excitement in playing hockey against pro teams with the St. Nick's Club, half of whose players had personal valets in attendance. He took flying lessons out on Long Island, played polo, knew Eddie Rickenbacker, raced automobiles around Long Island, and ended up as a volunteer in the Lafayette Escadrille. The newspapers exaggerated his exploits, but he did shoot down three German planes. He rose to squadron commander and had the squadron's planes painted Princeton orange and black, with a tiger logo. On December 22, 1918, the war over, he test-flew a repaired Spad. The engine stalled, the Spad crashed, and Baker died.

Well, Baker knew very well what to do under the circumstances of a stall, and he had taught his own pilots how to handle such a situation. The Spad was a sort of varnished cloth kite with a motorcycle engine. In a stall, you pushed the stick forward to gather some flying speed in a shallow dive, then pulled the stick back, and pancaked the thing. No problem. Spads had pancaked onto treetops. Some pilots had walked away from a dozen such landings. But Baker tried to glide back to the airstrip and, instead, crashed into the ground nose-first.

Was it a suicide? Professor Davies says absolutely not. Mark Goodman is not so sure.

v

The exuberance and accuracy of Mark Goodman's historical imagination are tremendously impressive, whether he is recreating pre-war Princeton and Manhattan or the Western Front. "It rained over most of northern France the day we buried Hobey Baker." A fine, simple, but resonant opening sentence. "The weather bore in from the North Sea well before dawn, silent and thick with mist. . . . The squadron—or what was left of it, more than a month after the Armistice—began to fall out for burial parade shortly after morning mess." Those are the opening sentences of the novel, Jeb Runcible speaking. They properly put Baker's death in the foreground and, not at all incidentally, recall Gatsby's burial in the rain—Gatsby, the last frontiersman, and Baker, the last Edwardian.

Mark Goodman's Book I, as I mentioned, deals with the pre-war college and social scene and with Baker as an ideal figure, and the author's prose is more than adequate to this task.

Hobey Baker, golden youth of autumn fields and winter ice. In that gilded age of the American romance, when our country marched into the new century vibrant and full-blooded, flexing its muscles and stretching its sinews, we worshipped our athletes in the robust conviction that they, not our great and fearsome machines, were the best we had to offer. They were, too. Willie Anderson, with a golf swing like a hawk leaping to flight; Jim Thorpe, the exquisite Carlisle Indian; . . . and my own hero, Christy Mathewson, who threw a small stitched sphere faster than the eye could follow. But none quite captured the national imagination like Hobey Baker, the athlete aristocrat, who played with a swift and innocent grace that seemed an affirmation of man's mortal divinity. "Here he comes!" they would cry as he flew up the ice with the puck cradled in his stick.

And, on the football field:

THUMP! The Harvard punt soars upfield toward our goal line, where Hobey waits, alone, his black jersey emblazoned with grime, his blond hair shining in the pellucid sunlight. He flexes on the toes of his cleats, hands fixed on his hips, as he gauges the ball's trajectory. He is perfectly still in the penultimate moment when the ball crests and begins to descend. Suddenly he backpedals three, four, five steps, plants, then dashes forward, his timing marvelous, to catch the punt on the fly.

This is the Hobey Baker who astonished the young Scott Fitzgerald, and there is surely no call for intellectuals to condescend to him. An athlete of that quality is an artist on a par with the great ballet dancers. Here is how Amory Blaine, the name derived from Baker's, sees Allenby—or Baker—in *This Side of Paradise* (1920):

Now, far down the shadowy line of University Place a white-clad phalanx broke the gloom, and marching figures, white-shirted, white-trousered,

swung rhythmically up the street, with linked arms and heads thrown back
[singing "Going Back to Nassau Hall"].... There at the head of the white
platoon marched Allenby, the football captain, slim and defiant, as if aware
that this year the hopes of the college rested on him, that his hundred-and-
sixty pounds were expected to dodge to victory through the heavy blue
and crimson lines ... and then the procession passed through shadowy
Campbell Arch and the voices grew fainter as it wound eastward over the
campus.

vi

But even in these silvery settings there are touches of shadow.
Jeb Runcible's intelligent but troubled girlfriend Julia Bremer—
troubled because she thinks she really wanted her brother to die of
polio—notices something enormously solitary about Hobey Baker.
She recalls him on the football field earlier on a Saturday: "There
was something spectacular and ... solitary about it. Is that the word?
Yes, solitary. As if he were the only person on the field. I mean, as
if he *felt* that way." And here we remember the child Hobey Baker
at St. Paul's, practicing alone on those dark frozen ponds late at
night; Baker, the solitary perfectionist.

The great revelatory moment comes in Book I when Runcible
sees Baker in his ultimate narcissistic solitude. It is like Nick Carraway seeing Gatsby for the first time, stretching out his arms toward
the green light.

It happened one evening when I returned early from the library and
suddenly found Hobey stripped to the waist before his mirror. His back was
to me, and as I stood there for a startled moment, he held his arm extended
and flexed, watching its ripple with a ferocity of wonder I have never
encountered in another human being. His eyes caught mine in the mirror.

"Just look at that arm," he whispered. "Do you know what that arm can
do?"

Then, as if he had just realized my actual presence, he quickly dropped
the pose and made some remark of humorous disparagement.

The incident went forever unmentioned. But as long as Hobey lived, I
never, never forgot the glittering intensity in those eyes, cold and bright as
diamonds, as he stood captive to the silver mirror.

Let it be said, though, that with that arm and its mate, Hobey could juggle
five balls in the air at a time. He could run the hundred-yard dash in ten
seconds, make any muscle in his body jiggle to the accompaniment of a
dance tune—and, to be sure, dress up in white tie and tails and join a
delightful dinner company walking on his hands.

These were the things that Hobey Baker could do.

In Goodman's interpretation—and remember that this is fiction—Hobey Baker, while absolutely correct around women, always Edwardian in his manners, averting his gaze from all the back-seat rumpus, and never participating in the callow sexual bull sessions, was also emotionally odd. "What's it like, Jeb?" he asked earnestly. "I mean, what does it actually feel like, to be in love with someone?" After some exchanges, during which Runcible stumblingly tries to explain the feeling, Hobey replies: "I'm not sure I could ever feel that way about someone.... I'd feel I was losing control. I hate that.... I can't stand not being in control of ... things." This exchange occurs in a chapter of Book I entitled "Roll Me Over / In the Clover."

When Baker and Jeb graduate from Princeton in 1914, Goodman pays his wry respects to his fictional mentor, Scott Fitzgerald:

Suddenly, while he poured and we drank, a rather square-cut underclassman with startling green eyes ran up to us and planted himself in front of Hobey.

"Excuse the intrusion, Mr. Baker," he began breathlessly, "but on behalf of our class I wanted to congratulate you on a splendid career. You were a source of inspiration to all of us, and it was an honor to have the privilege of seeing you play."

"Why, thank you," said Hobey, plainly taken aback.

"Then"—the youngster's hand shot out—"all the luck in the world to you, Mister Baker."

Gravely Hobey shook the outstretched hand; then the lad was off like a powder flash.

"Who the devil was *that?*" Hobey asked after a stunned pause.

"That's young Fitzgerald," I said, remembering. "You know, Hobe—the fellow who quit freshman football the first week?"

We all watched the eager youngster disappear into the crowd.

"Well," Spratling said at length, "he *does* go on, doesn't he?"

vii

After Princeton and a dispiriting taste of "real" life at the Morgan Bank, Hobey takes to the air, and in a fine scene Goodman depicts his farewell, flying over the Princeton stadium in formation.

It was an extraordinary sight, Hobey Baker flying point for a V formation of mechanized geese, flying south to Princeton for November. They came over high, stretched out against the darkening autumn sky, then banked and swooped in low over the stadium. As the bobbing planes receded upward, Hobey broke off from the formation and passed over the stadium one last time, dipping his wings in a final salute as the crowd rose and cheered.

Soon thereafter we are into Book II and France, with Runcible a flyer now too. Goodman is a master of the strong opening sentence: "Of all Nungesser's stories, my favorite was the tale of Albert Ball," the great and eccentric British ace. And now we find out what the mysterious title of this novel means.

Word of Guynemer's death got around quickly. . . . We all got pretty well oiled up. Toward the shank of the evening, when everyone was in full funereal throttle, one of the British captains who had known Guynemer stood up on the bar and led the group in a chorus of "Hurrah For the Next Man Who Dies."

> So stand by your glasses steady
> For this world is a world of lies,
> Here's a toast to the dead already
> And hurrah for the next man who dies.

The flyers, however, though indeed they frequently died, remain literally and emotionally above the war. Hobey is very good at what he does, high above the clouds, which he refers to as "cloud fields." He resists the reality of the whole thing. He and Runcible walk down the road from their chateau billet to enjoy a good meal with a French peasant couple. Hobey asks the peasant woman whether they have any children. "They was in the army," she said. . . . "One was shot in the head at the First Marne. The other was blown to pieces at the Somme." Hobey cops out by talking to the peasant woman about the merits of the Allied cause.

Jeb Runcible comes down out of the clouds both literally and figuratively in one of the epiphanies of the novel, shot down and crash-landing in no man's land as a German attack is imminent. He manages to leap and crawl, dodging mortar fire and snipers, to the British lines. Both the attackers and the defenders break out in national songs, and even the bagpipes skirl, as the grey-uniformed wave sweeps forward. Runcible is put inside the command post.

Outside, the shrieks and clang of metal told me the Germans had reached our trench. I jumped behind the desk as the dugout door was flung open. A skewered apparition, faceless, came hurtling into the room. It was a Tommy with a bayonet run clear through his back. The bayonet disappeared as he crashed into the table, half screaming, half gargling. Then he pitched forward to the floor. Standing over him, gore dripping from his recovered bayonet, was a German soldier. He could not have been more than sixteen years old. I remember his intense youth, and his startled look before I fired the pistol and ripped most of his face away.

Runcible has been feeling increasingly distant from Baker by this time, and the break comes when he finally gets back to the chateau, where the atmosphere is much like that of the Ivy Club at Princeton.

I slammed my drink down on the bar, sending broken glass skittering across the surface. "Hobey, will you for the love of God *please shut up?*"
The room stopped dead. Hobey looked at me closely, as if he hadn't noticed me before. . . .
I pointed vaguely eastward. "Do you understand this, Hobey? *That's not the bloody fucking Yale game out there.*"

viii

Then the death of Baker. Like Professor Davies, Mark Goodman wisely does not commit himself to a theory, but, as is his privilege as a novelist, he does push further. His narrator, Jeb Runcible, provides plenty of material for reflection.

As abundant evidence indicates, Hobey was bored with his peacetime role in Manhattan. "That's because you're afraid to die, Jeb. My problem is—what if I live" . . . "You know, Jeb," Hobey finally said, "I really am afraid to go back home. I just don't see what there is for me back there."

But then there is that scene, which actually happened, of Hobey Baker narcissistically regarding himself before the mirror. As Goodman portrays him, he can experience camaraderie of the Ivy Club variety, and also with his squadron. But he is not at all comfortable with women. He finds himself engaged, also a historical fact, to the veteran prom-trotter and post-debutante Mimi Scott. She pursues him to France as a Red Cross nurse and forces him into an engagement. "One weekend proved so disastrous that Hobey cut short his leave and returned to the squadron Saturday night to fret on my shoulder. 'I certainly am good with girls, aren't I?' "

There is so much talk about homosexuality these days that the subject itself has become a stupefying bore. And yet—remembering, always, that Goodman is writing fiction, an *interpretation*—there is enough here that is soundly based in fact to suggest that Baker had great difficulty in relating not only to women but to anyone outside himself. He was always somewhat apart from the boys at Princeton and then the men of the squadron, though happier with both groups than in a wider society.

The war takes its toll upon Baker in this novel. He thickens at the waist and begins to grow bald. Perhaps Goodman's Baker has some intimation of his darker sexual impulses and fears their disclosure, especially so considering the ambience within which he grew up. Gatsby, Kurtz, and now Hobey Baker—for Mr. Goodman has given us a complex tragic hero indeed. And perhaps he has come as close as is possible to the historical truth itself.

When Baker is buried on that rainy day in France, the dirge is really for the end of the era that produced him.

> ... Still I will always be
> Nearer, my God, to Thee,
> Nearer, my God to Thee,
> Nearer to Thee.

Mercifully the dirge ended, and a stillness lay for the moment over the misty French graveyard. Then the honor guard fired a final salute, and the ceremony was over. The generals and mayors and newspapermen climbed into their cars and went back to wherever they came from.

The dirge recalls to mind the one improbably said to have been played by the band as the *Titanic* went down in 1912, and an author as gifted as Mark Goodman surely was aware of the connection and what it means. Hobart Amory Hare Baker was, from our present perspective, a college man from another planet—no, from another galaxy. As Yeats wrote in his great elegy on Major Robert Gregory, "What makes us dream that he could comb grey hair?"

Goodman's Hobey Baker is a representative American hero in the sense that Ahab, Gatsby, and Joe DiMaggio are representative, though of course not average. Their aloneness is a part of the intense focus of their individuality. And it is not often, to say the least, that there comes before us a novel as interesting, accomplished, and powerful as this one.

ix

Quite probably the long line of American gentlemen ran out during the period following World War II, when WASP American aristocrats—untitled, of course, but solidly established—temporarily shaped the world. The American governing class was highly permeable, but certainly identifiable then. Walter Isaacson and Evan Thomas have provided a moving epitaph for this now-historical mode of being in *The Wise Men: Six Friends and the World They*

Made (1986), an account of six men, now called cold war liberals, who designed the international equation within which we currently live.

Almost a caricature of the breed was Dean Acheson—Groton, Yale, and Harvard Law graduate, finally Secretary of State, "present at the creation" of NATO and the Truman Doctrine—who announced after nine days of senatorial grilling over the firing of MacArthur that he was going to test the human capacity for absorbing alcohol. *The Wise Men* also includes Charles "Chip" Bohlen, who was kicked out of St. Paul's, Hobey Baker's school, for playing football with an inflated condom, but who went to Harvard anyway and became a leading Russian expert and ambassador to Moscow. There was also Robert Lovett, a Hill School and Yale graduate who led the Yale unit of the Reserve Flying Corps during World War I and was tapped for Skull and Bones not on the Old Campus but at a naval air station in West Palm Beach. He was later to play a key role as secretary of defense. During the Berlin airlift, he amused himself with amateur oil painting. John J. McCloy was born on the wrong side of the tracks in Philadelphia. On his deathbed, McCloy's clergyman father said, "Have John learn Greek." There followed the Peddie School, Amherst, football and tennis, and the positions of high commissioner for post-war Germany and president of the World Bank. McCloy's personal ideal: Periclean Athens. Finally, *The Wise Men* depicts George Kennan, ambassador to Moscow and architect of Truman's containment policy, and Averell Harriman, millionaire, Harvard graduate, and ambassador.

The kind of social and political crystallization described in *The Wise Men* does not seem today to be even remotely conceivable as a real option. The institutions, from prep schools to the Ivy League to the Episcopal Church, that helped to create and sustain these individuals have entirely and essentially changed. There is almost nothing left within these institutions of serious cultural substance. Any revival of substance will require an enormous act of cultural re-imagining. And even in the loving account of these six "wise men," it is possible to detect signs of vulnerability. There is a profound sense of alienation in Kennan and Bohlen, there are the severe drinking problems of Bohlen and Acheson, and Harriman is apparently bewildered in his negotiations (he really seems to have thought they were negotiations in the old sense) with the North Vietnamese. There was also Acheson's famous flub of placing South

Korea outside our defense perimeter, a goof that cost fifty thousand American lives. Was he drunk? And his misplaced loyalty to Hiss after his conviction, in effect for spying, was a peculiar lapse on Acheson's part.

It was the end of the line, and the mold has now been broken. Out of it 'ere night.

Empiricism, Metaphysics, and the Recovery of the Whole

In Robert Frost's late and great poem *Directive,* a mysterious guide, who may be Frost, escorts his companion, who may be the reader, to a clear stream up in the New Hampshire hills. The guide then offers his companion a broken drinking goblet, "like the Grail," and invites him to drink and be "whole again beyond confusion." That clear spring water is almost certainly Frost's own poetry, and the poem claims salvational qualities for it. More generally, perhaps the spring water represents the clarification that comes from true understanding.

The "confusion" Frost invites us to be "whole again beyond" certainly exists as a feature of our common experience and often seems to pervade the entire spectrum. We experience moral confusion, but also philosophical, religious, educational, legal, economic, and political confusion, and part of it all—indeed, at its center—is the sense that something is *missing,* that the whole is somehow less than the sum of its parts, that there is no center, no structure, no anchor, and no core. Yet I wish to propose, Frost-like, that there is a clear stream of understanding that can clarify the issues in these multiple confusions and enable us to see our way beyond them. An understanding of the sweep of modern history and modern thought, roughly since the Renaissance, will take us far toward such a clarification.

Sometime during the fifteenth century, the great and glorious project of modernity was launched in earnest. To put it briefly: whereas ancient Greek and Roman cultures, with their extension and modification in medieval Christian culture, sought to understand the world and live according to that understanding, the mod-

This article was originally published in the Free Congress Foundation's *Essays On Our Times.* Reprinted with permission.

ern project sought not to understand the world in its totality but to control it and use it. The ancient and medieval project issued in metaphysics, which attempted a full understanding of reality, part of which remained mysterious. The modern project issued in empiricism, which narrowed the focus of inquiry to the world available to the five senses, with the explicit intention of mastering it.

It is not surprising that empiricism has produced a sense of evanescing meaning, for empiricism never promised to deliver meaning of any sort, let alone ultimate meaning. It had no use for those intuitions and visions and purported revelations that had been addressed by metaphysics. Empiricism had nothing to say about the foundations of being or the structure of moral authority. Indeed, in its most advanced twentieth-century form, empiricism regards all such as "pseudo-statements." Empiricism promises something else altogether, and speaking both metaphorically and literally, it delivered the goods: material abundance and enhanced physical well-being through the progressive mastery of nature.

Now, it is necessary to bear in mind that virtually all philosophical options have been available to the Western mind since the pre-Socratics and, no doubt, even earlier in unrecorded prehistoric reflection and ritual. All the options have "always" been available at least in potentiality, in their concentrated kernels. As far back as we can go, we find theism and atheism, idealism and materialism, flux and the unchanging, skepticism and faith. Materialism and skepticism are not modern. The Roman poet Lucretius was a materialist, and a thoroughgoing one at that. What is truth? asked jesting Pilate, which can stand as a synecdoche for ancient skepticism. Heraclitus perceived the unchanging within the flux, the still center of the turning wheel, an intimation of the Logos that would be refined in later Greek philosophy.

The permanent possibilities of Western thought make their appearance very early and undergo a process of modification and refinement that explores their ramifications—from the pre-Socratics to James, Wittgenstein, and the rest of modern philosophy. It is highly unfashionable to say it, but the fact is, no other civilization has possessed anything approaching this tradition of disciplined reflection, a product, in my estimation, of the creative tension between reason and revelation, Athens and Jerusalem, that is at the heart of the Western tradition and that has proved continuously unsettling and creative.

ii

Let us return to that momentous change in the West sometime in and around the fifteenth century and add the idea that one or another mode of thought becomes dominant given specific historical circumstances. As argued above, all modes of thought are *available.* The dominant one at any given time is the one that is *needed.*

We are all familiar with the famous Victorian "crisis of faith," as a result of which tens of thousands of people passed from Christian belief to some form of unbelief. Certainly formal philosophy played a part in this development, along with the work of biologists, anthropologists and archaeologists, and also biblical critics. But the currency of these modes and their power may have been as much a result as a cause of the emerging world view. It would be naive to assume that the crisis arose because David Hume threw doubt on miracles or because the biblical scholars of Tübingen analyzed codices. All these currents of thought became powerful because the way had been prepared for them; there were cultural decisions behind them that gave them their resonance. The conclusions of biblical scholarship are esoteric and shifting, and the skepticism of Hume or Voltaire can be met—if there is any desire to do so. Indeed, the ancient tradition of platonic idealism in philosophy lived on, with a fitful existence, in Cambridge Platonists such as the seventeenth-century philosopher Henry More and even into the twentieth century with Ernst Cassirer, for whom More was a hero, and others, including the astounding Eric Vogelin. And a great variety of supposedly outmoded philosophical possibilities have been expressed by the poets from the Renaissance through to the present. But for the last half millennium, or close to it, what swept forward to ever greater prestige and spectacular practical accomplishment has been, in its philosophical aspect, what we call empiricism and, in its popular aspect, what John Courtney Murray called the "bourgeois atheism of the marketplace." The two levels are intimately related.

Sir Francis Bacon, Thomas Hobbes, John Locke, Jeremy Bentham, John Stuart Mill, and the other formulators of the new empiricist world view did not engage or refute Plato, Aristotle, Anselm, or Aquinas; they merely mocked and dismissed them and turned to matters that, from their own point of view, were more important. The new direction, Bacon's *novum organum,* was able to go forward and gain speed because, as Santayana once remarked, we

progress less by what we have learned than by what we have forgotten.

The great project of the empirical thrust was not a comprehensive
understanding of the world but power over it: how to navigate in
it, cure disease, build bridges and canals, disseminate knowledge
through the new printing presses, build sewers, construct more
powerful and efficient engines—in short, how to master the visible
world. Anselm's metaphysics, profound reflections on the nature
and ground of being, do not much improve the trade in spices or
tobacco—but the science of navigation certainly does. This entire
shift toward the visible world represented a profound civilizational
choice.

During the fifteenth century, the Chinese provided an instructive
contrast. They sent a fleet to India, and it returned with exotic
animals for the parks and zoos of the wealthy, along with other
curiosities. There was no second voyage. The ships never went back.
But after Portuguese ships rounded the Cape and reached Asia,
tens of thousands of European ships followed. In 1492, Columbus
thought he might reach China and its wealth. When he reached the
New World, he reported that he had found the biblical Earthly
Paradise. King Ferdinand was not interested in that—he wanted the
gold—and Columbus landed in jail. By the seventeenth century,
successful British trading voyages were returning dividends of 4000
percent to their investors. The great country houses went up. In
due course, Handel emigrated to England.

In the short run, metaphysical reflection was irrelevant to the job
at hand, to the mastery of the visible world. The empirical and
utilitarian philosophies that systematized the vast project were, at
least in the short run, triumphantly successful.

It is enormously exciting, even today, to breathe the fresh intellectual air of the new project and to experience the total self-confidence
of its great formulators. Sir Francis Bacon dismisses the entire corpus
of medieval philosophy with a derisive smile, regarding it as beneath
him to engage it in serious argument. As he writes in *The Advance-
ment of Learning* (1605):

And indeed, as many solid substances putrefy, and turn into worms, so does
sound knowledge often putrefy into a number of subtle, idle, and vermicular
questions, that have a certain quickness of life, and spirit, but no strength
of matter or excellence of quality. This kind of degenerate learning chiefly
reigned among the schoolmen; who having strong and subtle capacities,

abundance of leisure, and but small variety of reading, their minds being shut up in a few authors, as their bodies were in the cells of their monasteries, and thus kept ignorant of both the history of nature and times; they, with infinite agitation and wit, spun out of a small quantity of matter, those laborious webs of learning which are extant in their books. For the human mind, if it acts upon matter, and contemplates the nature of things, and the works of God, operates according to the stuff, and is limited thereby; but if it works upon itself, as the spider does, then it has no end; but produces cobwebs of learning, admirable indeed for the fineness of the thread, but of no substance or profit.

For Bacon—and he certainly had a point about late medieval scholastic thought—the goals of learning are absolutely clear, and he writes in tones that indicate that they are equally clear to all discerning men:

But the greatest error of all is, mistaking the ultimate end of knowledge.... Nor do we mean, as was said of Socrates, to call philosophy down from heaven to converse upon earth: that is, to leave natural philosophy behind, and apply knowledge only to morality and policy; but as heaven and earth contribute to the use and benefit of man, so the end ought to be, from both philosophies, to separate and reject vain and empty speculations, and preserve and increase all that is solid and fruitful.

Sweep away the cobwebs of idle speculation. Attend to what is useful. Again and again this note is struck in the empiricist tradition—in Hobbes, in Locke, and in the others. The most comprehensive and influential of them all was John Locke, who wrote decisive works on philosophy, psychology, government, and religion, all with a style so graceful and assured that his readers must have felt complete concurrence to be the only possible or even decent response. Listen to the great *Essay Concerning Human Understanding* (1690):

I suppose it may be of use to prevail with the busy mind of man to be more cautious in meddling with things exceeding its comprehension, to stop when it is at the utmost end of its tether and to sit down in quiet ignorance of those things which, upon examination, are found to be beyond the reach of our capacities.

This is downright and practical, and if much of traditional Western philosophy goes out the window—well, so be it. We are to get on with solid, verifiable knowledge that will be of use to the world. At the end of the road will be affluent nations of free and contented citizens—a goal worth all the dubious "speculations" of Plato's academy or the medieval schoolmen.

iii

As might be expected, so powerful a cultural force as empiricism became pervasive in its effects, not only in philosophy but in psychology, in religion (Locke's *Reasonableness of Christianity*—that is, Christianity is largely morality), and in literature. Ian Watt has argued persuasively in *The Rise of the Novel* (1957) that the novel is the fictional embodiment of empiricism (the literary expression of the new world view) and comes into being with *Robinson Crusoe* in 1719. As Watt argues, the world of the novel is the world of the five senses. Reality is defined as what we see, hear, smell, touch, and taste.

There had been much prose fiction before 1719—in Chaucer, Boccaccio, in the ancient world—but the novel is something genuinely new. It establishes time and place much more precisely than did any previous literary genre. We find no sea coasts of Bohemia in *Robinson Crusoe,* but rather an island established in compelling concreteness. Because the novel as a genre is so precise in description, it establishes individuality with special sharpness. Homer never describes Helen; we simply know that she is the most beautiful woman in the world. We do not know the color of her hair or the slope of her nose. A novelist cannot work that way. It would create a hole in the texture of his reality, and he cannot count on common understanding.

Like empiricism, the novel is secular. Gods and angels are completely excluded from its reality, and if miracles are allowed in, a novelist must provide alternative naturalistic explanations. The novel, as Allen Tate said, puts man "wholly into his physical setting." It is the epic, said Georg Lukacs, of a world forsaken by God. It presents, in the phrase of de Sade, "*le tableau des moeurs seculaires.*" And this remains true of the *form* of the novel, whatever the private opinions of the novelist might be.

In *Robinson Crusoe* (1719) we sense the sheer excitement of that early, vigorous, and self-confident empiricism. The West was possessing the material world imaginatively, even as its ships were possessing it militarily, commercially, morally. The world of fact in Defoe is as fresh as a newly minted coin. Crusoe's ship is obliged to anchor:

The sixth day of our being at sea we came into Yarmouth Roads; the wind having been contrary, and the weather calm, we had made but little way since the storm. Here we were obliged to come to anchor, and here we lay, the wind continuing contrary, viz. at southwest, for seven or eight days, during which time a great many ships from Newcastle came into the same roads, as the common harbor where the ships might wait for a wind for the river.

Nor is it an accident that the great century of the European novel was the nineteenth, the novel growing in length and power even as a triumphant empiricism provided the basis for the economics and technology that would extend European power over the face of the earth.

iv

This great success story has some humorous and little-known features. As customarily recounted, the story features enlightenment and progress winning the day against medieval superstition. In fact, the medieval period was relatively rational. Its folklore and fairy tales, its giants and dragons, were known to be fictions. It was the Renaissance that was riddled with superstition. Bacon and the empirical thrust, while, indeed, making their way against Aristotle and the medieval schoolmen, also worked against a world of their own in which the French royalty was guided by Nostradamus, where there was likely to be an alchemist or an astrologer in the next apartment, and where audiences flocked to plays about Faust or Prospero or to plays in which the opening featured witches or commands from a ghost. The Renaissance not only recovered Homer and Virgil but the underground occult writings of the ancient world as well.

The appeal of magic both black and white during the Renaissance clearly reflects that will to control, a desire analogous to that of the new empiricism. Faust flew through the air long before the Wright brother did, and Nostradamus claimed to be predicting the major events of the next seven thousand years—and he was taken seriously. Francis Bacon said no, just the facts, please; though in his *New Atlantis* he did foresee, in a Nostradamus moment, a scientific utopia.

v

As I touched upon when mentioning the persisting vein of philosophical idealism, the sweep of empiricism did not go unopposed, especially in literature. The principal British writers of the Restoration and eighteenth century, from Dryden through Swift, Pope,

Johnson, and Burke, are religious and cultural traditionalists who
express attitudes of varying ambivalence and hostility toward the
new empiricist *Weltanschauung.* John Dryden belonged to the
Royal Society of Scientists but was far from confident about the
ultimate meaning of the march toward science and reason, as shown
in the opening lines of his *Religio Laici* (1682):

> Dim as the borrow'd beams of moon and stars
> To lonely, weary, wand'ring travelers
> Is Reason to the soul; and, as on high
> Those rolling fires discover but the sky,
> Not light us here, so Reason's glimmering way
> Was lent, not to assure our doubtful way,
> But guide us upward to a better day.

Alexander Pope thought that the new empiricism might be lethal
to traditional civilization, and in a negative version of Virgil's *Fourth
Eclogue,* he wrote of the deadly goddess at the end of *The Dunciad*
(1743):

> Thus at her felt approach, and secret might,
> Art after Art goes out, and all is Night.
> See skulking Truth to her old cavern fled,
> Mountains of Casuistry heap'd o'er her head!
> Philosophy, that leaned on Heaven before,
> Shrinks to her second cause, and is no more.
> Physic of Metaphysic begs defence,
> And Metaphysic calls for aid on Sense!

In *The Battle of the Books* (1704), in which he took the side of
the classical authors against the antitraditional moderns, Swift took
Bacon's spider passage and stood it on its head. In Swift, the spider
is not the medieval scholastic philosophers but rather the moderns,
who ignore the permanent truths of tradition:

So that in short, the Question comes to all this; Whether is the nobler Being
of the two, That which by a lazy Contemplation of four Inches round; by
an over-weening Pride, which feeding and engendering on it self, turns all
into Excrement and Venom; producing nothing at last, but Flybane and a
Cobweb: Or That, which by an universal Range, with long search, much
Study, true Judgement and Distinction of Things, brings home Honey and
Wax.

As Swift's classicist bee sums up the matter:

The Difference is, that instead of Dirt and Poison, we have rather chose to fill our Hives with Honey and Wax, thus furnishing Mankind with the two Noblest of Things, which are Sweetness and Light.

The later phrase, to embody Swift's point, had a venerable history in classical literature, and the spider-bee fable was meant to recall Aesop, whom Swift erroneously believed to be an ancient.

Samuel Johnson's sense of tradition in literature is analogous to Burke's sense of tradition in society. Both appeal to accumulated experience. Johnson believes Shakespeare to be a classic because he has been considered one for more than a century. Here is the applicable criterion; important enough to bear repeating here:

To works, however, of which the excellence is not absolute and definite, but gradual and comparative; to works not raised upon principles demonstrative and scientifick, but appealing wholly to observation and experience, no other test can be applied but length of duration and continuance of esteem. What mankind have long possessed they have often examined and compared, and if they persist to value the possession, it is because frequent comparisons have confirmed opinion in its favor.

The claim to literary greatness must rest on a consensus extending over time and thus transcending momentary fashion. And these traditionalists hold in common another theme that came out of the Renaissance: that literature, in the form of the classics and of modern writers such as Shakespeare, who have become classics, is the principal carrier of the values of civilization. In other words, they were humanists in the older sense of that much-abused word. As I embodied the conception in the opening paragraph of my book on Henry St. John, *Viscount Bolingbroke* (1965), a statesman, a friend of Pope, and a humanist:

A painting attributed to Melozzo da Forli, and now in the Queen's collection in Windsor, brings before us a scene which embodies one of the most important ideals of the Renaissance. The Duke of Urbino, Frederigo da Montefeltro, wearing his robes of state, sits in a large rectangular hall, his left hand resting on a folio. Guidobaldo, his son, about eleven years old and dressed in yellow damask trimmed with pearls, stands at the Duke's knee. Behind the Duke and his son, on a raised platform with a desk before it, sit three men. One wears the red suit of a prelate; the second, black ecclesiastical garb; the third, secular clothes. Servants and courtiers stand nearby unobtrusively. All are listening with great attention to a grey-haired humanist, dressed in black robes, who sits in a pulpit opposite the Duke. Open before him is a large book bound in crimson and adorned with silver clasps. We see that the humanist is reading aloud to his distinguished audience, no doubt from some classical or Christian author, and, as was the practice, commenting on the text as he proceeds.

It is the humanist who is in the pulpit. The man of letters instructs not only the head of state, the Duke, but also the clergymen and the courtiers in the background. This scene at the Court of Urbino thus reflects an assumption central to the humanist program and to the culture of the Renaissance—that education, a literary education derived in large part from classical sources, might succeed where the medieval curriculum no longer seemed quite adequate, might succeed in establishing a just social order and in taming the dark impulses in men's hearts.

The traditional Christian humanists lost out, at least in the short run. It is possible that Christian humanism was inherently unstable, as it occurred historically, and indeed the very label "Christian human-ism" suggests one reason why it may have been so. In this label, the term "Christian" is adjectival; the term "humanism," substantive. The secular classical-humanist component thus tended to edge the Christian component aside, as it did in the late humanist Edward Gibbon.

However that may be, the humanist program lost out, and empiri-cism, science, and their culture carried the day. First Greek, then Latin passed out of the required curriculum, then even English classics and classics in translations went out, a development that may now have reached its furthest point. That there is widespread uneasiness about all this is attested to by the immense interest recently generated by Allan Bloom's *The Closing of the American Mind.*

vi

In my own view, however, we may be reaching the end of the great era of empiricism, coming to another decisive shift in Western thought and consciousness. Of course, empiricism will persist as a method, and its accomplishments will unfold still further, but it will cease to be an exclusive habit of mind. We are beginning to perceive the inherent limits of empiricism and to experience the inevitable moral, religious, philosophical, and political confusions that arise from empiricism's programmatic narrowing of focus. The signs of this confusion are becoming widespread: at the popular level, in a sense of meaninglessness and attendant feelings of anxiety, and also at the highest levels of intellectual reflection. There follow a few striking examples among the many that could be adduced.

It is one of the ironies of twentieth-century thought, for example, that Ludwig Wittgenstein's *Tractatus* (1921), arguably the most important work of philosophy produced in this century, at once expresses and sums up the most advanced form of the empirical tradition and then, reaching its utmost border, turns decisively against it. An extreme form of empiricism, the mode of philosophy known as logical positivism arose in Vienna between the wars and rapidly spread throughout the Western world. It became dominant in the academy, and the professional philosophical organizations were dominated by its partisans, though they were harassed by dissidents of various philosophical sorts. Logical positivism is a scientific philosophy and asserts that only empirically verifiable statements are true. It also submits all statements to rigorous logical analysis, classifying as "pseudo-statements" all those that do not meet these stern tests. As Otto Neurath of the Vienna school wrote in 1931:

All the adherents of a rigorous empiricism reject anything that smacks of the "absolute," whether the subject matter relates to the world of the *a priori,* or the world of the categorical imperative.... The representatives of a scientific [approach to the world] know only science and the clarification of scientific methods, and this clarification is all that remains of old-fashioned "philosophizing." What can not be regarded as unified science must be accepted as poetry or fiction.

The next year, Rudolph Carnap, another member of the Viennese circle, wrote in *Erkenntnis*:

Through the development of modern logic it has become possible to give a new and sharper answer to the question of the validity and justification of metaphysics.... In the realm of metaphysics (including all value-theory and norm-science) logical analysis leads to the negative conclusion that *all the alleged statements in this area are totally meaningless.*

Though these torpedoes were aimed principally at Heidegger, the logical positivists meant to construct a philosophy to end all philosophy, a streamlined Bauhaus-style philosophy from which virtually all of prior Western philosophy was *ipso facto* excluded. No Corinthian columns were permitted here to make Plato and Aristotle comfortable. By the strict terms of positivism, the statements of Plato and Aristotle are mostly "meaningless."

But something marvelous and strange happened to logical positivism in Wittgenstein's *Tractatus.* The most brilliant mind of the Vienna group, Wittgenstein had a distinctive, sometimes monklike personality. After the First World War, he worked at menial jobs as a hospital porter and orderly. The *Tractatus,* his only work published during his lifetime, is a strange object indeed for a major philosophical work. In length, it runs to about ninety pages. Most of it consists of a terse, dazzling exposition of logical positivism, a virtuoso demonstration of the Vienna method. This part of the *Tractatus* was what people like Rudolph Carnap and, in England, A. J. Ayer and Bertrand Russell took seriously. But the climax of the *Tractatus* comes in the last ten pages where, having pushed the method to its outermost limit, Wittgenstein affirms that there is something (actually, much!) more. Here he speaks of mystical or higher reality (*das Mystiche, Hocheres*) that exists outside the "world" knowable by the methods of logical positivism.

Wittgenstein had evidently had a powerful mystical experience sometime before World War I, perhaps such an experience as Socrates had had. The *Tractatus,* accordingly, while fully giving positivism/empiricism its due, then turns into a cultural-critical work—indeed, a work of older philosophy—with a final theocentric form. In a memoir of Wittgenstein, Paul Englemann recalled that in contrast to the local positivism, Wittgenstein "passionately believes that all that really matters in human life is precisely what, in his view, we must be silent about." Well. From Vienna and logical positivism to St. John of the Cross and the *via negativa.* Stop talking, Neurath, Carnap, Russell, Ayer!

Wittgenstein himself commented that the logical system of the *Tractatus* outlines the coastline of an island only to get a better view of the boundary of the ocean. The exquisite intellectual beauty of the *Tractatus* lies in the fact that by pushing the logical positivist method to its very limits, the *Tractatus* comes to the outer edges of empiricism—and knows that there is more. We are not surprised to learn that Wittgenstein admired St. Augustine, considered Kierkegaard the greatest nineteenth-century thinker, and sometimes thought about entering a monastery. There are more things in heaven and earth, Carnap, than are dreamt of in your philosophy. The greatest of all the logical positivists was really a rabbi.

vii

In a remarkably analogous way, modern astronomy—an extension of empiricism through instruments—has come to its conceptual edges. We now know that the universe had a *beginning,* an idea so disturbing to some minds that it was bitterly resisted until the proofs came in. Einstein, for example, held out for the everlastingness of the universe and even made mathematical errors in his desire to demonstrate this. Einstein felt uncomfortable with the alternative, to say the least. But we now know that the universe began about twenty billion years ago with a gigantic explosion, the radiation from which has been measured by scientists at Bell Laboratories and the time span calculated with remarkable precision. The fact of the Big Bang, as it is now familiarly called, has been confirmed by measuring the speed at which stars are moving away from the epicenter of the explosion.

But what was there before the beginning? Here again we reach the limits of empiricism—and again, exquisitely, through a very sophisticated empiricism itself, courtesy of the radiation experts at Bell Laboratories, empiricism, as in Wittgenstein, falls silent. As scientist Robert Jastrow of Dartmouth has put it, the scientists laboriously climbed a mountain and, upon reaching the peak and looking over, saw on the other side the theologians, who had been there for centuries. "In the beginning . . ."

viii

There is yet another strange instance that brings us up against the frontiers of empirical knowledge. I speak here with considerable hesitation about the so-called Shroud of Turin. I would like to request at this point a momentary suspension of disbelief; that is to say, I would like to request an attitude of *real* skepticism. Just what *is* this object?

Recent carbon dating tests have indicated that the linen cloth dates from the fourteenth century and therefore is not, as many had previously supposed, the burial cloth of Jesus. But the image on the garment is assuredly that of a man who had been crucified. A pollen dating test indicates a first century origin. The details on the cloth were not available to us until 1898, when the cloth was photographed and hitherto invisible details appeared on the negatives. Photography was unknown to any hypothetical forger. The anatomical knowledge indicated by details on the image was not available in Europe in the fourteenth century. We have no record of a crucifixion in Europe after the fourth century.

Scientists from the Jet Propulsion Laboratory in Pasadena have performed various operations connected with the Shroud. This work represents a remarkable conjunction of the most modern techniques with an ancient mystery. They have used computer techniques developed for mapping the topography of Mars to study the image on the Shroud. According to Dr. Donald Lynn, there is no "linear directionality" in the Shroud image, which means that it could not have been painted on. Furthermore, the three-dimensional image produced at the laboratory demonstrates that the marks on the cloth correspond to those that would be obtained from a sheet laid over a body.

But how was the image on the Shroud produced? The answer is: we do not know. All kinds of experiments have been carried out without coming close to reproducing the equivalent of the image. And here, once again, we appear to be standing at the outermost edges of empiricism. It seems more plausible that the Shroud actually was the burial garment of Jesus than that a medieval artist somehow faked it. Genuine skepticism would enjoin a fully open mind concerning this peculiar object.

There have also been important and, for the Shroud controversy, pertinent developments in serious biblical criticism. Such scholarship has recently been coming to very different conclusions from those resulting from nineteenth-century scholarship, what Matthew Arnold called the science of *Tübingen,* which caused such dismay among the Victorian faithful. Very roughly speaking, serious biblical scholarship during the past 150 years has resembled a parabola. For a long time, this scholarship arrived at conclusions we can associate with Albert Schweitzer and Rudolph Bultmann. No, this scholarship told us, we have little knowledge about the historical Jesus. It may be that he never existed. It may be that a religion swept the eastern part of the Roman Empire in the first century and fabricated a divinity.

In a charming scholarly episode, some serious scholars doubted that the town of Nazareth existed in the first century. There was no evidence that it existed before the fourth century. Was the town of Jesus itself a fiction? In 1955, archaeologists found it, when excavating beneath the Church of the Anunciation. In 1961, an inscription was discovered in Caesarea dating from the early Roman period in which the name "Nazareth" is there for anyone to inspect.

This episode is representative. The consensus in recent biblical scholarship is summarized in such eminently fair books as Stephen Neill's *Interpretation of the New Testament: 1861–1961* (Oxford, 1964) and A. E. Harvey's *Jesus and the Constraints of History*

(Westminister, 1982). These books, and others, discuss the careful work of biblical scholars in recent years, most of them unknown to the general educated public. The latter work of analysis has gone forward with a great sense of intellectual responsibility, and much of it is highly technical. It comes, however, to the conclusion that the synoptic gospels must be taken very seriously as *history*. We may know as much about the life and death of Jesus as we know about the life and death of Cicero.

The habits of mind established over almost half a millenium are very difficult to disturb. To question or even to modify settled assumptions is a painful business. Empirical habits of mind have dominated the West at least since Sir Francis Bacon. The prevailing view of reality, even among highly educated people, is often like that of a businessman after a good lunch. The empirical world, the world of the five senses, is all there is. Yet, we have seen that a convergence is coming into being—a convergence in philosophy, in astronomy, in the on-going investigation of the Shroud, and in modern biblical criticism.

Of course, what lies before us in our own *fin de siecle* most emphatically is not the abandonment of empiricism. Nostradamus and Cagliostro are not welcome here. Before empiricism, there was no medicine, no effective diffusion of knowledge, no efficient transportation, and only the most arduous communication. Life often approximated Hobbes' famous description of the state of nature: solitary, nasty, poor, brutish, and short. What lies before us, in my view, is a disciplined cultivation of a radical skepticism, an effort to carry skepticism a final step. Indeed, something of this order happened in Wittgenstein's *Tractatus.*

The modern secular and empirical consciousness is not skeptical, but selectively skeptical. It has been skeptical about classical philosophy and about Christian claims. It has not often been skeptical about its own presuppositions. Now, suppose we were not selectively skeptical but really skeptical, skeptical across the board, entertaining no prior theoretical assumptions about the nature of actuality, no preconceptions about what is possible or thinkable. We would simply clear the intellectual decks and depend upon the evidence, no matter how unsettling. There would be no official truth, no respectable truth.

A very different and much less relativistic landscape would begin to emerge under the sunlight of this comprehensive skepticism. In

this way, we would appreciate and pursue empiricism, but, moved
by the evidence and not by mere wishful thinking, our intellectual
net would be cast much wider, and we would find relief from our
present sense of utter cultural and intellectual banality.

In Athens, while Paul was awaiting them, his spirit was exasperated within
him as he saw that the city was full of idols. And he would have discussions
with Jews and the worshippers in the synagogue and in the market place
every day with anyone he happened to meet. And some of the Stoic and
Epicurean philosophers encountered him, and some of them said: What
might this vagabond be trying to tell us? And others said: He seems to be
an announcer of foreign divinities. Because he brought the gospel of Jesus
and the resurrection. So they took him in hand and led him to the Areopagus,
saying: Can we discover what is this new teaching of which you are telling
us? You are bringing something new to our ears. . . .

Then Paul, standing in the middle of the Areopagus, said: Gentlemen of
Athens, I perceive that you are in every way more god-fearing than others;
for as I went about and observed your sanctuaries I even found an altar
inscribed To the Unknown God.

What you worship without knowing what it is, this is what I proclaim to
you. God, who made the world and everything in it, being Lord of Heaven
and earth, does not live in hand-built temples, nor, as one who needs
anything, is he ministered to by human hands, since he himself gave life
and breath and everything else to all. . . .

When they heard about the resurrection from the dead, some scoffed
but some said: We will listen to you again concerning this matter.

So Paul went from their midst; but some men attached themselves to
him and believed, among them Dionysius the Areopagite and his wife, who
was named Damaris, and some others with them.

> *Acts* 17–18, trans. Richmond Lattimore,
> *Acts and Letters of the Apostles* (1982)

Bloomsday

It has been said that the man who wishes to find God has already found Him. Professor Allan Bloom of the University of Chicago wishes to recover Western civilization amid the rubble. The tremendous excitement here is that maybe he has done so. His disorganized, idiosyncratic book, the ultimate heroes of which are Socrates, Nietzsche, Plato, Locke, and Publius, has sold a breathtaking three hundred thousand copies in hardcover and has been at the top of the *New York Times* best-seller list for months. The book quite possibly marks a historic turning point in the rediscovery of Western thought.

The Closing of the American Mind has an unforgiving disorganization. Trying to recover something from it is like trying to recover something from Montaigne's essays. The book is really Bloomsday in the Joycean sense—Allan Bloom, intelligent beyond any ordinary human measure, roaming through the specific diseases of the academy, through popular culture and popular language, coming at the reader with a long and brilliant monologue on Nietzsche's influence on the modern world as filtered through Freud and Max Weber plus an assortment of the British utilitarians.

Finally, toward the end, we learn where Bloom is headed. He believes in intellectual and spiritual heroes who have explored the ideal territory of human thought and feeling, people who call us to our best selves, or even beyond. Professor Bloom wants the university to resemble, ideally, Plato's *Symposium,* in which *friends*—tremendously important concept in ethical thought—discourse on the great questions of beauty, truth, love, death, immortality, and God. Thought itself is ecstasy and human completeness.

But in the foreground is the university we actually have. Bloom's description of it is horrifying. From his perspective of what the ideal

This article is reprinted from a book review entitled "Bloomsday," by Jeffrey Hart, which appeared in the Fall 1987 issue of *Policy Review. Policy Review* is a publication of The Heritage Foundation, 214 Massachusetts Avenue NE, Washington, D.C. 20002.

university could be, Bloom has seen the brutal truth about what it actually is. Bloom knows and tells his readers how this nation, and the West, is being morally and culturally gassed by its intellectual and academic elites.

Let us look first at how Bloom thinks about the university—as noble, powerful, and poetic a statement as any hymns to Oxford written by Cardinal Newman or Matthew Arnold: "When I was 15 years old I saw the University of Chicago for the first time and somehow sensed that I had discovered my life. I had never before seen, or at least had not noticed, buildings that were evidently dedicated to a higher purpose, not to necessity or utility, not merely to manufacture or trade, but to something that might be at an end in itself." When he entered into his enormous idea, he found that it "protected the tradition, not because tradition is tradition but because tradition provides models of discussion on a uniquely high level." Allan Bloom knows that "the facile economic and psychological debunking of the theoretical life cannot do away with its irreducible beauties."

Bloom is so intelligent, so philosophically adept, that it must be exhilarating to take a course under him at Chicago. Okay, so Freud posits sexuality as the basis of everything, all creativity. Fine. Is repressed sexuality the basis of Freud's own thought? Next question. Mr. Marx, you say that economic interest explains all human action. Fine. What economic interest explains your own thought, Mr. Marx? Bloom is absolutely brilliant at exposing the assumption within the answer.

ii

Bloom paints a vitriolic portrait of today's "student." In my own teaching experience at Dartmouth, I would say that, notwithstanding some outstanding and infrequent exceptions, Bloom is entirely accurate.

These opening sentences may well deserve to be ranked with the opening sentences of *A Farewell to Arms*: "There is one thing a professor can be absolutely certain of: almost every student entering the university believes, or says he believes, that truth is relative." Enter Professor Bloom, fully armored with all the earned weapons of Western philosophy:

The students, of course, cannot defend their opinion. It is something with which they have been indoctrinated. The best they can do is point out all the opinions and cultures there are and have been. What right, they ask, do I or anyone else have to say that one is better than the others? If I pose the routine questions designed to confuse them and make them think, such as "If you had been a British administrator in India, would you have let the natives under your governance burn the widow of a man who had died?" they either remain silent or reply that the British should never have been there in the first place.

As Bloom puts it in his subtitle, higher education has failed democracy and impoverished the souls of today's students. But Bloom gets it only half right with his discussion of "openness." Modern education, he writes, "pays no attention to natural rights or the historical origins of our regime, which are now thought to have been flawed and regressive.... It is open to all kinds of men, all kinds of life-styles, all ideologies. There is no enemy other than the man who is not open to everything." Well, that is the public face of the ideology. "Openness" applies only to the left though. We are to be "open" to Castro or to Stalin, but Hitler has become a religious category, a guarantee of the existence of evil. The left always offers the possibility of a better world.

Bloom shows the intellectual underpinnings of this "openness." As he shrewdly points out:

At the root of this change in morals was the presence in the United States of men and women of a great variety of nations, religions and races.... Openness was designed to provide a respectable place for these "groups" or "minorities"—to wrest respect from those who were not disposed to give it—and to weaken the sense of superiority of the dominant majority (more recently dubbed WASPs, a name the success of which shows something of the success of sociology in reinterpreting the national consciousness). That dominant majority gave the country a dominant culture with its traditions, its literature, its tastes, its special claim to know and supervise the language, and its Protestant religions. Much of the intellectual machinery of 20th-century American political thought and social science was constructed for the purposes of making an assault on that majority.

Like Buddhist monks in Saigon, the WASPs immolated themselves culturally. They lost their nerve completely, and the entire idea of the gentleman died. Any tom-tom beater is as good, now, as anyone. Says Bloom:

Sexual adventurers like Margaret Mead and other who found America too narrow told us that not only must we know other cultures and learn to respect them, but we could also profit from them. We could follow their lead and loosen up.... We would go to the bazaar of cultures and find reinforcement for inclinations that are repressed by puritanical guilt feelings. All such teachers of openness had either no interest in or were actively hostile to the Declaration of Independence and the Constitution.

Young Americans, even Bloom's elite students at the University of Chicago, "know much less about American history and those who were held to be its heroes" than past generations did. There has occurred a homogenization of American culture. "Practically all that young Americans have today is an insubstantial awareness that there are many cultures, accompanied by a saccharin moral drawn from this awareness: We should all get along. Why fight?"

It is fashionable for the elite universities to require a course in "non-Western" culture. But as Bloom shows, "If the students were really to learn something of the minds of any of these non-Western cultures—which they do not—they would find that each and every one of these cultures is ethnocentric. All of them think their way is the best way, and all others are inferior."

Right there is the intellectual turn within the turn. The very anthropological perspective that allows us for one moment to relativize and "appreciate" these cultures is itself Western and "higher." There is no Chinese anthropology that "appreciates" and "respects" Vietnamese culture. There is no Moroccan or Albanian anthropological perspective. In its academic apotheosis, Western culture is the only culture that does not celebrate its own ways and its own achievements. It keeps looking for some Zimbabwean Mozart. Bloom says: "It is important to emphasize that the lesson the students are drawing from their studies is simply untrue. History and the study of cultures do not teach or prove that values or cultures are relative. All to the contrary."

And yet we have undergone a civilizational lobotomy. "By the mid-sixties universities were offering [students] every concession other than education, but appeasement failed and soon the whole experiment in excellence was washed away, leaving not a trace." Serious reading, foreign language, and other academic requirements were jettisoned; the Ivy League, with Brown University in front of the Gadarene swine, led the way.

A partial list of the sacrifices made by the students to morality will suffice to show its character: they were able to live as they pleased in the university, as *in loco parentis* responsibilities were abandoned; drugs became a regular part of life, with almost no interference from university authorities, while the civil authority was kept at bay by the university's alleged right to police its own precincts; all sexual restrictions imposed by rule or disapproval were overturned; academic requirements were relaxed in every imaginable way, and grade inflation made it difficult to flunk; avoidance of military service became a way of life and a principle. All these privileges were disguised with edifying labels such as individual responsibility, experience, growth, development, self-expression, liberation, concern. Never in history had there been such a marvelous correspondence between the good and the pleasant.

iii

Bloom's great theme throughout is that ideology has invaded the academy to an absolutely unprecedented degree, *closing* the American mind—at least the academic American mind—to the truths about human nature as it actually is and has aspired to be. The center of his book, which I doubt many of his three hundred thousand purchasers have made their way through, is a brilliant University of Chicago lecture on the history of recent philosophy, though without reference to William James (very likely the most important philosopher of our era) or to Charles Sanders Pierce (the power and subtlety of whose thought is only beginning to be felt). Nor does he say much about Whitman or T. S. Eliot or Emily Dickinson. Oddly enough, Professor Bloom, the rhapsodist of Chicago and its university, is relentlessly European in his intellectual reference.

Bloom himself seems torn between Locke, Madison, and the heights and depths of Continental philosophy. He writes:

"God is dead," Nietzsche proclaimed. But he did not say this on a note of triumph, in the style of earlier atheism—the tyrant has been overthrown and man is now free. Rather he said it in the anguished tones of the most powerful and delicate piety deprived of its proper object. Man, who loved and needed, God, has lost his Father and Savior without possibility of resurrection.

Bloom thinks that the buzzwords of our articulate and semi-articulate culture come out of Nietzsche's abyss, filtered through Weber and Freud and packaged in a carton of cornflakes. The terms "commitment" (instead of love), "life-style" (which is designed to legitimate the bourgeois as they venture beyond good and evil), "sexual orientation" (instead of male and female), "identity" (instead of who you are and what you do), "relationship" (again, instead of love) represent Nietzsche turned upside-down, the bourgeoisification of the proposed *Uebermensch,* the hero as a feminized Dagwood Bumstead. In the presence of Nietzsche, talk about *values* is "twaddle." Nietzsche thought that God was dead, that there was no nature and objective structure of ethical meaning, and that therefore we had to reinvent ourselves in a heroic way. The old wide-sweeping classical conception of "nature"—that is to say, what is objectively true about human nature—was "dead."

On the strange fish that thrash about in the sea of this generation, Bloom is consistently coruscating. His *obiter dicta* during a lecture at Chicago must themselves be worth the price of the tuition. Bloom has a mind like a whirling sparkler, but it is deeply grounded in the classical conception of "nature." For example, here is Bloom on feminism:

The souls of men—their ambitious, warlike, protective, possessive character—must be dismantled in order to liberate women from their domination. Machismo—the polemical description of maleness or spiritedness, which was the central *natural* passion in men's souls in the psychology of the ancients, the passion of attachment and loyalty—was the villain, the source of the difference between the sexes. . . . A host of Dustin Hoffman and Meryl Streep types invade the schools, popular psychology, TV and the movies, making the [feminist] project respectable. Men tend to undergo the re-education somewhat sullenly but studiously, in order to avoid the opprobrium of the sexist label and to keep peace with their wives and girlfriends. And it is indeed possible to soften men. But to make them "care" is another thing, and the project must inevitably fail.

Bloom is especially brilliant on the subjugation of eros, that once powerful god, in our debilitated culture. "The student who made fun of playing a guitar under a girl's window will never read or write poetry under her influence. His defective eros cannot provide his souls with images of the beautiful, and it will remain coarse and slack." Like the ancient philosophers, Bloom knows that "nature" decrees a male "lust" for knowledge, for the good and the true, for the beyond. "Aristotle said that man had two peaks, each accompanied by intense pleasure: sexual intercourse and thinking. The human soul is a kind of elipse parabola, and its phenomena are spread between its two foci displaying their tropical variety and ambiguity."

Bloom is powerfully drawn to the nineteenth-century German philosophers. He knows how great a thinker Nietzsche was, and Bloom honors his attack upon Socrates and "reason." After all, Nietzsche did see that "reason" in itself never built a civilization. All civilizations are rooted in religion and myth. Nietzsche looked over the brink, rationally seeing that reason was not enough. Up against John Locke and Thomas Jefferson, the agonized Nietzsche wins the purely philosophical contest by a knockout.

But from the Nietzschean brink Professor Bloom does, as he should, draw back. Without answering Nietzsche on a philosophical level, he turns from the nihilistic *Strum and Drang* of nineteenth-century German philosophy to the practical political world of the Founding Fathers:

Freedom of thought and freedom of speech were proposed in theory, and in the practice of serious political reformers, in order to encourage the still voice of reason in a world that had always been dominated by fanaticisms and interests. How freedom of thought and speech came to mean the special encouragement and protection of fanaticism and interests is another of those miracles connected with the decay of the rational political order. The authors of *The Federalist* hoped their scheme of government would result in the preponderance of reason and rational men in the United States. They were not particularly concerned with protecting eccentric or mad opinions or life-styles. Such protection, which we now often regard as the Founders' central intention, is only an incidental result of the protection of reason, and as it loses its plausibility if reason is rejected. These authors did not respect the many religious sects or desire diversity for its own sake. The existence of many sects was permitted only to prevent the emergence of a single dominant one.

It is not exactly clear from Bloom's book how the university can escape its present cultural and spiritual anarchy. His answer is essentially Matthew Arnold's, though informed with greater philo-sophical knowledge than Arnold had at his disposal. Professor Bloom puts his faith in the "saving remnant" who will lead the philosophical life within the American academy. He regards the activity of philoso-phy as a good in its own right, and the activity of thought must be informed by the great books:

The model for all such efforts is the dialogues of Plato, which together rival the *Iliad* and the *Odyssey*, or even the Gospels. . . . Plato turns the personages of *The Clouds* into one of those civilization-constituting figures like Moses, Jesus or Achilles,who have a greater reality in men's souls than do their own flesh-and-blood contemporaries. . . . Socrates is the teacher of philosophy in an unbroken chain for two and a half millennia, extending from generation to generation through all the epochal changes. Plato insured this influence, not by reproducing Socrates' philosophy, in the manner of Aristotle or Kant, but by representing his action, more in the manner of Sophocles, Aristophanes, Dante, and Shakespeare.

It is the philosophic *life* to which the saving remnant must aspire, the continuing reexamination of those great questions, the activity of reexamination itself constituting the peak of civilization.

And yet the very book that looks to the university for salvation contains one of the most savage indictments of the contemporary American academy. It is conceivable but not very plausible that the civilization of the West will be revived by some impulse from these centers of moral and intellectual corruption. There are, no doubt, great isolated professors life Allan Bloom, but modern universities are, quite simply, out of business, at least for the time being.

I have a second caveat here, and it is not a minor one. Yes, indeed, it is highly desirable to refine the great questions of love, beauty, friendship, truth, loyalty, and so on, and it is highly desirable to keep the best examples of such discussion forever before us. All of this is certainly far superior to Women's Studies and the rest of the dreck that now clogs the university curriculum.

But there will be readers who object that Western thought is not simply an on-going conversation, ever renewing itself. Western thought *got somewhere*. In the Agora, the public forum at Athens, there was an inscription "To the Unknown God." That is as far as Greek philosophy, which means philosophy itself, had reached at that time. For the religious believer, however, God is not unknown. Bloom's brilliant dissection of the ills of relativism is weakened by his inattention to religious truth.

What the Hell
Was Socialism?

For my own part, I must say that the experience of ideas in the
air is an exciting one.

Lionel Abel

Reviewing William Barrett's memoir *The Truants: Adventures
Among the Intellectuals* (1982), Hilton Kramer began with some
general observations about the influence of coteries.

It is often a source of wonder and consternation for the powers that preside
over the great opinion-making organs of our society—in government, in
culture and in the media—to discover that the views so fluently dissemin-
ated by their vast enterprises have had their origin, more often than not, in
the ideas and controversies of obscure intellectual coteries.

Such coteries, he thinks, "have come—for better or worse—to exert
a decisive influence on the course of culture and society."

Yes, in many cases, that is so. One thinks of the Clapham Sect and
the Fabians, the Viennese psychoanalysts, the *philosophes* of the
eighteenth century, of original supply-siders of a few years ago, and
even of the Twelve Apostles. Hilton Kramer, however, is writing
about Barrett's book, which is about the "New York intellectuals,"
writers, most of whom, were associated with *Partisan Review* after
its founding in 1934.

One immediately feels a sense of unease about Kramer's associat-
ing these writers with groups that assuredly did make a large difference in politics and culture. First of all, William Barrett's memoir is
entitled *The Truants,* and he means precisely that they were by and
large truants from reality and responsibility. His memoir contains
largely affectionate portraits of Phillip Rahv, William Phillips, Lionel
Trilling, and especially Delmore Schwartz, but it looks back on the
whole cultural episode not only with affection but with condescen-

sion, though soaked in a Virgilian music. He certainly makes no
sweeping claim for their continuing cultural and political influence.
As his account tells us, they were "truants" fooling around with ideas
like "Marxism" and "socialism" and "revolution," ideas that have
little purchase on American reality. Furthermore, Barrett deals re-
spectfully and analytically with Lionel Trilling, whom he considers
the most intelligent of the New York intellectuals, but his treatment
of Trilling is to some degree a dissection. Barrett, a philosopher,
knows precisely the limitations of Trilling's naturalism and Freudianism and the disabling effect they could sometimes have on his
criticism—though he thinks that important themes in Trilling were
also precursors of neo-conservatism.

But there are more problems concerning Mr. Kramer's claim of
sweeping influence for this particular coterie in its radical phase. In
another essay on the subject, he argues, surely correctly, that the
great popularity of *Partisan Review* came during the years after
World War II, or maybe a little earlier, and continued well into the
1950s, when it "emerged for the first time" as the leading literary
and critical journal of the day. During that phase, however, there
was little trace in the magazine of the old radical militancy. When
in 1952 *PR* published a celebratory symposium called "Our Country
and Our Culture," which ran through four consecutive issues, the
only really virulent anticapitalist and anti-American contributions
came from two younger writers, Norman Mailer and Irving Howe,
who sounded in this context like visitors from some time warp who,
against all odds, had somehow managed to keep their Trotskyite
pieties completely quarantined from the experience of history.

As Mr. Kramer says, during the period of its greatest currency,
the politics of *PR* were anticommunist, antitotalitarian (with Hannah
Arendt the leading theorist), and reflective of a sharp awareness of
the death camps. It is precisely here that one would think the New
York intellectuals had their greatest impact, but Kramer has another,
and an interesting, idea.

The whole matter has now received recent and serious academic
assessment by Alexander Bloom and Terry A. Cooney, the latter
ending his book inexplicably with the year 1945. Alexander Bloom
is a young professor of history at Wheaton College, gently New Left
in sentiment, and he has done prodigious research. Even William
Phillips says that he learned some things from Bloom's book. But
the book apparently was extruded from a trunkful of five-by-eight

cards, is not well written, and has a wholly inadequate grasp of the changes that occurred in this coterie and why the changes came about. For Mr. Bloom, the really heroic days of the New York intellectuals were their earlier radical and Marxist ones. They had a fling with the Communist Party, broke with it—thought they remained radical—then, alas, became established and famous and, alas again, no longer radical. Some actually became anticommunist or neo-conservatives. The plot is a tragic one, as he sees it: material rise and moral fall.

It is an extraordinary development, this New Left sensibility, that now floods the younger professoriate. Marxism and communism are associated with innocence and virtue, while, at the same time, no thought whatever of practical action follows. Bloom and the myriad like him—some far worse—are in effect pastoral poets. It appears as if the changes in the views of the New York intellectuals had nothing to do with history—the Moscow purges, the murder of Trotsky, the Hitler-Stalin pact, Pearl Harbor, the Soviet betrayal of the Yalta promises over Poland and the seizure of Eastern Europe— let alone the huge fact that democratic capitalism, after a decade of depression, suddenly seemed viable. Events of that order do tend to concentrate the mind, but not for Professor Bloom.

ii

In a 1946 essay called "In Retrospect: Ten Years of *Partisan Review*," founders William Phillips and Phillip Rahv gave a concise account of the origins of *PR*. "Conceived in the fall of 1933 and born in February 1934, the magazine emerged from the womb of the Depression crying for a proletarian literature and a socialist America." The first nine issues, under the auspices of the New York John Reed Club, were avowedly communist. But Phillips and Rahv were also drawn to the modernist movement in literature, and from the start, tension built up between Communist Party orthodoxy and literary quality. Phillips and Rahv broke with the Party amidst much recrimination, found alternative financial backing, and started up a "new" *Partisan Review* in December 1937, adding to the editorial board Mary McCarthy (who was sleeping with Rahv), Fred Dupee, and Dwight Macdonald. The magazine was still socialist and revolutionary and undertook highly unproductive negotiations with Leon Trotsky in Mexico. (Trotsky turned out to be as rigid as the official Party Stalinists and, not accepting the role of "contributor" to the magazine, instead moved—of course—to take it over.) Ever polishing the purity of its socialism, *Partisan Review* envisioned a grand literary program in terms of Three Generations. Arising before World War I, there had been an authentic American radicalism, as in, for example, Dreiser, Anderson, Veblen, Robinson, and Sandburg. This native radicalism, reinforced by an emergent Depression Marxism, had brought proletarian literature into being—Mike Gold, Josephine Herbst, and the rest. These latter, however, were crude and propagandistic. Superior literary techniques had been developed by the great modernists, such as Joyce, Yeats, Pound, and Eliot, though these were hardly radicals or progressive. *Partisan Review* thus envisioned a purified socialism employing the refined techniques of the modernists and issuing in a grand, Third Generation 1930s synthesis. Needless to say, nothing much ever came of this ambitious program.

iii

But what, back there in the 1930s, did "socialism" really mean for these New York intellectuals?

Sidney Hook was close to the *Partisan Review* circle at the time and a principal adjudicator of Marxist questions for them. He was also for a brief period close to the Communist Party and was even approached by Earl Browder about committing espionage. In his recent political autobiography, Hook is helpful in his account of his socialism.

In my case, as in so many others, allegiance to socialism at first appeared to be primarily an articulation of a feeling of moral protest against remediable evils that surrounded us. . . . The appeal of the idea was threefold. First was its apparent rationality. . . . Second, and perhaps the most profound source of the Socialist appeal, was its moral concern, its sense of human fraternity. . . . Third, and this appealed strongly to the young, was its heroic element. Human beings, instead of being creatures of circumstance beyond their control . . . could now become, within the limits of nature, master of their own fate.

Hook, however, in time became acutely aware of the weaknesses of a socialism so described. "A curious feature of the socialist faith before World War I was its trust in—perhaps it would be more accurate to say its absence of scepticism about—state power." Such socialists "scrupulously defined socialism to exclude dictatorship even before the terrifying visage of bolshevism appeared." In other words, the socialist dream neglected to bother about one of the fundamental questions of political philosophy—whether you go to Aristotle or Madison.

Lionel Abel in his recent collection of essays entitled *Important Nonsense* (1987) has shrewd things to say about Hook's relationship to socialism. He notices that Sidney Hook replaced Hegel with John Dewey in the Marxist matrix, dropping the Hegelian metaphysical "religion" in favor of contemporary instrumentalist "science." Then the fusion of Dewey and Marx blew to smithereens, Dewey obliterating Marx. Another way to put it might be that Hook simply found "democracy" and "socialism" to be incompatible and chose the former. As Hook kept reinterpreting Marxism in the direction of Dewey, says Abel, the Marxism of *Partisan Review* "in practice tended to include any critical approach that showed an interest in social and historical context."

Irving Howe was less analytical and less detached. For him, socialism remained a "passion," even as in subsequent years he tried without much success to redefine it so that it had contemporary relevance. Alfred Kazin's youthful socialism became something he calls radicalism, difficult to define or apply, except as a rhetorical stance.

William Barrett, who entered the *Partisan Review* circle through his close friendship with Delmore Schwartz and became an editor in 1945, was a socialist during the 1930s but later rejected it.

The Great Depression hung over our heads, and socialism seemed like a simple and inevitable answer. I have to think now, however, that the same reasonably intelligent and alert youth I then was would have every reason today to be wary of socialism. The whole experience of our century weighs heavily against it; and if we are not going to learn from that history, our position is indeed desperate.

This theme is a recurrent one in *The Truants.* In 1946 Albert Camus rebuked Barrett for calling himself a Marxist. Now Barrett writes,

I think Camus was dead right. Our kind of Marxism was a luxury; it never had to sully itself by coming to power, and did not even have to ponder the problem of power generally and its crucial concentration in the modern state; on the other hand, we could keep the purity of our dissent by being detached from what we regarded as the wickedness of American capitalism. . . . But in fact we were treading on air.

iv

Nevertheless, if their then passionately affirmed Marxist and revolutionary commitments look vaporous and even comic from our present perspective—"intellectual follies," to cite Abel's title—the particular cosmopolitan perspective of the group was important and almost certainly counted in terms of influence.

One important feature of the magazine's agenda was a successful effort to try to enrich the American literary consciousness with the best recent European writing. Frequent in its pages were contributions from, or critical elucidations of, Eliot, Joyce, Rilke, Mann, Gide, Proust, Sartre, Kafka, Auden, Spender, Koestler, Orwell. To put it in negative terms, the cosmopolitan style of *Partisan Review* helped to make derisory the declamatory-sentimental Americanism of MacLeish, Anderson, Sandburg, Brooks, and the like.

Partisan Review cosmopolitanism meant more than acknowledging good European writing. It meant urbanism as against the rural (in a famous episode, Trilling managed—but only just—to bury the hatchet with Frost); it meant science, secularism, rationalism, and a correlative rejection of the mystical and religious, the nationalistic, the rigid and static, and the antitheoretical. Edmund Wilson, whom the *Partisan Review* writers much admired but who kept his distance from the magazine (which he at least once called the *Partisanski Review*), argued provocatively that politics had little to teach literature, but that literature might well have something to teach politics, and that "Flaubert was superior to Marx." In their intellectual development—indeed, in their allotment of space in the magazine—the editors tacitly agreed.

Naturally the *Partisan* critics took delight in polishing off the sentimentally Americanist art of "The People, Yes" Popular Front period. They called it *kitsch,* a term first applied by Clement Greenberg, or "cultural Bolshevismus," a Dwight Macdonald coinage, and saw it as using sentiment to cover up the truth of the liberal-Stalinist alliance within the Popular Front. One of the most powerful statements ever made against the liberal-communist obfuscating alliance was a 1946 editorial written by William Barrett entitled "The Liberal Fifth Column." Reviewing Malraux's Popular Front novel *Man's Hope,* Fred Dupee found it propagandistic, flawed in its grasp of reality, sentimental, and a sign of Malraux's intellectual decay. Rahv was suspicious of Silone's growing mysticism, and Abel found in Silone a dismaying shift from the head to the heart, which coincided with the surrounding evasions and emulsifications. Leslie Fielder thought that Hiss and his defenders were typical products of the Popular Front period, and he was undoubtedly right. Sometimes this criticism may have gone too far, as in Trilling's attack on Dreiser. On the surface at least, the New York intellectuals were firm democrats and committed to the highest values intellectually.

v

For about fifteen years or a few more after World War II, a tough-minded and combative antitotalitarianism was the normal position among the New York intellectuals, and socialist themes virtually disappeared from *Partisan Review*. Indeed, *Dissent* was founded in 1954 as "a reaction to the gradual but steady disintegration of the socialist movement." Meyer Schapiro, a founder, saw *Dissent* simply as critical of the right and of the Soviet Union. But *Dissent* socialism, whatever its content, never established itself as having the appeal and clout of *Partisan Review*.

Lionel Trilling, Phillip Rahv, William Phillips, Leslie Fiedler, and other *Partisan Review* contributors, along with Irving Kristol, a bit outside the immediate circle, and Daniel Bell, gave antitotalitarian themes varying degrees of prominence in their work. Trilling, for example, certainly rejected socialism by teaching by example the truth of multiplicity and complexity. In his later phase, he even distanced himself from the great modernists in a famous essay that repeated the title of an Arnold essay, "On the Modern Element in Literature." Trilling, always ambivalent, seemed to feel more at home among the Victorians. In the magazine he founded, *Politics*, Dwight Macdonald excoriated the 1948 fellow-traveling presidential campaign of Henry Wallace.

But around the year 1958, something strange happened to the New York intellectuals. *Partisan Review*, which had always and under every circumstance taken a virtually puritan insistence on the very highest standards in literature and which had indeed broken with the Communist Party over modernist literary excellence, suddenly seemed to throw such standards overboard. It embraced the New Left/New Sensibility of the period, as exemplified by Susan Sontag's famous essay on "Camp," which amounted to a brilliant legitimation of trash. Sontag's essay was so provocative that any editor would have been proud to publish it, but an editor might have thought to answer her argument by saying that, after all, there is a difference between Mozart and Andy Warhol. Worse followed. Mary McCarthy found her way from "Our Country and Our Culture" to—of all places—Hanoi and wrote up her experiences there absolutely ga-ga. So much for her celebrated "intelligence." Phillip Rahv reappeared as a professor at Brandeis and a born-again Leninist, with a townhouse on Beacon Hill. He launched a new and evil magazine called *Modern Occasions*, in which, among other things, he printed a vicious attack on Lionel Trilling as a man who had sold out the radical cause.

All of this gave credibility to Norman Podhoretz's later summary:

I now realize that neither *PR*'s anti-communism in the thirties nor its defense of "our country and our culture" in the fifties was powerful enough to overcome its unshakable commitment to the Left. *That*, it turns out, was what truly defined the tradition of *PR*: the struggle to maintain solidarity with the Left even when one recognizes that the Soviet Union was (yes) an evil empire and that the United States was with all its faults a decent society.... The vision of this utopian Left is, it has now become clear, far more precious to all of them than the real civilization in which we live in the here and now.

Hilton Kramer agreed:

While enthusiastically embracing the rewards which their new status brought them—professorships in the universities, staff jobs on the *New Yorker*, and the loving attention of the media—they were none the less haunted by the specter of the radical vocation and possessed by the rhetoric it had bequeathed to them. Which is why the political and cultural upheavals of the Sixties represented such a crisis for the New York intellectuals, and in fact marked the termination of their movement.

Too many of them had not abandoned the Left at all, at least not emotionally.

In his fine memoir, Lionel Abel places the end of the New York intellectuals as a group in the year 1958 in a scene of high comedy and also, perhaps, intellectual tragedy. Meeting in the Manhattan townhouse of millionaire leftist Joseph Buttinger was a representative group: Dwight Macdonald, Mary McCarthy, Harold Rosenberg, William Phillips, Norman Podhoretz, Paul Goodman, Hannah Arendt, Eric Bentley, Meyer Schapiro. The issue was Boris Pasternak. He had won the Nobel Prize but had been denied permission by the Soviets to go to Stockholm to receive it. The business at hand was the formulation of a joint statement protesting, at least in the name of literature, the treatment being accorded Pasternak. The group could not agree on the simplest statement of support for Pasternak, Abel says, because of the fear that what one did or said might be regarded as contrary, and even harmful, to the Left. . . . Also, there was not one person in the room who then knew with any degree of clarity just what it was still possible to mean by the term "Left." . . . And the fact is that the New York intelligentsia came apart simply because it could not agree that it was in the interest of anything that could be called the Left to protest Pasternak's treatment by the Russians.

Thus the New York intellectuals began in 1937 with a key decision by Phillips and Rahv that Yeats and Joyce were more important than the Communist Party, and so we had the *Partisan Review.* But in 1958, Boris Pasternak was not more important than a ghostly "Left" that could not even be defined. Socialism started out as a idealistic protest against remediable conditions, seriously flawed though its theory was. It ended in pure funk and cultural self-intimidation. This may well be, as Hilton Kramer thinks, its continuing legacy.

vi

There are many fine things in these memoirs and in the academic studies of them, and one finishes them with a sense of fine intelligence and, especially, verve derailed to a considerable degree by the socialist fantasy, which remained an emotion even when emptied of specific content. More memoirs are forthcoming, including Diana Trilling's recollections of her husband, and one wishes that we had James Burnham's own memoirs of the period—Burnham, that mild and temperate rationalist whom Alexander Bloom thinks moved to "the extreme right" (as if he had become some sort of Bircher, so skewed is Bloom's political perspective; Burnham in fact supported Nelson Rockefeller on several occasions, including his vice presidency).

But for many pleasures and matters of interest along the road, let one of them do service for the rest. It occurs in William Barrett's *The Truants,* when he discusses Trilling's naturalism and Freudianism, very firmly held positions, in connection with Trilling's famous essay on Wordsworth's "Immorality Ode." Barrett writes:

It is only on repeated reading that one becomes aware how uncompromisingly naturalistic and Freudian Trilling's outlook is. . . . He begins, for example, by telling us that Wordsworth's ode is not about immortality at all. This would be news to poor Wordsworth unless he was altogether woolgathering when he gave the poem its title.

The perspective of the New York intellectuals, as a group, had its philosophical limitations, and Barrett, a philosopher, sees them.

Willmoore Kendall
American

Willmoore Kendall remains, beyond any possibility of challenge, the most important political theorist to have emerged in the twenty-odd years since the end of World War II. Nevertheless, he was, for all the immense sanity of his genius, a strange and solitary figure, isolated not only from the academic establishment—though he was a great teacher and profoundly changed the lives of some of his students—but from any establishment whatsoever. It is only the first of the terrible polarities with which he grappled that he was, personally and intellectually, so solitary and yet also the rediscoverer of the historic American political orthodoxy.

There are many ways in which Kendall was deeply indeed, almost terrifyingly American, but surely his isolation was one of them. It was undoubtedly an isolation inextricable from his genius itself, from his capacity to think his way through convention and assumption finally to arrive at the irreducible and crystalline truth. By talking with him or reading his essays, one could see that his was, so to speak, a "typical strangeness," analogous to that of the pioneer pushing West alone, developing idiosyncrasies, yet never doubting his own American "orthodoxy," or to the captain of a whaler—Ahab, say—moving through strange and lonely seas. One side of the American character is its optimism, its capability, its health and gregariousness. But how often it is that the American genius is isolated and driven by obscure furies—Melville, Hawthorne, Hemingway. Kendall was in this vein, and of this rank. Yet even Thorstein Veblen, in any comparison of the two, seems almost a genial conformist.

I first met Willmoore Kendall in Paris in the fall of 1965 when I was driving up from Catalonia on the way to an academic winter at

Oxford. He was living in a rather grim Paris suburb, Meudon-Belle-vue, and working on Rousseau. I had admired his essays and we had corresponded; I looked him up. I also knew his legend, and so I was entirely unprepared for the considerate and civilized individual, elegant to the point of self-consciousness, whom I met: a black turtleneck shirt and splendid checked sport coat on a tall, handsome, almost courtly man, though also in visage worn and deeply lined. We had drinks in a left-bank cafe and went on to dinner in a Greek restaurant where the food was superb.

For this initial impression I was, as I say, totally unprepared, for I was aware of the legend. It was said at *National Review* that Kendall was never on speaking terms with more than one member of the group there at a time, though the identity of that one favored individual changed from month to month, Kendall disengaging from one person and, simultaneously, sending out feelers to the next one. His drinking feats were referred to with awe. He had been replaced as book editor of the magazine, it seemed, because he had been obliged to defend his conduct of the section *after* lunch. And, embedded in the major mythology of the U.S. Congress is the time he passed out noisily in the House dining room. Once, it is also said, he was arrested for speeding on the Jersey turnpike only to inform an incredulous judge that, no, your honor, he had no driver's license— never, in fact had had one—and, no, now did not feel the need of one. The judge, in despair, or perhaps in touch with the incommen-surate, let him go.

At Yale Kendall has also passed into the realm of legend, for as a member of the faculty, he was absolutely unique. From his first appointment in 1947 he was embroiled in controversy, and, though tenured, he was never given a promotion or a salary raise. His personal impact upon his colleagues was so shattering that he was encouraged to take frequent leaves of absence and never, in fact, remained at Yale for more than two consecutive years at a time.

Nevertheless, he was one of the most popular teachers on the scene and had a decisive effect upon the lives of many students. Everywhere he appeared, he was a felt force. One well-known but uncomprehending journalist described him as a wild Yale don, of extreme and highly abstract views, who could get a conversation into the shouting stage faster than anyone within memory. This description does suggest something of Kendall's violence of personality but is misleading as to the character of his "views." They were civilized, central, and startingly gentle.

In 1961, Yale said goodbye. The episode was bizarre and, so far as I know, unique in academic history. Kendall, on one of his frequent leaves, had settled in Spain and, as the humor struck him, had phoned the administration and said, well, you don't seem to be able to take me; how about paying me off and calling it quits? The check was instantly on the way. Yale bought back his tenure for $25,000 and gratefully bade farewell.

Of all this bizarre history there was not so much as a hint in the scholarly and urbane gentleman with whom I sipped cool drinks in the Paris dusk that fall. The waiters bustled about. Over *there* was the site of Cluny, whence pilgrims had journeyed south to Santiago da Compastella in the northeast corner of Spain, one of the great, and civilizing, pilgrimages of the European Middle Ages. What would Europe have been without Cluny, without Santiago? Did I realize that Camus' *Plague* was a parable of the Social Contract? We must all go to the San Fermin next spring in Pamplona. He might visit us in Oxford. It would be good to see Pembroke College again. But the, almost in passing came the touch consonant with his legend: he was, it seemed—and he was impatient with the delay—processing his first two marriages simultaneously through annulment proceedings before the Vatican Rota. Ah, his Roman lawyer was a pedant. And, to be sure, though others—one man perhaps two—had had *two* marriages annuled, he was the *first* in the two thousand year history of the Church to try to annul two *simultaneously*. He thought he would succeed. We speculated about the astonishment of Paul VI.

Later that year he visited me and my family at Oxford. While he was there, it became apparent that he was suffering from a dangerous heart condition and could sustain himself only through sudden recourse to nitro pills. He loved Oxford. He had been an precocious student, and his Rhodes Scholarship in 1932 had brought him here to Pembroke, introduced him to political philosophy, and changed his life. Nevertheless, he was a terribly sick man. I remember once walking along High Street with him; he suddenly stopped and said go on. He leaned against the New College wall and took a nitro pill, which revived him temporarily. Still, it was a marvelous week or so. He had brought his evening clothes, and he went back to some ceremonial event at his old college. He found to his immense delight that his peers there knew his work and knew his stature. The dons, he thought, were much less ideological than American academics.

Meanwhile, his marvelous talk went on. "What *was* the relationship between the Philadelphia Constitution—the Preamble especially—and the Bill of Rights, which seems to embody an entirely different theory of government? Not the whole Bill—really only the First Amendment. The rest are common-law specificities. And *what* do *you* think is the relationship between these two documents and the Declaration's abstractions? What *individual* rights do *you* have under the Constitution? And how would you sustain them against legislation by the *Congress*?" Great, deep questions opened up. He seemed to roll the matter back to the terms in which it must have been considered by the Founders. "What do you make of the fact that the Preamble *deliberately* puts 'justice' and the 'domestic tranquility' in rhetorical balance—neither having primacy? How does that fit in with the *theory* of the Constitution?"

That year, as American perplexities in Indochina were deepening, I remember one startling thing he said. At the time I thought it part of the violence of emotion that lurked in some corner of his being. I was full of Strausz-Hupé and protracted conflict, of Maxwell Taylor and graduated response, of both Kissinger and Kahn and the impulse to analyze international conflict in terms of game theory. Kendall brushed this aside. No, neither the American character nor the American *system*, he said, could wage protracted conflict, not year-after-year, grinding boring conflict. Such would be bound to fragment the consensus upon which American institutional authority rests. He then terrified the workmen around us in an English pub. "Only two countries today," he said, "can plausibly contemplate atomic war. And only one can seriously contemplate it," said leeringly.

ii

Another time we sat in an inn called the Rose about ten miles from Oxford, where the Thames is a fresh and tiny river, actually patrolled by swans. Matthew Arnold country. I learned that he had been born in a small town in Oklahoma, his family having come westward from Kentucky. We have lately been hearing a great deal about middle America, but for Kendall it was a felt fact, part of his mind and his identity. He liked to call himself an "Appalachians-to-the-Rockies patriot." The overwhelming emotional fact of his life was his father, a blind Methodist minister, clearly a formidable mind, whose ministry took him from one small Oklahoma town to another as he attended to the needs of their independent citizenry. His father's blindness and consequent need for someone to read to him accelerated what would in any event have been a precocious development. The boy taught himself to read by the time he was two by picking out words and then sentences on a typewriter he had been given as a toy. By the time he was four, he was able to read aloud to his father from adult texts, and to this early habit of oral reading may be traced the spoken quality of his own later prose, one of the most distinctive stylistic achievements of twentieth-century writing. In other ways, too, the blind minister had a lasting effect upon his son. As a mature man, Kendall retained undiminished the awe a child is likely to feel for his father, and so exacting was the standard he felt his father to have set that until the last years of his teaching career he did not presume to lecture extemporaneously—everything had to be organized and in correct proportion; everything had to be *there* on the page.

Kendall graduated from high school at the age of thirteen, a year earlier than most students enter it, and became the youngest freshman ever, until then, to enter Northwestern University. Simultaneously, he became the youngest full-time reporter on the Chicago *Herald and Examiner*. When he completed his Bachelor of Arts degree, he toyed with the idea of many careers—he would teach, he would go to Europe, he would enter the foreign service or become a drama critic. At length he decided to do graduate work in Romance languages, first at Northwestern, later at the University of Illinois, where he completed the coursework for a doctorate. At this point, a Rhodes Scholarship, taking him to Oxford where he read politics and economics, turned him in a new direction. Henceforth his language skills—he spoke Spanish and French and read Russian, German, and Italian—would be ancillary to his work as a political theorist. In 1938 he returned to the University of Illinois with his Oxford Bachelor's and Master's degrees and finished his doctorate in political science. His dissertation, *John Locke and Majority Rule* (1941), has become a classic in the field of political theory and points to what would become the dominant theme of his political thought: what conditions must prevail for majority rule to produce good government?

This question was deeply rooted in his background and experience. The America in which he had grown up had as part of its identity its historical experiences as a free—that is, as a self-governing—people. It had shown the world that majority rule could work. But how, and under what theoretical conditions?

Earlier than most American intellectuals, Kendall had become aware of the threat posed to the people's liberties by alien ideologies, for his academic career was punctuated by jobs that took him to South America and to Spain as a journalist. Initially in Spain he supported the Republic, but he quickly became aware of the extent of the Communist influence on the government side and thereafter favored the Nationalists. Subsequently, when the hard choice was between communism and some right-wing authoritarian regime, he chose the latter as by far the lesser evil. Despite the fury shown toward them by the American press, the right-wing regimes were generally much less oppressive than the communist alternative, and above all, they posed no threat to the United States whereas the expansion of communist power most certainly did.

Kendall's provisional support for such foreign authoritarian regimes, however, did not at all abate his allegiance to the unique system of government established by his beloved Constitution. The American system *must* be made to work, all of his writings say in effect, and, to be sure it does work, we *must* understand its principles; for if our system does fail, the alternatives are only too clear:— the abandonment of self-government in favor of an authoritarian government of the Left or the Right. In the last paragraph of the last essay he ever wrote, he concludes:

What I do take sides on is the thesis of the *Federalist Papers*, namely: That America's mission in the world is to prove to the world that self-government—that is, government by the people through a representative assembly which, by definition, calls the plays—is possible. What I do take sides on is our solemn obligation, as Americans, to value the good health of the American political system—the system we have devised in order to prove to the world that self-government is possible—above the immediate demands, however just and right, of any minority. What I do take sides on is government by consensus, which, I repeat, requires of minorities demanding drastic change that they bide their time until they have pleaded their case successfully before the bar of public—not merely majority—opinion. What I do take sides on is the Preamble of the Constitution, which gives equal status to justice and domestic tranquility, and so pledges us to pursue them simultaneously and not even in the "case" that seems "dearest" to a protesting minority, subordinate domestic tranquility to justice.

iii

For all his urbanity and cosmopolitanism, Willmoore Kendall cherished the vernacular, and especially regional habits of speech. They preserved, in their own way, the particular and the concrete and could strike through more polished, more conventional, and more academic words to convey a feeling of recognition. His own prose style is characterized by a sort of dialogue between the vernacular and the polite, the long sentences with their oral rhythms winding and unwinding between the two modes. It is much to the point here that his first publication was a book called *Baseball: How to Play It and How to Watch It*. He like to use, as I recall, a striking and oddly disturbing phrase that I had never heard before and have never heard since, but that probably he recalled from his Oklahoma childhood. The American people, he would remark, continue to live their political tradition "in their hips." He meant that although they continue to live according to their traditional modes and orders, they have forgotten in their articulate life what those modes and orders are. In the life of the nation, a gap had opened between *doxa* and *episteme*—between, on the one hand, unconscious assumption and practice and, on the other, conscious idea. The division was reflected, Kendall saw, in the "two majorities," presidential and congressional. Typically the president appealed to the regnant abstractions; he adumbrated vast new "frontiers" and "great societies"; he spoke of the unfinished agenda of democracy, of things like "equality of opportunity": and idealistic goals abroad. Moreover, *both* presidential candidates, competing for "swing" constituencies in the large states, were likely to employ this mode. Presidential rhetoric was much more in tune with the language of the academy and the media, and the thrust of presidential action was likely, though not always, to be in the direction this rhetoric adumbrated. Congress, on the other hand, represented a different constituency. The congressman was closer to local feeling and interest. His concerns were less sweeping and ideal and did not as easily go with the customary rhetoric of idealism. Congress, he saw, was much less articulate but also much more successful. It usually prevailed, to the endless frustration of ideologues desiring to actualize the abstractions.

Kendall's brilliant discussion of "equality of opportunity" in his late essay on "Basic Issues Between Conservatives and Liberals" provides a concrete instance of the way this works. On the one hand, in the public forum, no articulate resistance exists to the idea that "equality of opportunity" is at the very top of our political agenda. The man who challenged it openly would soon find himself publicly discredited. On the other hand, writes Kendall,

Any way you look at it, progress on the equalization of opportunity front, if there be progress at all (which I doubt), is glacially slow. Newborn babies in the United States are *not* born to the equality of opportunity that liberals claim for them as, literally, their birthright, but what is more, nobody thinks they are. More important still: even measures that might move things just a little towards making good the supposed right to equal opportunity are stoutly—and on the whole successfully—resisted all along the front. Most important of all: really drastic measures on behalf of equality of opportunity are not even proposed—not, I imagine, because they wouldn't be in favor of such measures, but because sound strategic instinct tells them that such measures are not politically possible.

The paradox thus is surfaced: equality of opportunity is the only morally respectable stance in the public forum, but it is politically impossible. It is not that a counter-argument does not exist, but that it is "silent"—both known and not known—and never articulated. The "congressional majority" defeats or tables or ignores liberal measures when they do come before it, but it does so without articulating a "position."

An important aspect of Kendall's political writing is his effort to give voice to that silent side—to the majority position. Edmund Burke once compared the English people to oxen grazing in a meadow. Large and silent, they fill the meadow with their bulk and their numbers, but it is the swarm of tiny crickets that fills the air with its chirping. Kendall's view of the American people was similar, and he tried—with brilliant success—to sound the argument in opposition to the crickets.

For example, here is the known but unarticulated case against equality of opportunity.

The equality of opportunity goal, the majority would say, is unrealistic, impossible to achieve, *utopian*—and because utopian, *dangerous*. In order to equalize opportunity in any meaningful way, you would have, first of all—as clear-headed political philosophers have always seen—to neutralize that great carrier and perpetrator of unequal opportunity, the *family*, and you can do that, really do it, only by abolishing the family, which we will not let you do because that would be wrong. You would have, in the second place, to abolish poverty, and we do not believe anybody knows how to do that . . . and the schemes one hears of now and then for making the pie big enough to go around do not commend themselves to us, either intellectually or morally; usually they involve one kind or another of *socialism*, about which we believe *both* that it is morally wrong and that it won't work—that it will in fact impoverish people rather than improving their lot. In a word, you can't equalize opportunity, and it is wrong to talk as if you could—wrong, to go no further, because you encourage many people to think themselves entitled to things they cannot have, to think they are being treated unjustly when in fact all is being done for them that can be done—more, indeed, in many cases, than ought to be done because more than is good for them. All that creates unnecessary and unwarranted resentment and causes dissension among us, kicks up trouble. Finally, we repudiate your equality of opportunity goal because it rests on a false reading of the all-men-are-created-equal clause and makes us forget, keeps us from acting on, the true meaning of those words.

To perceive the split between *doxa* and *episteme*, Kendall saw, led logically to an investigation of its sources. Where and when did it occur? Was it always part of our political history, or did it appear at some point or other? What *was* our political tradition? What really was, in the above passage, "the true meaning of those words,"—the all-men-are-created-equal clause?

iv

The "ordinary" books—as Kendall liked to call them—on American political history, books like those of Farand, Curti, Hartz, or Rossiter, assume as a matter of course that we have a single political tradition enshrined in the Declaration of Independence the Constitution, and the Bill of Rights. At the center of Kendall's work is the recognition that profound problems exist as regards this received assumption, that in these "founding documents"—at least as *conventionally* interpreted—there exists a contradicition in political theory and, further, that this contradiction, if fully explicated, defines the political issues that now divide us. Kendall concludes that contemporary students of American politics must begin by analyzing this apparent contradiction, and in this I think there can be little doubt that he is correct.

Though the bulk of Kendall's writing consists of a complex meditation upon the issues to be raised here, his most extended treatment of the matter occurs in a series of lectures he delivered several years ago at Vanderbilt University, and published by the Louisiana State University Press under the title *The Basic Symbols of the American Political Tradition* (co-authored with George W. Carey; 1970). He observes, to begin with, that the Philadelphia Convention in 1787 almost unanimously opposed the adoption of a Bill of Rights, and he raises the question of whether a Bill of Rights—or, more precisely, the theory of inalienable individual rights—is compatible with the government established by the Philadelphia Constitution or with the political theory of the Preamble. He notices that though the Declaration does talk about inalienable rights and about equality, the Preamble, which sets forth the purposes for which the new government is being established, says nothing at all about rights or equality—though surely this was the place to talk about them if it were thought proper to do so.

Is the American tradition, then, one of protecting individual rights and of equality, or is it that of the Preamble? The question presses itself upon us, for it is obvious enough that in a given situation the goals of the Preamble might come into conflict with a "right." Which takes precedence—the goal of "domestic tranquility" or the supposed "right" of free speech? Suppose the goal of equality, allegedly implicit in the Declaration, comes into conflict with the obligation to provide for the common defense? or the maintenance of a more perfect union? The goals set forth in the Preamble might come into conflict at any number of points with the rights said to be enumerated or implied in the Declaration or in the Bill of Rights, especially in the First Amendment. Kendall also reminds us that the men who were prominent at the outbreak of the War of Independence and who might be called the "rights" men—Sam Adams, Tom Paine, Patrick Henry, and so on—tended to recede from view as the war went on and to give way to another breed altogether. Patrick Henry refused to attend the Philadelphia Convention. Other "rights" men walked out and refused to sign—George Mason is a prominent example—and the Constitution itself was widely accused of betraying the "spirit" of the Declaration.

I would like to set aside for just one moment the question of whether the contradiction adduced here is real or only apparent; Kendall at length concluded that it was apparent and that it has its source in a later misinterpretation of the key documents. But even that misinterpretation, it is clear, derives from something profoundly true about American culture. No misinterpretation that becomes not only widespread but also pervasive could come from nowhere—its roots must be deep in the national identity. And the sense of contradiction, apparent or real, that Kendall defines in these documents has a familiar ring to the student of American literature, for

that literature tells us that the very form of American experience is
one of contradiction and polarity, that it exhibits, as Henry James
remarked, a "rich passion for extremes." In his well-known book on
the American novel, Richard Chase observes—indeed, it is the thesis
of his book—that "the best and most characteristic American fiction
has been shaped by the contradicitions and not by the unities and
harmonies of our culture." He adduces a number of such polarities,
beginning with those of New England Calvinism and its opposition
of the kingdom of light and the kingdom of darkness, or election
and damnation. Elsewhere Chase, sharpening a formulation of Lionel
Trilling's, describes American culture as divided between conservative feeling and radical idea, a contrast that might well seem to be
adumbrated in the contrast between the government established by
the Constitution, designed to reflect a deliberate sense of community, and the universals and absolutes allegedly to be found in the
Declaration and the First Amendment.

Kendall has a number of profound things to say about this contradiction, but in his Vanderbilt lectures and in his later writings he
reaches the following conclusion: yes, there are at *present* alternative political traditions virtually at war in America; but, no, when
read carefully and in the context of their own time, the founding
documents do not in fact reveal the contradiction and thus do not
themselves provide the basis for our current ideological war. It is
true, he says, that the language of the Declaration has been read as
asserting a "right" of "equality," but it was Abraham Lincoln who in
fact first articulated such a reading and *made* it part of the political
tradition—or rather, part of one of the two political traditions. In
its own time, the language did not carry this meaning and need not
necessarily be so read today. The Declaration means to say only that
men are created equal in their right to set up a system of government, by which they then shall be governed by majority consent,—
not that the task of that government shall be thenceforth to render
them equal. One of the paradoxes of the American system, in fact,
is that although men are "equal" in the sense that they equally grant
or withhold consent, they are part of a social system that has always
been hierarchical. Kendall traces this paradox back to the beginnings, to the Mayflower Compact: all the free men aboard the ship
gave their consent to the Compact, but only eleven out of forty-one
were called "Mister."

If read as stipulating a right of equality, the Declaration does contradict the theory of the Preamble; if read, correctly, as affirming men's equality in having their consent solicited, the clause is logically ancillary to the Constitution and not at all in conflict with it. Men are equal in their right to govern themselves through a representative assembly and to enjoy, as individuals, those (but only those) rights that the assembly confers in its pursuit of the general good. When the clause is read as implying a mission to establish an overall equality of condition, Kendall argues, this is clearly something quite different from the intent of both Declaration and Preamble and, in fact, is one of our leading heresies. It expresses itself not by appeal to the meaning of the founding documents but to a series of quasi-messianic leaders—Washington, Jefferson, Lincoln, Roosevelt, Kennedy—"each of whom sees more deeply into the specifically American problem, which is posed by the all-men-are-created-equal clause of the Declaration of Independence. America will build a New Jerusalem which will be a commonwealth of free and equal men, free men yes, but especially equal men, and will cause it to spread over the face of the entire earth." If that requires the remaking of human nature, making the unequal equal, well, no task is too great for the genius of the messianic and, significantly, *suffering* leader. Through Him we shall be reborn.

But what of the other famous right, the right of free speech? One reading of the First Amendment, Kendall point out, would mean definitively that the United States is an "open society," that no questions are in fact closed and that sanctions of any sort against the right of free speech are illegitimate and unconstitutional. This might be called the Hugo Black reading of the Amendment. Yet the language of the Amendment, Kendall points out, mentions no such right, is careful *not* to, and cannot legitimately be construed as sustaining one. "Congress," indeed, "shall make no law . . . abridging the freedom of speech." But the Tenth Amendment makes it clear that this statement applies specifically to *Congress,* not to the state governments, and that the thrust of the Amendment as it stands is to strengthen the authority of the state government as against the central one, *not* the individual against all government. The First Amendment, says Kendall, gives the states a legislative monopoly in the area of speech. Thus James Madison, the author of the Bill of Rights, could validly claim in answer to its opponents that the Amendments would not "endanger the beauty of the government" established by the Philadelphia Constitution and would not "weaken its frame or abridge its usefulness"—would not, that is, introduce a theoretical contradiction. The contradiction comes to the fore only when the later idea of the "open society" is read back into the original language.

To bring these issues to the fore in this way illuminates the argument at the center of our political conflict at the present time. Is the American government committed to the establishment of equality among its citizens? Does the First Amendment mean that America is an "open" society, has no "orthodoxy"?

Related to this argument are contrasting conceptions of the role of the different branches of government. What is the form of the American government that, according to Kendall, emerged from the founding documents? His answer is complex, original, and convincing. The Philadelphia Convention (as indeed the *Federalist* explains) established a government not, as we are now generally told, of three independent and equal or "balanced" branches, but a government of legislative supremacy—a supremacy now inhibited by individual rights. In the last resort, Congress has final weapons that it may use against the other two branches and that they lack against it. Does the Supreme Court have the last word on a given issue? Most certainly not. Congress can remove an act from the jurisdiction of the Court, can "pack" the Court, can initiate the amendment process, can impeach justices and can refuse to pay them.

Why, then, does the Court so often have its way? Why does Congress so seldomly employ a weapon of the last resort, as it did when the Court declared the income tax unconstitutional? Kendall proposes a variety of explanations: that the issues generally are not of sufficient urgency, or that the Court, aware of the power of Congress, tailors its decisions so as not to force a showdown. But more importantly, he concludes, we have in historical fact been governed by an "understanding" of the Constitution that enjoins "restraint" upon the three branches. Congress does not forget that it possesses ultimate weapons, but it believes that it should not throw its weight around, and that its restraint enforms a similar restraint on the part of the other branches. In Kendall's view, this morality of restraint is articulated in the *Federalist* and has become the political ethos according to which the branches have historically functioned. The Constitution will work to permit the emergence of the deliberate sense of the nation only if the three branches move together on the great issues.

But there exists an alternative to this historic working of the Constitution, an alternative rooted in the theory of absolute and inalienable individual rights. The Court might assert such a right without consulting the deliberate sense of the nation. If the court deems the "right" to exist and to be inalienable, it need not wait upon the deliberate sense. The Court might thus force a showdown, which it could not win but which would fracture the ethos of restraint according to which we have historically been governed. Such a danger is implicit in the entire "rights" theory of government and in the aggrandizement of the Court and its mystique. Kendall considered the Court to be embarked upon a course that would lead to such a confrontation; he prayed that it would forbear.

But, it might now be asked, what prevents Congress—if, under the central or orthodox American tradition, Congress is really supreme—what prevents *Congress* from violating the deliberate sense of the community? Kendall gave his answer in several places—in the Vanderbilt lectures, in his famous essay on "The Two Majorities in American Politics," and in various other essays. The Founders deliberately designed Congress (and Congress has so evolved) so that it would resist the transmission to its floors of "waves of popular enthusiasm." Congress is bicameral; its upper chamber is not apportioned according to population; its elections are staggered; and it has developed procedures such as the committee system, the filibuster, and the seniority system that frustrate action by a temporary majority. The congressional process thus slows down any decision on important matters until the deliberate sense of the community may be discerned. On important matters—so the Founders clearly thought—a majority position must remain in being over a considerable length of time before being embodied in legislation. On important matters, the system really provides for government by consensus and not by slender majorities. Finally, because Congress by its nature is so deeply involved with particular and local interests in its constituencies, it functions to de-ideologize and de-fanaticize the issues before it. The orthodox American political tradition, wrote Kendall in his last essay,

says to the movement seeking drastic change through the rewriting of the nation's laws: you must cool your heels in, so to speak, the legislative antechamber until (a) the legislation you demand can pass Congress, with overwhelming majorities, and until (b) the legislation can go into effect with the acquiescence not merely of Congress but of the President and the

Supreme Court. Put the other way 'round, the system says to the movement seeking drastic change through governmental action, you must settle, from moment to moment, year to year, decade to decade, for whatever the three branches of our government (one of them, I repeat, acting by overwhelming majorities) are willing to give you; for whatever, in the first instance, the generality of our Congressmen and Senators can get together on. And that means, in practice: you must settle, from year to year and decade to decade for just as much, just as much and no more of your "objectives" as you can "sell" to the generality of politically active men and women out in American society.

It is on this line that Kendall takes his stand against modern liberalism as he understands it. Acting through their representatives, the American people have resisted, on the whole quite successfully, the set of policies that constitute the liberal program. The greatest breaches in the defenses of the "deliberate sense" conception of the governing of America have in fact most recently been made by the Supreme Court. The advocates of the liberal policies recognize the foot-dragging character of the "deliberate sense" mechanisms set up by the Constitution and embodied in the Congress. Like James MacGregor Burns in his *Deadlock of Democracy*, they are committed to a set of policies and are determined that those policies will be effectuated; the question then arises of what must be done *to* our political institutions and habits in order to break the "deadlock" that keeps them from being effectuated. "What is *really* new in Burns," as Kendall writes,

is on the one hand the problem to which he reduces American political theory, and on the other hand his repudiation, no less flat and un-ambiguous than that of Machiavelli himself, of the whole range of concerns, principles . . . and above all inhibitions handed down to him from the past. The nation's political regime is, for Burns, the *ancilla* of a set of policies that he and his friends have declared good. Let the liberal program prevail, and *ruat coelum*!

The substance of justice and common good is preserved, in the orthodox American political tradition, through loyalty to a pro-cess—a process the delicate design of which reflects the Founders' perceptions regarding human nature and the nature of the body politic, perceptions continuous with the traditional wisdom of the West. The political heretic desires to short-circuit the process in the interest of a set of prescribed absolutes that reflect a different and opposite conception of human nature and politics. The confrontation as inherently revolutionary.

V

But in the last resort the representative assembly, Congress, no matter how carefully buffered against waves of popular enthusiasm, no matter how systematically designed to insure consensus government, does respond to the will of the people. The system presupposes what Kendall calls, consciously employing the categories of our first "founding" document, the Mayflower Compact, the "virtue" of the people—that combination of civility, Christian conscience, and recognition of a higher moral law that was a principal presumption of the founding documents. Supppose the presupposed "virtue" is lost. Suppose the people become "corrupt." In a sense, Kendall says in his essay on Richard Weaver that there is a missing *Federalist* paper, for *Publius* never answered the question, How are the people to be kept virtuous? The people are to be kept virtuous, Kendall answers, by *teachers* who keep alive—or, if necessary, recover— the nation's "historical memory," the nation's knowledge of its own traditions, "lest, in ignorance of them, they forget, like madmen, what and who they are." The teachers, then, who care enough for the past, not just because it *is* past but for what it knows, those teachers can keep the people "virtuous." (It is good to have that word, with its ancient roots, cleaned off, purified of all priggishness. The Latin *virtu*—strength, ability, knowledge, courage—is one of those deep and complex words.)

Willmoore Kendall was such a teacher. He knew instinctively, and he succeeded in historically resurfacing, the American political tradition. In his last year, his academic wandering ceased; he was, in fact, ready to admit that his difficulties had been in part those of a difficult personality, but only in part. He knew, too, how intense the ideological animus had been. The University of Dallas, however, proved hospitable, and he founded there a graduate program that is reminiscent in modern terms of the curriculum of the Renaissance humanists, a doctoral program in politics and literature. The students go back to fundamentals in political theory, and they also partake of the moral insights of the poets and novelists. In modern terms, it is the equivalent of the program advocated by Erasmus, Sir Thomas More, or Sir Thomas Elyot, and taught at Milton's St. Paul's. It is "rhetoric" and "logic" plus historical consciousness. At Dallas, both professionally and personally, everything seemed to come together for Kendall: he said that his days of wandering were at an end. He was surrounded by promising students and a first-rate staff; he at last was happily married.

One senses here a liberation. He had even begun to lecture extemporaneously, not laboriously writing everything out. The small child's awe of the blind but powerful father no longer operated to overpower. He knew, and he knew that he knew.

One almost parenthetical note is necessary here. Kendall was, for excellent reasons, almost defiantly American. He talked of being an Appalachians-to-the-Rockies patriot; he liked Dallas for itself and because it was only a few hours' drive from his Oklahoma birthplace. But though this middle America was part of his identity and part of his historical sense—he knew how America is hated, even by some Americans—he knew that the American crisis was part of a broader Western crisis. He did not want *Americans* to be *Burkeans*, but he knew Burke's power as a diagnostician of the disease. Nowhere is it more clear that Kendall, precisely as an American, saw himself as a part of the West than in the concluding paragraph of his review of Leo Strauss' book on Machiavelli. Again the role of the "teacher" is central. Machiavelli, Strauss had shown, was a very great teacher, a very successful teacher, but also a great negator. How is he now to be counteracted?

Strauss's silence on this point is perhaps as explicit a statement as the "situation" and the "quality of the times" call for, and what it says is: the mischief can be undone only by a great teacher who feels within himself a strength and a vocation not less than Machiavelli's own, who possesses a store of learning not inferior to Machiavelli's own, who will take the best of the young, of this generation and future generations, and, leading them by the hand without arguing with them, habituate them to the denial of Machiavelli's denials.

Kendall's was a great and a generous ambition, an ambition conceived in national and even world-historical terms. In his students and in his writings, he would negate the negation. I do not know, of course, but I think he will win in the end.

On June 30, 1967, at the age of fifty-eight, he decided to take an afternoon nap and died in his sleep. For some months he had been functioning at full capacity, and he had recently felt a special vitality and confidence in the importance of what he was doing. He died after a most ordinary academic day—he gone down to get his mail, he read, talked with one of his students about a term paper, and laid himself down to rest.*

*The foregoing account of the final phase of Willmoore Kendall's life is indebted to an unpublished memorial sketch by Professor Leo Paul de Alvarez of the University of Dallas.

Frost and Eliot

As the first half of the twentieth century begins to recede and acquire shape as history, Robert Frost and T. S. Eliot loom ever larger on the landscape of American poetry. Each complements the other. They are related dialectically, and the achievement of each is enhanced by that relationship.

Twenty-five years ago one would not have been inclined to say "Frost and Eliot." Eliot was by far the dominant figure. But it is accurate to say that during the past generation Frost has been gradually reperceived. Truly first-rate Frost criticism remains relatively rare compared with the sustained and intense attention accorded Eliot. On Frost we have only a handful of first-rate essays, by Randall Jarrell, James M. Cox, William Pritchard, and a few others, plus some academic work, but the biography by Lawrance Thompson has been important. Above all, the poetry has gradually established its own claims as a major body of work. If one reads Frost's and Eliot's volumes in the order of their appearance, from *A Boy's Will* (1913) and *Prufrock and Other Observations* (1917) through *Four Quartets* (1943) and *In the Clearing* (1962), Frost is by no means overwhelmed by Eliot.

Different as the two poets are in many ways, and though Frost conducted a kind of private war with Eliot, it is possible to discern interesting resemblances beneath the obvious contrasts. In both men the central theme is metaphysical desolation. Both poets are profoundly at odds with the current of secular optimism flowing from the Enlightenment through the nineteenth century. Frost's New England landscape, spare, hard, and usually unyielding, inhabited by its declining Yankee stock, can be taken as an extended metaphor expressive of that desolation. In Frost's poetry the central persona or dramatic voice speaking the poems finds ways to live with that desolation. In Eliot's poetry the central persona lives through and finally beyond the desolation.

This article first appeared in *Sewanee Review* and is reprinted with permission.

Both Frost and Eliot were, in the broad sense of the word, conservatives, though of very different kinds. Frost liked to deliver querulous remarks regarding the New Deal, but at bottom his conservatism had to do with both the valid claims of the self and his sense of limits, limits of near but not altogether complete intractability. There are limits in the form of psychological and physical barriers between people ("Home Burial," "Into My Own," "Mending Wall," "A Hundred Collars"), the limits implicit in the act of choice ("The Road Not Taken," "Stopping by Woods on a Snow Evening"), the barriers between man and nature ("Two Look at Two," "Storm Fear," "The Need of Being Versed in Country Things"), the limits that make a mockery of political idealism ("New Hampshire"), limits to the value of science ("The Star-Splitter"), limits to the wisdom of the world ("Provide, Provide"), limits to what we can know about the past ("Vanishing Red"), the limits implicit in mortality ("Out, Out—"). If it is accurate to say, with Kenneth Minogue, that the liberal sensibility is distinctively concerned with the claims of victims, real and imagined, then we find in Frost something quite different and opposed: a resolute defense of the valid claims of the self ("Love and a Question," "Two Tramps in Mud Time," "A Considerable Speck"). In contrast to Eliot, the central figure in Frost does not "develop." Instead he increases in solidity and weight through a kind of dramatic accumulation. The drama consists of his changing relationship to those limits. The limits are real; that is the un-utopian given. But there are moments when he gets past or through them.

In Frost the voice of reason and of skepticism is paramount, the "sound of sense," but Eliot is a thaumaturge, mesmerizing us with mysteries and incantations, the "sense of sound." He once remarked that poetry began with a savage beating a drum in a jungle, and for all of its learning, one senses the presence of the primitive in Eliot's poetry. He engages us in an enormous act of recovery, reaching back beyond the present to "the mind of Europe"—not only "from Homer to the present" but also to the spiritual perceptions recoverable from the great myths. *The Golden Bough* he read "as a revelation of that vanished mind of which our mind is a continuation."

ii

Beginning in 1923 with the collection *New Hampshire*, Frost conducted a kind of literary guerrilla warfare against Eliot. If Frost took the offensive, however, he was also engaged in defending the validity of his own poetry. Frost plainly believed in 1923 that he had to offer a rejoinder to the author of *The Waste Land*, which had been published in 1922 and had immediately become one of the most influential works of the modern movement.

When *New Hampshire* appeared, Frost, at forty-eight, was a well-known and frequently honored poet. The title poem "New Hampshire" constitutes a Frostian manifesto and contains an almost explicit attack on Eliot as one who "took dejectedly / His seat upon the intellectual throne." It is striking to note that "New Hampshire" (414 lines) is almost the same length as *The Waste Land* (434 lines) and that it defines, as does *The Waste Land*, the imaginative world of the poet. *New Hampshire* is Frost's answer to Eliot's desert.

The notes Eliot appended to his poem were of course notorious; the second section of Frost's volume, following the long title poem, consists of shorter poems with the collective designation *Notes*. In the first edition, the title poem contained footnotes referring to the later poems. Frost seems to be implying several things here, playfully but also seriously: that he is a poet, not a pedant; that "New Hampshire," in contrast to the desert, "gives birth—the poems included as *Notes* often amplify some theme or incident in the title poem. The third and final section of the volume was originally called *Grace Notes*, a declaration, I take it, of further fecundity, with perhaps a a pun intended on the word *grace* to offer an ironic comment on Eliot's religious preoccupations.*

In the poems that follow and are frequently related to the title poem, the glances at Eliot are frequent. "The Census-Taker" brings the Frostian sensibility to a waste land, here a deserted logging site, a tarpaper shack surrounded by an autumn landscape of tree stumps. Negation echoes through the poem:

> I came as census-taker to the waste
> To count the people in it and found none,
> None in the hundred miles, none in the house.

Frost here confronts his own version of the waste land and pointedly remarks that you do not have to go abroad to engage spiritual experience:

*Louis Untermeyer quotes Frost as remarking early in 1940: "Eliot and I have our similarities and our differences. We are both poets and we both like to play. That's the similarity. The difference is this: I like to play euchre. He likes to play Eucharist."

> This house in one year fallen to decay
> Filled me with no less sorrow than the houses
> Fallen to ruin in ten thousand years
> Where Asia wedges Africa from Europe.

The poem characteristically concludes, not with the expectation of theophany as in *The Waste Land*, but with an assertion of will specifically, an earthly will, against the void.

> The melancholy of having to count souls
> Where they grow fewer and fewer every year
> Is extreme where they shrink to none at all.
> It must be I want life to go on living.

There may be more in his poetic universe than the human will, but here Frost insists on at least that element.

Other poems in the *New Hampshire* volume glance unmistakably at Eliot. "Wild Grapes" is a kind of rewriting of the earlier poem "Birches" with an Eliotic rebirth theme woven in. The poem playfully glances at myths. Frost's sacred wood lies in New Hampshire. Other poems in the volume, read individually, do not carry the implicit allusion to Eliot, but read in their context they easily do so. Consider in this light "Fragmentary Blue," "To Earthward," "Fire and Ice," and even the familiar "Stopping by Woods on a Snowy Evening." The tough-minded conclusion of the last poem, "The Need of Being Versed in Country Things," can be read as a rejoinder to the urbane Eliot immersed in his "unreal city." Poem after poem in *New Hampshire* carries this resonance, even such an unlikely candidate as "The Pauper Witch of Grafton." *The Waste Land* is full of sexual defeat. That is its subject, both in itself and as a metaphor for a larger sterility. In "The Pauper Witch of Grafton" Frost in effect replies that he can write a triumphant poetry of sexual fulfillment.

iii

Returning now to "New Hampshire," I will confine myself to Frost's central act of self-definition. The poem as a whole is immensely rich. Frost fashions the state of New Hampshire before our eyes into a poetic world of many modes and many voices, a poetic quarry from which the subsequent poems are drawn, a quarry of apparently inexhaustible resources. In its central section Frost addresses himself to the subject of New Hampshire's mountains—the opposite of a desert flatland. A bit earlier, Frost had quoted Emerson to the effect that "the God who made New Hampshire / Taunted the lofty land with little men," and he returns (in line 308) to the theme of the mountains and makes of them a symbol of the poetic imagination in operation.

> If I must choose which I would elevate—
> The people or the already lofty mountains,
> I'd elevate the already lofty mountains.

His poetic imagination will go to work on those mountains and in the process give birth to a kind of personal myth. Frost begins by inquiring:

> What has given me assurance
> To say what height becomes New Hampshire mountains,
> Or any mountains?

He goes on to consider, and reject as far as he is concerned, several common accounts of the nature of art. He suggests that the idea of enlarging the mountains originated in a mistake on an old map, "the sad accident of having seen / Our actual mountains given in a map / Of early times as twice the height they are." A large creative act, we understand, can be triggered by trivia, by accident. Our attention thus naturally shifts away from the trivial occasion to the creative act itself, which, with a dramatic heightening of the tone, blank verse turning to rhyme, Frost performs before our eyes:

> Whereas I never had a good idea
> About improving people in the world,
> Here I am over-fertile in suggestion,
> And cannot rest from planning day or night
> How high I'd thrust the peaks in summer snow
> To tap the upper sky and draw a flow
> Of frosty night air on the vale below,
> Down from the stars to freeze the dew as starry.

Here he steps forward explicitly as the creator of his own poetic world. His "New Hampshire" is not the actual state but a poetic artifact. We see him creating part of it. That pun on the poet's name—a "flow / Of frosty night air"—is surely intentional. There is a chill in Frost's poetry, and he knows it; that chill is the imaginative signature *Frost*. He embodies it here in his symbolic myth of his own art. To the heat of Eliot's symbolic desert, burning, burning,

Frost offers by way of contrast the cold summer snows of those imagined mountains.

In the final section of "New Hampshire," Frost gives us his declaration of independence as a poet, and he defines the persona that will be and has been its dramatic expression. He rejects both the inhibitions of the older genteel tradition and the new fashion of wallowing in misery. He scorns " the new school of the pseudo-phallic," by which he presumably means the cult of Lawrence and the popular versions of Freud current in 1923. Attacking Matthew Arnold, he also hits obliquely at the author of *The Waste Land*. In "The Scholar Gypsy," Arnold had written about the despondency pervading Victorian intellectual life and about "One"—perhaps Tennyson, whose *In Memoriam* had been published in 1850 when he succeeded Wordsworth as poet laureate:

> and amongst us One,
> Who most has suffer'd, takes dejectedly
> His seat upon the intellectual throne;
> And all his store of sad experience he
> Lays bare of wretched days;
> Tells us his misery's birth and growth and signs.

This great poet of despair may be the author of *In Memoriam*; the pronoun may also include the author of *Dover Beach*, who contemplates his buried life or alter-ego in the form of the Scholar Gypsy. In 1923 Frost's allusion could hardly fail to suggest the author of *The Waste Land*, another great poet of despair,—but it also defines Frost himself as a kind of Scholar Gypsy:

> For early didst thou leave the world, with powers
> Fresh, undiverted to the world without,
> Firm to their mark, not spent on other things;
> Free from the sick fatigue, the languid doubt.

The public self he chooses does have affinities with the Scholar Gypsy of the Arnold poem. In choosing this persona, he carefully calls attention to the fact that this is an act of choice, an imaginative creation: "I choose to be a plain New Hampshire farmer."

iv

When the critics and literary people equipped to understand Robert Frost finally recognized that he belongs among the most powerful poets of our time—a recognition that came absurdly late, when Frost was in his seventies—when, that is, informed recognition finally arrived, there was still something askew about it, something out of focus, some disabling distortion in the very terms of its definition. Frost was no cracker-barrel philosopher, we were reassured. No, he was a "terrifying" poet, a spirit out of the abyss, a journeyer into the heart of darkness. In that famous speech on Frost's eightieth birthday, Lionel Trilling, very consciously (even self-consciously) reacting against the popular cracker-barrel Frost, presented us with the Revised Version. "I think of Robert Frost as a terrifying poet," he said. "The universe that he conceives is a terrifying universe. Read the poem called 'Design' and see if you sleep the better for it. Read 'Neither Far Out Nor in Deep.'" This vein of criticism concentrates on these and other such "pessimistic" poems as "Acquainted with the Night," "The Most of It," and "Desert Places" to fashion that terrifying and so recognizably—and reassuringly—modern Frost. Frost, Trilling was saying, is really all right despite the unpromising first impressions.

Like the popular version of Frost, this one too misses the point. Surely the point of Frost is that he precisely refuses to be terrifying; his refusal is virtually programmatic. Terror, at least in literature, is—though not comforting—at least enhancing. Literary terrorism moves us and thrills us, and as it does so, it confers a certain sort of stature. The circumstance or the person capable of generating terror becomes through that very capacity dramatic, important, striking. But Frost refuses us this experience. He stops just short, points, and draws back. In drawing back, he forces us to confront something in its own way worse than terror. There is a bleakness, a barrenness in Frost that corresponds to something bleak and barren in the American reality, sensed not only in the dying Yankee culture that is the subject of his poetry, but with equal intensity in a Los Angeles suburb or on the plains of the Midwest. It is somehow also a presence in American history, whether one thinks of the grinding bleakness of that advancing frontier or of, say, one of Grant's relentless campaigns. Frost's poetry deals with a pervasive aspect of American reality, something inescapable, but it is not terror.

Frost's refusal, sensed everywhere in his poetry, to comfort us with something grand, with the purgation of terror and tragedy, is connected with his skepticism and his rationalism, though these are to be understood as habits of mind, not anything systematic. This frame of mind hence constitutes a kind of chastity of the imagination. Temperamentally he is rooted very much in the eighteenth century, that eighteenth-century New England with its spare white churches and chaste classical facades, as well as in the Lockean eighteenth century with its distrust of enthusiasm and its analytic suspicion of similarities, analogies, metaphors. Things have *differences*. Frost is as wary of metaphor as Swift or Dryden or Pope. Like them, he is unwilling to give the emotions their way completely, to say my love is like a red red rose, to permit the awful daring of a moment's surrender. The chill of reason is always there, the Frostian chill, and he is aware of the pun. There is always the cooling touch of humor or irony, or perhaps a single deflating word.

Consider one of his characteristic "dark" poems, "Desert Places," which might be cited to sustain the claim that Frost is a "terrifying" poet. The scene is the familiar one of "Stopping by Woods on a Snowy Evening," but here the falling snow and the gathering night possess none of the real, if also sinister, attractiveness that they have in that poem. The whiteness gradually covering the earth is pure negation—repulsive, blank, and benighted. It has no expression, nothing to express; nature is alien, numbing, meaningless. The poet thinks of the similar barrenness of the stars and of the famous sentence from Pascal's *Pensées*: "The eternal silence of these infinite spaces terrifies me." But he changes his Pascal, using instead of *terrifies* the homely and diminishing word *scare*. He knows about the "desert places"—Eliot's *Waste Land* is just offstage in this poem—but he is not mastered by the desert, overwhelmed, terrified. By the time we reach the last line, we realize that the subject of this poem is just that refusal to comfort himself and the reader. He can "scare" himself—he has it in him to do so—but in fact he won't. He knows the meaning of that desert, but the reason and the will remain in charge.

Similarly, the entire tone and meaning of the poem "Acquainted with the Night" are conditioned by the single word *acquainted*. The poem is about loneliness, fear, hysteria—the emotions traditionally associated with night taken as a symbol—and the poem convinces us that the poet is no stranger to them. But in this poem he uses the word *acquainted*; whatever his past experience with them, he now will admit openly only to acquaintance: the formality of the word distances that terror. Once again the point is his resistance and refusal. The reason and will remain in control, if only by the narrowest margin.

V

The characteristic movement of skepticism and rationalism in Frost's poetry is back to earth. In "New Hampshire" Frost created a myth in which the "frosty" night air flows *down* to the vale below, "down from the stars to freeze the dew as starry." From the early "Trial by Existence" to the very last poems, this insistence on the primacy of earth (as against the transcendent) is one of Frost's principal themes. It is fundamental to his imaginative differences with Eliot. The early and immensely popular "Birches," which can be read as a Frostian manifesto, glances toward transcendence, then turns back to make room for a different kind of affirmation.

In "Birches," the poet begins by recalling that he has seen birches permanetly bent by the ice that collects on them in the winter, and then he toys with a pleasant fancy. When he looks at birches bent in this way, he "like[s] to think some boy's been swinging them." But he knows that this is not true—that the trees bent by ice all winter are permanently bent and that swinging does not do this, and he withdraws the thought almost as soon as it is offered. In this seemingly casual discourse, a serious point is being broached: truth has asserted its claims at the expense of fancy. Ice, not a boy playing. But fancy is not defeated. It comes forward again in the form of a playful simile.

The trees, bent by the ice, now arch in the woods

> Like girls on hands and knees that throw their hair
> Before them over their heads to dry in the sun.

Only "like" girls.

The poet returns to the ordinary world of prosy reality:

> But I was going to say when Truth broke in
> With all her matter-of-fact about the ice-storm
> I should prefer to have some boy bend them
> As he went out and in to fetch the cows.

The resistance to the metaphorical mode throughout the first part of the poem is important—indeed, it is the subject of the poem. The Frostian skepticism will admit no easy beauties, and this skepticism prepares us for the emblematic passage that follows. The poet himself, we hear, was swinger of birches when a boy, and now, when "weary of considerations" and when "life is too much like a pathless wood, "he dreams of going back: "I'd like to get away from earth awhile / And then come back to it and begin over."

Frost's "pathless wood" in this poem can hardly fail to remind us of Dante. Frost too has been lost in that wood. He would like to get away from earth awhile—but only for awhile. Frost will not go on with Dante to the *Paradiso* and the heavenly love of Beatrice; the movement is back to earth, a movement analogous to those lines in which Truth successfully asserted its claims against fancy:

> May no fate willfully misunderstand me
> And half grant what I wish and snatch me away
> Not to return. Earth's the right place for love:
> I don't know where it's likely to go better.
> I'd like to go by climbing a birch tree,
> And climb black branches up a snow-white trunk
> *Toward* heaven, till the tree could bear no more,
> But dipped its top and set me down again.
> That would be good both going and coming back.
> One could do worse than be a swinger of birches.

It is the point of the birches that they climb toward heaven but also return the poet to earth, for "earth's the right place for love: / I don't know where it's likely to go better." The skepticism is pervasive and works both ways: *he* does not know where it is "likely" to go better. Issues of epistemology and probability lurk behind the line. We are in the mental climate of eighteenth-century skepticism and among eighteenth-century philosphical issues; we think of Locke and Berkeley and Hume. And this eighteenth-century skepticism, this resistance to metaphor and analogy, takes on an ultimate importance in Frost, for all philosophical theology, all affirmation of connection between time and eternity, man and God, depends on some form of analogy: it gets us from here to there and back again.

Despite his pervasive skepticism and despite the experience evoked in the lines about the pathless wood, Frost makes his affirmation—not only that "earth's the right place for love" but that, as in the childhood joys of swinging birches, earth enables us to climb "toward" heaven. Whether we ever get closer or not, our approach is from earth. These affirmations, moreover, are all the more potent because they are earned amid surrounding skepticism. The final two lines develop enormous power: good both going away *and* coming back to earth. Then, in the seemingly casual throwaway: "One could do worse."

Read in this way, "Birches" asserts the claims of Frost's skepticism and sense of human limits against the desire for transcendence and the sense of mysterious possibility. His goal is to wring a great poetry out of an irreducible minimum, to triumph over the possibility of desolation, which is always present and is never finally transcended. The triumph is in its way as impressive as Eliot's.

vi

If the Frostian mode characteristically keeps things separate, insisting on their differences, the central impulse of Eliot's poetry is to achieve coherence by perceiving identities. The disparities of his early poetry become the final identities of *Four Quartets*. Eliot has suggested that Shakespeare's plays can be read as a single long poem. So can Eliot's oeuvre be read. It moves from the fractured metaphor with which "Prufrock" begins,

> Let us go then, you and I,
> When the evening is spread out against the sky
> Like a patient etherised upon a table,

to the culminating conceit in which the most disparate things are perceived as one: "The fire and the rose are one." The parts of a world have been put together, but not wholly in time's covenant.

Eliot's poetry also moves through a succession of voices to the final purified voice of "Little Gidding," where no persona is left to be shed. Thus J. Alfred Prufrock refuses to be the great poet of *The Waste Land*. He might, but cannot, say

> I have gone at dusk through narrow streets
> And watched the smoke that rises from the pipes
> Of lonely men in shirt-sleeves, leaning out of windows.

That is, he cannot be the great poet of modern urban truth. And he might, but cannot, say: "I am Lazarus, come from the dead, / Come back to tell you all, I shall tell you all." Prufrock will not tell us what it is like to be dead. He ends as a minor romantic sensibility: "I have seen them riding seaward on the waves." But another voice later takes up the challenge thus refused. "April is the cruellest month." Lazarus will tell us all, after all.

For the American aspect of Eliot's journey I would like to focus on "The Dry Salvages, "which can be read as his "answer" to Frost and to America. I accept in general the thesis proposed in a famous essay by Donald Davie. In *Four Quartets*, "The Dry Salvages" sticks out like a sore thumb. It does contain some magnificent passages, but also some conspicuous ineptitudes, in both form and content. This "American" quartet is deliberately defective, and the defects express a judgment.

Davie notices, for example, the conspicuous awkwardness of the sestina, as in the sequence of rhymes: "motionless," "emotionless," "devotionless," "oceanless," "erosionless." The poet or persona here is clearly overcome by the demands of form. And telltale ineptitudes abound throughout. We have the inert cliche "worshippers of the machine," the flaccidity of "watching and waiting," the vague idea that the rhythm of the river "was present in the nursery bedroom." The allusion to Krishna may also be a signal to the intellectually wary: " I sometimes wonder if that is what Krishna meant." Earlier, at Harvard between 1911 and 1914, Eliot had applied himself to oriental studies, which had recently had a considerable American vogue. As he later said, "Two years spent in the study of Sanskrit under Charles Lanman, and a year in the mazes of Pantanjali's metaphysics under the guidance of James Woods, left me in a state of enlightened mystification." Yeats once remarked on "those translations of the Upanishads, which it is so much harder to study by the sinking flame of Indian tradition than by the serviceable lamp of Walt Whitman." And Whitman turns out to be a presence in "The Dry Salvages," in "the rank ailanthus of the April dooryard" and in the Whitmanesque "fare forward, voyagers" refrain of section 3. In *T. S. Eliot and Walt Whitman*, Sydney Musgrove observes of this passage that "Eliot has employed Whitman's material and manner in order to reject his philosophy. For Whitman, time stretches away in one infinite linear direction . . . . For Eliot, the sense of direction is illusory; time is an eternal present." "The Dry Salvages" explicitly rejects other themes easily associated with the nineteenth century and with American secular optimism generally:

> It seems, as one becomes older,
> That the past has another pattern, and ceases to be a mere
>   sequence—

> Or even development: the latter a partial fallacy,
> Encouraged by superficial notions of evolution,
> Which becomes, in the popular mind, a means of
>   disowning the past.

And it offers a comment on the trivialization of culture that results from this mistaken conceptualization of time:

> To communicate with Mars, converse with spirits,
> To report the behaviour of the sea monster,
> Describe the horoscope, haruspicate or scary,
> Observe disease in signatures, evoke
> Biography from the wrinkles of the palm
> And tragedy from fingers.

"The Dry Salvages" is parodic, a deliberate mixture of the true and the false, the beautiful and the inept, insight and confusion. As Davie puts it, "It is hardly too much to say that the whole of this third quartet is spoken by a nameless persona; certainly it is spoken through a mask, spoken in character as an American. This, and nothing else, can explain the approximations to Whitmanesque and the other pre-symbolist American verse procedures." That persona is recognizable as a compound American ghost: the echoes are of Mark Twain, Whitman, Melville, perhaps Emerson and Henry Adams. "It is thus," Davie says, "that the incompetence turns out to be dazzling virtuosity; and the inhumanity of the conclusion reached turns out to be only a parody of the true conclusion reached in 'Little Gidding,' which is thoroughly humane in its insistence that all varieties of human folly and imperfection are the conditions for apprehending perfection, that the world is therefore necessary and to that extent—even the worst of it— "good." The "strong brown god," suggestive of nineteenth-century pantheism, is not the transcendent God of *Four Quartets*. The strong brown god has nothing to do with the moment in and out of time. The "American" quartet presents a false resolution set against the true resolution of "Little Gidding," in which Eliot leaves America and moves back behind the nineteenth century and the Enlightenment to the English seventeeth century.

After the deliberate ineptitudes, formal and conceptual, of "The Dry Salvages," the final quartet brings the sequence to its triumphant conclusion, the verse in its concentrated power one of the peaks of twentieth-century achievement. Transcending spiritual desolation, the voice in "Little Gidding" concludes with lines of haunting beauty, full of the Eliotic sense of mysterious significance, but now the reverberations offer a complete contrast to those of "April is the cruellest month":

> We shall not cease from exploration
> And the end of all our exploring
> Will be to arrive where we started
> And know the place for the first time.
> Through the unknown, remembered gate
> When the last of earth left to discover
> Is that which was the beginning;
> At the source of the longest river
> The voice of the hidden waterfall
> And the children in the apple-tree
> Not known, because not looked for
> But heard, half-heard, in the stillness
> Between two waves of the sea.
> Quick now, here, now, always—
> A condition of complete simplicity
> (Costing not less than everything)
> And all shall be well and
> All manner of thing shall be well
> When the tongues of flame are in-folded
> Into the crowned knot of fire
> And the fire and the rose are one.

The imagery here recapitulates earlier themes in the poem, giving them a final resolution. It reaches back autobiographically to Eliot's own earliest memories: the "remembered gate," the "children in the apple-tree," the "waves of the sea." Whitman is also present in the theme of exploration, but to un-Whitman-like purpose.

vii

Transcendent reality plays no comparable role in the poetry of Robert Frost. But though the poetry remains "in time," signals do occur—and more frequently than is generally recognized—that the total reality may contain much more. In such major poems as "After Apple-Picking," "West-Running Brook," and "For Once, Then, Something," Frost peers beyond the epistemological barriers, presses against Hume, Kant, and Wittgenstein, and sees into a glass not altogether dark. We have seen the importance of barriers, the recognition of a sense of limits in Frost's poetry, but there is a counter-movement as well, and the dialectic set up between them makes for much of the drama present in the poetry. This is particularly striking in those poems addressed to questions of ultimate meaning. The Frostian consciousness normally resides in the time-space contin-uum and finds it extremely difficult to move behind or beyond the world of ordinary appearances. Sometimes, however, while remain-ing drenched in skepticism, that consciousness catches glimpses through the epistemological veil of what may be a signal of transcen-dence. It hears, in Peter Berger's memorable phrase, rumors of angels.

The Frostian consciousness thus moves back and forth between the experience of skepticism and the experience of possible meta-physical affirmation. "After Apple-Picking" intimates a resurrection that completes the analogy of springtime awakening. "The Onset" may easily be read analogically and its April seen as an assertion against Eliot's cruellest month. Let me focus, however, on "For Once, Then, Something" from *New Hampshire* (1923), a more serious effort in every respect than the late quasi-theological "masques" of reason and mercy.

The first sentence of this poem, extending over six lines, describes the speaker kneeling at a well-curb. The posture might suggest prayer, but the image the speaker gazes at, the reflection on the surface of the water, is himself: "Me myself in the summer heaven godlike." At least two possibilities of interpretation are present. The literally superficial view may be an anthropomorphic god, projected by man's vanity into the heavens. But the view suggested may be humanism of the sort that contains in its conspectus nothing higher than man. "Me myself" contains some mockery. So does the human face looking down from the summer heaven "out of a wreath of fern and cloud puffs." It may be that both anthropomorphism and the humanism of "man the measure" are branches of the same tree: a vanity that is "wrong to the light."

The poem pivots on the italicized "*Once*" with which line 7 begins, and it offers an alternative to the superficial view of the first part. Once the epistemological barrier represented by the surface of the water permitted the speaker to see "a something white, uncertain, / Something more of the depths." A metaphysical rumor, I take it. Though the speaker holds out the skeptical possibility that the "whiteness" could be a "pebble of quartz," the insistence of the first part of the poem on turning itself into a parable goes against the conclusion that the whiteness *is* merely a pebble of quartz. On the literal plane it may be; on the parabolic, that is unlikely. If the speaker in the first seven lines were merely looking into wells, "others" would have no reason to "taunt" him over the results of so trivial an activity. The poem retains skepticism, but it also steps beyond it.

In one of his last major poems, the mysterious and haunting "Directive" from *Steeple Bush* (1947), Frost returned once more to his oblique quarrel with Eliot. In *New Hampshire* (1923), Frost had asserted his own claims against the author of *The Waste Land*. In "Directive," he takes on the author of *Four Quartets* and in particular of "Little Gidding," which had appeared in 1942.

It is illuminating to set the concluding lines of "Little Gidding" beside Frost's "Directive." The latter poem also records a quest; it too is a journey backward in time that ends with a clarification. In Eliot the abandoned Chapel Perilous of *The Waste Land* becomes the past-haunted chapel where prayers have been valid. Frost takes us not to a haunted chapel but to an abandoned and haunted farm, where the dead are felt as unseen presences. "Directive," like "Little Gidding," has its "children" and even its "apple tree." "Little Gidding" is thus very much present in "Directive," but present by way of contrast. The central image in "Little Gidding" is fire, the transformed fire of *The Waste Land*, the refining fire that in the last line becomes one with the rose of divine love. Ice provides the contrasting image in "Directive," the chill of Frost. We find it first in the lingering sense of the glacier's presence. The chill of the glacier and the hard realities of rock and iron assert themselves powerfully against the poetic analogy, in which the glacier "braced his feet against the Arctic Pole." The personification of the glacier becomes just a manner of speaking. The claims of metaphor are chilled.

The chill persists, informing the climactic line of the poem, in which metaphor is reborn.

> Your destination and your destiny's
> A brook that was the water of the house,
> Cold as a spring as yet so near its source,
> Too lofty and original to rage.
> (We know the valley streams that when aroused
> Will leave their tatters hung on barb and thorn.)
> I have kept hidden in the instep arch

Of an old cedar at the waterside
A broken drinking goblet like the Grail
Under a spell so the wrong ones can't find it,
So can't get saved, as St. Mark says they mustn't.
(I stole the goblet from the children's playhouse.)
Here are your waters and your watering place.
Drink and be whole again beyond confusion.

We again enter the world of parable. The brook suggests Frost's own poetry. It is "cold"; it is "too lofty and original to rage" in the manner of the lesser "valley streams." Perhaps we are meant to think again of Eliot, and of the "exasperated spirit" who proceeds from "wrong to wrong," prior to the refinement of the fire. Frost is not unaware of the gifts reserved for age or the place where a story ended.

First there's the children's house of make believe,
Some shattered dishes underneath a pine,
The playthings in the playhouse of the children.
Weep for what little things can make them glad.
Then for the house that is no more a house,
But only a belilaced cellar hole,
Now slowly closing like a dent in dough.
This was no playhouse but a house in earnest.

It is not necessary or even perhaps desirable to read these lines autobiographically, but behind them it is surely possible to see Frost's own "house in earnest"—the loss of three children (one through suicide) and the intermittent near-madness and sudden death of his wife. The word *confusion* in the final line of "Directive" awakens echoes. Frost in a famous definition described poetry as a "momentary stay against confusion." But in "Directive," the claim made for the cold stream of Frost's poetry appears to be larger: "Drink and be whole again beyond confusion." Perhaps we can say that Frost moves between the two formulations, as he moves between skepticism and affirmation, between simile and metaphor. Poetry may offer only a momentary stay. But perhaps it *can* make us whole again beyond confusion.

Finally, "Directive" is Frost's last manifesto on how to read him. The opening lines suggest one way: as the popular and beloved poet of a simpler rustic past, the spokesman for enshrined pieties, a kind of New England Sandburg. But the past was not simple, we learn later in the poem, and this poet knows that it was not. The prevailing sense of Frost as the national hand-holder is an error. At the end we come to the cold stream of the true poetry. That poetry is not simple either, nor is it topical or subject to fashion. It is "lofty and original." Pure, it escapes labels. Indeed that poetry now seems less dated than much identifiably "modernist" poetry.

viii

In a curious way, the sociology of knowledge may shed some light on the differences between Robert Frost and T.S. Eliot as regards knowledge of the metaphysically transcendent. One of the fundamental propositions of the sociology of knowledge holds that the plausibility of a view of reality depends upon the social support it receives. We obtain our notions about the world largely from other people, and these notions continue to be plausible to us because others continue to affirm them. The signals of transcendence in Frost are intermittent and tend toward the ambiguous. The consciousness in Frost's poetry is resolutely individualistic. It discovers its truths on its own. It maintains those truths on its own. In terms of the sociology of knowledge, this individualistic consciousness receives very little collective reinforcement. Its "plausibility structures" are all internal.

Eliot, in contrast, does inhabit a supportive "community"—only it exists in time rather than in space. Eliot's spatial community is the ordinary, secularized, urban Western world. But in "Little Gidding," Eliot's "neighbors," so to speak, are Juliana of Norwich, Nicholas Farrar, George Herbert, Charles I, John Milton. Such intimations of the transcendent as are available to Eliot's own consciousness receive continuous support from that Christian community. As the sociology of knowledge tells us, such support increases the plausibility of the individual's insight. Eliot himself says as much in "East Coker":

> And what there is to conquer
> By strength and submission, has already been discovered
> Once or twice, or several times, by men whom one cannot hope
> To emulate—but there is no competition—
> There is only the fight to recover what has been lost
> And found and lost again and again: and now, under conditions
> That seen unpropitious.

The Poet of Europe

Have you seen the Pope's gentle remarks to the Modernists?
They are indeed noble! I could not have done it better myself.
He gently hints they can't think, which is true. The old Heretics
had guts, notably Calvin, and could think like the Devil, who
inspired them. But the Modernists are inspired by a little minor
he-devil, with one Eye and a stammer, and the result is poor.

Belloc to Dorothy Hamilton
October 8, 1907

In England before the First World War it seems (in historical
reverie) always to have been a summer afternoon. This may owe
something to half-conscious effects lingering in the mind of scenes
in Impressionist paintings, their joy in light and foliage and, above
all, their virtually uninterrupted affirmation of gaiety and color
and pleasure. It may owe something to late nineteenth-century
poetry and its celebration of landscape. Certainly it owes much
to the fact that, since the First World War, the emotions of the
West have undergone a shattering confrontation with a barbarism
far worse—colder and more malignant—than anything in previous
Western experience.

In this historical reverie, pre-war England is a place of long, sunlit
summer afternoons and bandstands, of little boys in sailor suits and
weekends at spacious country houses with lawn parties and baccarat
and billiards and riding to hounds, of lazy punting trips down the
Thames from Oxford and picnics at the Rose and Crown. It is the
world of Saki and Beerbohm and Rupert Brooke (a world which
James, because of his greater depth, loved even more than they did),
and of Compton Mackenzie's Oxford, with its dreaming spires, still
the aristocratic Oxford of Arnold and Newman and Benjamin Jowett.

It is as a part of that England that Belloc first comes clearly into

This article first appeared in *Triumph* and is reprinted with permission.

view, Belloc of Balliol and the Oxford Union. It was there, in that particular milieu, that he could flourish. For all his quarrels with it, the England of that time was his proper home. His central views were all formed before 1918. The very terms of his quarrels belonged to pre-war England. This is very far from saying that Belloc is a figure of "merely historical interest," as the saying goes. Indeed, it is because he was so firmly rooted in that pre-war world, and therefore connected in so many ways with a continuous European past, that he remains so important.

Hilaire Belloc was born in France, but he was raised in England; he attended Newman's Oratory School, then presided over by Newman himself—a sensitive, remote, fragile, august man in the full glory of his last phase. There is a symbolic quality to Belloc's presence at Newman's school. Both devoted their lives to bringing the truths of the past to bear on the present; both were gifted with deep historical consciousness; both were soldiers in a sense— Newman with the rapier of dialectic, Belloc with the "sound of the guns," a phrase that occurs often in his work, at Valmy, at Waterloo, at the Marne. Yet, though they were very different, one cannot quite say that they were opposite kinds of men, for both knew, as Manning remarked to Belloc, that "all human conflict is ultimately theological." Once, in Belloc's Latin class, Cardinal Newman burst into tears over some haunting passage in Virgil and had to leave the room. It is staggering to learn that the boys called him "Jack."

And after the Oratory came Oxford itself—Balliol and the Union. At the Oratory, Belloc had imbibed Catholicism and the classics. At Balliol, he read history, and the three things came together in his powerful mind. The classics, Catholicism, and history; Europe, the Church, and the West—kind of analogue of the Trinity itself; the three things were one.

When Belloc went up to Oxford in 1893, the Oxford Union was still in its great period. Today, a feeble-minded uplift and a low sincerity ruin all prospect of thought. But then the art of debate was assiduously cultivated and practiced for sheer intellectual pleasure. Such debate was only possible under conditions of disinterestedness: there was a whole range of ideas that could be entertained, and no one's life—more precisely, status—was at stake. The snarling, violent, moralistic mobs of the democratic campus had not yet made their appearance in history. The Union of 1893 was the Union of

F. E. Smith and John Simon—and then, suddenly, of Hilaire Belloc.
As Basil Matthews recalls:

> It was one of those rare nights in the Oxford Union when new ideas are
> discovered. Simon had denounced the Turk in Thessaly and Smith had held
> up the Oriental to admiration. Men whispered to each other of the future
> Gladstone and Dizzy whom Oxford was to give to the nation. No one would
> be fool enough to speak after such brilliant rhetoric . . . . Suddenly a young
> man walked to the table. He was broad of shoulder and trod the floor
> confidently. A chin that was almost grim in its young strength was sur-
> mounted by a large squarely-built face. Over his forehead and absurdly
> experienced eyes, dark hair fell stiffly. As he rose, men started up and began
> to leave the house; at his first sentence they paused and looked at him—
> and sat down again. By the end of his first sentence, with a few waves of his
> powerful hands, and a touch of unconscious magnetism and conscious
> strength, the speeches of J. A. Simon and F. E. Smith were as though they
> had never been. For twenty minutes the new orator, Mr. Hilaire Belloc,
> who was soon to sit in the seat of Gladstone, Salisbury, Milner, Curzon, and
> Asquith as President of the Union, held his audience breathless.*

Some of this was theater, of course, but for the most part it
represented a genuine curiosity about what intelligence could do
with a particular subject. The egalitarian and cloddish impulse to
"commitment" about everything under the sun was absent.

Of course, politics in its way was a serious thing, and it attracted
men of surpassing abilities. Simon and F. E. Smith went on to notable
parliamentary careers. The Liberal ministry that came to power in
1906 was the most brilliant ever to assemble at Westminster: As-
quith, Grey, Campbell- Bannerman, Haldane, Bryce, Winston Churchill. Yet it was the last time that most men agreed on most things.

Governments of both parties agreed, for example, that money
should be allowed to "fructify in the pockets of the people." Because
government had not extended itself into the very texture of existence, government was not awfully controversial. It was not yet in
every hamlet, kitchen, and schoolroom. As the marvelous symbolic
story has it, Simon and F. E. Smith, before going down from Oxford
to London, tossed a coin to determine which would be Liberal,
which Tory. There was no sense in entering the same party. One
might block the other's path. If a crank called Marx had written
some tracts in the British Museum, what of it?

---

*For this quotation and for much of the following, I am indebted to Robert
Speaight's authoritative *Life of Hilaire Belloc* (1957).

ii

Of course, men could be serious about serious things, and politics before the First World War has a flavor—no, not a flavor, a distinctive character—that separates it from later politics. This point is worth pausing over. It was very much a part of the pre-war atmosphere that candidates were not universally expected to caress the voters, much less lick their feet. Holding office was not *that* important. When Belloc ran for Parliament in 1906, he was told that the voters of South Salford might not vote for a Catholic. This is how he handled the problem, making his first campaign address to a packed house:

Gentlemen, I am a Catholic. As far as possible I go to Mass every day. This [taking a rosary out of his pocket] is a rosary. As far as possible I kneel down and tell these beads every day. If you reject me on account of my religion, I shall thank God that He has spared me the indignity of being your representative.

After a shocked pause, Belloc was cheered to the rafters and, later, elected. (A comparison with John F. Kennedy before the Houston ministers is instructive here.) This incident is usually held up as evidence of Belloc's unique courage and integrity. Yet, though the incident is extreme and special, it is also in many ways representative. When John Stuart Mill was standing for Parliament, he once spoke before a tough crowd of Victorian workmen. In the midst of his remarks, a billboard was brought forward bearing the deadly words from his *Thoughts on Parliamentary Reform*: "*The Lower Classes, though mostly habitual liars, are ashamed of lying.*" The audience demanded to know whether Mill had written that. Said Mill clearly, "I did." The workmen cheered and stamped their feet, and their leader arose to say fervently that "the working classes had no desire not to be told of their faults; they wanted friends, not flatterers." Both episodes are very much in the vein of Burke's speech to the electors of Bristol. *Non serviam*!

Such an attitude is unthinkable today. Belloc and Mill and Burke would have disagreed on practically everything. Belloc had no time for Burke, and both would have looked on Mill as almost impossible. The essential point is that each believed that certain things were in fact true and that, beside the truth, any office was a bauble. The modern politician, in contrast, is other-directed. He finds out what is true by responding to his antennae. Mussolini's name now is mud, but largely because he was an ignominious failure; until 1940 his prestige in the West was very high indeed. His failure should not blind us to the fact that his technique of total reliance upon mass manipulation and mass appeal was not so different from modern politicians generally. In Ivonne Kirkpatrick's excellent biography of Mussolini, *Duce* (1964), we learn that he believed in almost nothing at all, at least not until his awful last month, and that at the height of his power he often made up his policy on the spot, even made momentous decisions, as he read the emotions of the crowd from the balcony of the Palazzo Venezia. Was Bobby Kennedy much different?

England before 1914 is usually called Liberal England by historians, after the name of the dominant party, but of course the word "liberal" had not yet reversed its meaning. Despite the overwhelming triumph of the Liberal Party in 1906, Liberal England was almost finished. Lloyd George was in the 1906 cabinet. In 1909 he would present his People's Budget with its sharp increase in taxes. Soon he would preside over the People's War of 1914–1918—the first war in history in which the use of mass civilian armies dictated a politics of mass manipulation at home. The future of mass taxation and mass government and mass emotion was suddenly radiant. At the center of the great empire, the end came almost unnoticed. In the spring of 1914 Belloc overheard the following conversation on a train going down to Horsham:

"Terrible news from the Balkans."
"Yes, but they're only barbarians."

During the weekend of June 29, he attended Mass at Salisbury. The congregation was asked to pray for the soul of the Archduke Franz Ferdinand, who had just been murdered at Sarajevo. Belloc had some sense but no immediately clear idea of the likely repercussions of the assassination on European peace. Then came the chilling moment. On July 20, cruising off Plymouth in the *Nona*, Belloc saw the British Grand Fleet, "like ghosts, like things made themselves out of mist", hastening eastward. He knew then there would be war—and the end of a world

The crippling event in Belloc's own career was his failure to get a post at Oxford. He expected one, and with good reason, for his record had been excellent. He had really been one of the great undergraduates of all time, and he loved Oxford to the point of idolatry. His powers were recognized to be formidable, yet he was passed over for candidates no one ever heard of again. Belloc was a natural don, a don par excellence, with his thorniness and his total inability to work as a team member—he was a disaster as a party politician and a total failure in corporate journalism. But he had the potential of being a great historian. On the evidence of the history he did write, it is safe to say that, given the leisure of an academic environment, he would have produced work of classic quality. His moment as a historian had arrived. He wished to demolish the then-dominant Whig interpretation of history, according to which history was the happy-ending story of the advance of liberty under Whig and Protestant auspices, with heroes and villains suitably arrayed back through the ages. Such a view, Belloc believed, was no longer tenable, and it operated as a block to the understanding. But Belloc was condemned to a lifetime of journalism, one-night lectures, and hurried writing. He could not concentrate his resources upon writing a few great works, and we have had to wait until 1959 for Herbert Butterfield to accomplish Belloc's appointed task regarding Whig history.

iii

Belloc was so much the natural don that he even had some of the weaknesses of the academic mind. As a historian and as a moral and religious thinker, he was admirably concrete, but when he wrote on current political and social matters, a don-like abstraction took over. He tirelessly attacked the English party system, arguing that because the governing class was linked by a web of family relations and because the parties always seemed to agree, they were therefore in conscious collusion and even agreed to alternate in office. The truth was more mundane. As a class and as members of a common culture, they did largely agree, but it is unlikely that any member agreed to lose an election out of collusion with his rival.

Similarly, in his book *The Jews*, he has many incisive things to say about the relations between Jews and non-Jews, but defining the Jews as a "dispersed nation"—which is, to a point, fair enough—he "reasons" to the absurd conclusion that English Jews ought actually to approximate a nation, have their own laws, courts, judges, be free from military service, taxes, and so on. This is a rationalist farrago. Belloc's plan might well accommodate the Jewishness of an individual, but it forgot all about his Englishness. In the real world, the

Jews maintained their distinctive social and cultural institutions within the ordinary structure of law.

Again, he had shrewd things to say in *The Servile State*. The capitalist system does tend to lead to collectivism. It does concentrate property in the hands of a few. It engenders wide insecurity. Yet, from this, he again "deduced" a servile system in which the capitalists would rule over forced labor. It is only by stretching the definitions all out of shape that Belloc's predicition can be seen as having any relevance to the real world of power relations today.

Belloc always believed that his rejection at Oxford was due to his Catholicism, and he was bitter about it to the end of his days. The subject crops up again and again in his conversation, and he even cultivated a deliberate attitude of anti-academicism. Actually, he probably was not rejected because of his religion. The fact is, he tended to be a monologist, and dominating brilliance, after awhile, can become a bore. In addition, he was obsessive on some points. The Fellows of an Oxford college might well hesitate a long time before submitting themselves to a lifetime of disquisitions on distributism and the Jewish problem. Whatever the truth here, Belloc ended up at Fleet Street and missed his calling. But Oxford was his home, and he should have had that fellowship at All Souls.

In consequence, his achievement was fragmentary, though not on that account ephemeral. His grasp of essential things was a firm one, as is manifest wherever we look in his work. F. D. Wilhelmsen's subtitle for his study of Belloc, an absolutely first-rate piece of modern criticism, is an accurate one: *Hilaire Belloc: No Alienated Man* (1953). For though Belloc was, increasingly, at odds with the twentieth century, he was not alienated from the Western tradition or from the sources of anything positive that remains in Western culture. He held in balance the necessary coordinates of the fully human existence. He symbolized these in a little book called *Four Men*, which he published early in his career. The book is an allegory, recounting the journey of four men across Sussex in an autumnal setting: Myself, Grizzlebeard, the Poet, and the Sailor. As the journey and the conversations unfold, we see that Belloc means for each of the three men accompanying Myself to represent an essential quality of the fully human. The Poet represents spiritual aspiration, vision, and the sense of belonging to a world not present to the senses. He embodies a religious impulse that goes back to Plato and beyond.

The Sailor belongs to this world, to its sudden landfalls and its hills against autumnal skies. His health saves man from mystical excess, solipsism, and decadence. Grizzlebeard is tradition incarnate: full of songs, lore, legends, and the wisdom of the past. Without Grizzlebeard's living connection with the past, man is isolated in time, a "stranger lost in a wilderness of pavements," as Wilhelmsen eloquently says. So thoroughly a part of the West was Belloc, so finely did he bring together these three essential elements that he found himself alienated from much around him. But the modern sensibility is alienated from itself; for it, as Wilhelmsen observes, nation, Church, and West, the past, roots, and origins are always wrong.

Looking at Belloc's work, we see that the three essential elements are always present, making each work an expression of the integral Western man behind it. He possessed the historical imagination as Eliot defines it: he wrote history with the past of Europe in his bones. History pervades his life at every point. Michelet was a friend of his father. A friend of his grandmother, a Mlle de Montgolfier, told him how as a girl she had been present at the storming of the Bastille. Belloc went over the roads and the battlefields of Europe foot by foot, and he attempted not only to record the past but to think his way back into it, to imagine it as it really was, when it was not past but present, and then to bring it forth re-created. He did not always succeed, and sometimes his imagination led him astray, but his method led to real discoveries. He knew, for example, that the eighteenth-century Whig oligarchy was not on the side of freedom. He knew that Cromwell had nothing further from his mind than religious liberty and that he would have been horrified by the thought of political liberty. He knew that James II had not been overthrown by any great wave of popular revulsion. Belloc's critical gaze liberated the past from the liberal dogmas of his present, and it did so at a moment when those dogmas, for sensitive minds, were in a state of dissolution. The main tendency of Belloc's historical polemic is now generally accepted by historians.

iv

Belloc was a poet of Europe's past, and his prose, gaining resonance from his meditative involvement, moves us, often, as Burke's does. When Belloc wrote the following passage, he was entirely on the side of the Revolution, yet listen to his epitaph for the French monarchy:

So perished the French monarchy. Its dim origins stretched out and lost themselves in Rome; it had already learnt to speak and recognized its own nature when the vaults of the Thermae echoed heavily to the slow footsteps of the Merovingian kings. Look up that vast valley of dead men crowned, and you may see the gigantic figure of Charlemagne, his brows level and his long white beard tangled like an undergrowth, having in his left hand the globe and in his right the hilt of an unconquerable sword. There also are the short, strong horsemen of the Robertian house, half hidden by their leather shields, and their sons before them growing in vestment and majesty, and taking on the pomp of the middle ages; Louis VII, all covered with iron; Philip the Conqueror; Louis IX, who alone is surrounded with light; they stand in a widening interminable procession this great crowd of kings; they lose their armour, they take their ermine on, they are accompanied by their captains and their marshalls; at last, in their attitude and their magnificence they sum up in themselves the pride and the achievement of the French nation. But time has dissipated what it could not tarnish, and the process of a thousand years has turned these mighty figures into unsubstantial things. You may see them in the grey end of darkness, like a pageant standing still. You look again, but with the growing light and with the wind that rises before morning they have disappeared.

Burke, Gibbon, Macaulay—and Belloc: in meditative evocation, he was their equal.

Yet although the past lived and was present to him, he possessed also his allegorical Sailor's intense communion with the world that is present to the senses. He knew the English landscapes, and he loved the English inns; he had walked through Normandy and Burgandy, and from Paris to Rome, and from Paris over the Pyrenees to Madrid. The physical world became a part of him, producing, as all intense experience of the senses does, both pleasure and melancholy. He did not see through things to something else—he saw the things themselves—and his attachment to them made him poignantly aware of transience. The elegiac note is not peculiar to the West, but it is integral to it, to its historicity and its sense of mortal limitation, to its knowledge that the world is immensely important, but that it is always dying.

His Catholic faith was, in its quality, also an extension of an older Europe. If he had been told that anyone could discuss the Resurrection as a "significant" thing without first inquiring whether it had actually occurred, he would have thought that he was hearing about a half-wit. Belloc had been born a Catholic and had attended the Oratory School. At Balliol his faith had been attenuated, but not lost. In his mature years it became crystalline. It was hard, irrefragable, based upon truth rather than on transitory relevance, on reason rather than on emotion. It had almost a military character. St. Dominic was his favorite saint. Belloc reasoned thus: Christ claimed to be divine. He was crucified, and three days later He rose from the dead. Such is the evidence, both written and traditional, and it goes back to eyewitnesses. Other views of the matter substitute theories, for which there is no evidence, for events for which there is much evidence. Faith does not rest on speculation or emotion— these may help or hinder it and are thoroughly marginal—but on evidence, available to everyone. Belloc's position is hard and sane and admirable.

v

As for the Catholic Church, here too he was a historian with the past of Europe in his bones. He knew that the Church, both in its liturgy and its creed, was traceable back to the origins, to those who had seen and talked with Christ, and that it was not a new thing but was continuous with those origins. He embraced the scandal of the concreteness of the Church in his famous formula, "Europe is the Faith and the Faith is Europe." Of course the proposition is phrased polemically: *contra* idealism. Belloc always insisted upon the historical reality, and the Church was, historically, European and followed European expansion. Theoretically, the Church is universal and might have emerged in the Egyptian empire or in China. Theoretically, God might have been born in Brazil. In fact, Christ was a Jew, and the Church is European. The history of Europe cannot be understood without reference to the central role of the Church, and the Church cannot be understood apart from its actual history in Europe. Belloc's scandalous formulation is really a way of saying that grace perfects nature and that Providence would not have rooted the Church in Assyria rather than in Rome. This is a scandal to idealists and universalists everywhere, and Belloc meant it to be one.

In Praise of Chesterton

G. K. Chesterton was a much greater literary critic than his current reputation would suggest and also a much greater man, one from whom there is a good deal to be learned today. Nevertheless, he is not much read or talked about now. What he was and what he stood for matter all too little to current opinion. His name is never mentioned in the quarterlies. Most of his books are out of print, and though Sheed and Ward recently brought out a few of his things in a new edition, it has been remaindered.

Several reasons for Chesterton's eclipse, spring to mind. One is surely the very diversity of his work. He was not only a literary critic, but also a historian and moralist, a social and political theorist, a poet, a journalist, a writer of fiction, a biographer, a religious thinker, and a notable wit. His wit, indeed, was essential to him; it was an aspect of his humility: he was certain, as he said, that Satan fell through force of gravity. Yet, even if we think only of his criticism, his range was almost unbelievable. He wrote books on Chaucer, Blake, Cobbett, Dickens, Stevenson, Shaw, and Browning, not to mention Watts the painter. He was the first critic in this century to defend Pope against the Romantic depreciation; he helped to rescue Chaucer from the philologists; he published three books on Dickens, one of them easily the best so far written on him. His book on Shaw, a good friend of his though an intellectual opponent, is the best thing on Shaw (sample: "Shaw is like the Venus of Milo; all that there is of him is admirable"). And when he turned his hand to Aquinas, he produced a study of which Etienne Gilson observed, "I consider it as being without possible comparison the best book ever written on Aquinas." One could go on and on in this vein, for Chesterton resisted triumphantly the tendency toward specialization of intellect all too familiar to us.

This article first appeared in *The Yale Review* and is reprinted with permission.

His range, just because it was so enormous, dawns slowly upon the reader. The first Chesterton I hit upon was *The Victorian Age in Literature,* assigned in a Columbia seminar taught by Jacques Barzun and Lionel Trilling. I thought the assignment a bit odd. The other books in the course were mainly by what might be called the classical authors of modern thought—Blake, Nietzsche, Hegel, Tocqueville, Freud. I was certain that Chesterton did not rank—or, rather, *belong*—with them. As it turned out, I very much admired this extraordinary book, and so did everyone else who read it for the class meeting. Knowing little else about Chesterton, however, I assumed, in a careless sort of way, that this was his best work, a lonely and even accidental masterpiece. The only difficulty with this theory was that each book I then read by him contradicted it, since each, improbably, seemed as good or better.

And yet, no doubt precisely because of his range, Chesterton seems a bit unmanageable. Even trying to buy his books becomes a chore. One ends up hunting through shelves marked History, Biography, Criticism, Essays, Religious Books, Travel, and so on. One of the largest book stores in New York has thrown up its hands, so to speak, and established an independent section marked "Chesterton." Even intellectually, I suppose—though we continue to make pious observations about the "universal man" of the Renaissance—we are more comfortable with a person who can fit into a category—he writes mainly about the Romantics or about Milton, or he is a New Critic or a biographer. To name a thing is one way of controlling it, of putting it in its proper, and limited, place in the mind. Not in the least able to control Chesterton in this way, we have been forced back upon the Chesterton anecdote and legend, upon the genial Fleet Street personality ("G. K.") of vast bulk who could be found in the pubs and chop houses improvising ballads with Belloc or tossing off essays, gurgling with good humor. We like to recall the stories about the cabs that he ordered to wait, and then forgot. All this reminiscing is fun, of course. But it tends to obscure the fact that he had an extraordinary mind.

There is also the barrier of Chesterton's Catholicism, a kind of Chinese Wall to most American intellectuals. Yet, this sort of provincialism *is* oddly American and surely will fade. Such non-Catholic Europeans as Hannah Arendt, Leo Strauss, and Ludwig Wittgenstein show no such reluctance in establishing relations with the Catholic tradition in thought, and they refer to Anselm or Aquinas as readily as to Plato or Marx. And why not? The peculiar American attitude is undoubtedly due in the main to the strains connected with social mobility, as well as to the special American attitude toward the past and to the fact that in America Catholicism has not, until recently at least, been associated with the upper classes. It would be a pity, however, to miss Chesterton for the sake of this adventitious taboo, and of course no one, in order to profit from him, need accept all or even any of his theological conclusions.

Still another barrier to the appreciation of Chesterton may be the cloudy impression that he was an anti-Semite. I have heard intelligent people say that he was, and George Orwell attacked him on such grounds, writing of "literary Jew-baiting, which in the hands of Belloc, Chesterton and their followers reached an almost Continental scurrility," and further, of "Chesterton's endless tirades against Jews, which he thrust into stories and essays upon the flimsiest pretexts." That such statements could pass as fact is in itself evidence of how little Chesterton has been read in recent years. Orwell, of course, has it quite wrong. Chesterton was not an anti-Semite, was not in any sense, as that expression implies, a racist. His comments on "racial" theories of behavior are consistently scornful. As far as Jewishness is concerned, Chesterton considered it a cultural phenomenon, and he wrote about it—which in all probability is what seems odd—without embarrassment or guilt. He wrote about the French also, and about the Irish, the Germans, and so on, and he found much to admire in each of these national and cultural groups. His most pejorative comments, in fact, were about the Germans.

Finally, it may even be that his prose style itself causes some difficulties, though he was one of the masters of English prose. Indeed, any essay on him is in constant danger of being overwhelmed by the desire to let him speak for himself. Chesterton, for example writes that John Stuart Mill "boasted none of that brutal optimism with which his friends and followers of the Manchester School expounded their cheery negations. There was about Mill even a sort of embarrassment. He exhibited all the wheels of his iron universe rather reluctantly, like a gentleman in trade showing ladies over his factory." That last sentence contains an entire cultural thesis. Or consider Chesterton on three other great Victorians:

Newman's strength was a sort of stifled passion, a dangerous patience of polite logic and then: "Cowards! If I advanced a step you would run away:

it is not you I fear. *De me terrent, et Jupiter hostis."* If Newman seemed
suddenly to fly into a temper, Carlyle seemed never to fly out of one. But
Arnold kept a smile of heart-broken forbearance, as of the teacher in an
idiot school, that was enormously insulting. One trick he often tried with
success. If his opponent had said something foolish, like "the destiny of
England is in the great heart of England," Arnold would repeat the phrase
again and again until it looked more foolish than it really was. Thus he
recurs again and again to "the British College of Health in the New Road"
till the reader wants to rush out and burn the place down. Arnold's great
error was that he sometimes thus wearied us of his own phrases, as well as
of his enemies'.

Though such passages as these demonstrate very well some of
Chesterton's powers as a prose writer, it is nevertheless true that
his prose can be, as I say, a barrier, not, as Edmund Wilson maintains,
because he is diffuse, nothing could be further from the truth, but
because he is so concentrated. There are pages in Chesterton, and
almost books—I have in mind *Orthodoxy, The Victorian Age in
Literature, The Everlasting Man*—in which virtually every sentence
sets forth some complicated and memorable idea. Chesterton cannot be read quickly. One cannot settle for the drift of the thing. In
no other English prose writer after the seventeenth century does
intellect seem so ascetically concentrated, and for sensibilities accustomed to, say, Edmund Wilson's leisurely diffuseness, this sort
of thing can be exhausting.

Chesterton's relationship to Matthew Arnold was a peculiar one.
He said that he early recoiled from Arnold's influence, feeling, among
other things, that "there must be (to use an Irishism) something
shallow in the depths of any man who talks about the *Zeitgeist* as if
it were a living thing." He disliked Arnold's tone; he disapproved of
what he considered Arnold's limited and gloomy stoicism. Yet, when
he came to define Arnold's strengths as a critic, he revealed a good
deal about his own strong points. Arnold, he wrote,

simply happened to know certain things that Carlyle didn't know, that
Kingsley didn't know, that Huxley and Herbert Spencer didn't know. He
knew that England was a part of Europe: and not so important a part as it
had been the morning after Waterloo. He knew England was then (as it is
now) an oligarchical state, and that many great nations are not. He knew
that a real democracy need not live and does not live in that perpetual
panic about using the powers of the State, which possessed men like Spencer
and Cobden. . . . He knew the Catholic Church had been in history "the
Church of the multitude": he knew it was not a sect.

One can find in this passage about Arnold a view of history that runs throughout Chesterton's own work and is responsible for much of its power. To some considerable degree, this view has now been accepted academically, but in Chesterton's day, it was eccentric. He did not think of the last four hundred years in England as exhibiting the gradual advance of liberty and democracy, but rather the contrary: he thought they exhibited the gradual, and at times not so gradual, advance of the oligarchy. Chesterton wrote the history of England much as Swift or Bolingbroke would have written it if they had known more about the centuries before the Tudors, and his view of the eighteenth century was similar to theirs. He thought that the common people, during the course of several centuries, had been bilked of their personal and communal property, of their farms and common land and, more recently, of their individual businesses, by a succession of rapacious moves on the part of the "best" people, first by aristocrats and then by the magnates. He cites as evidence the seizure of Church lands and the destruction of the guilds ("simply to say that the Guilds declined is about as true as saying that Caesar quietly decayed from purely natural causes at the foot of the statue of Pompey"), the Enclosure Acts, Poor Laws, Reform Bills, and so on. Chesterton argues, and he is right, that the reign of Queen Anne saw the end of real resistance to the oligarchy, that in those years the efforts of the Tories to prevent the triumph of a faction were decisively defeated. Anne's successor, George of Hanover, "was simply something stuffed into a hole in the wall by English aristocrats, who practically admitted that they were simply stuffing it with rubbish."

In his *Short History of England* (1917), Chesterton set forth this theory and, anticipating the work of Butterfield, Namier, Feiling, and other recent writers, provided an alternative to the increasingly threadbare "Whig interpretation of history." As always in Chesterton's work, this book is full of ideas, thrown out as if casually, that could easily be expanded into other books: as the power of the oligarchy increased, he observes, "the worst that could be said is that the English humourist has been driven slowly downward in the social scale. Falstaff was a knight, Sam Weller was a gentleman's servant, and some of our recent restrictions seem designed to drive Sam Weller to the status of the Artful Dodger."

Although Chesterton was anti-Whig and used the eighteenth-century word "mob" with genuine affection ("the rise of Dickens is like the rising of a vast mob"), he was not, in the tiresome modern way, antibourgeois. One of the most important things he ever said about himself was, "I cannot do my duty as a true modern by cursing everybody who made me what I am." If his history of England provides an alternative to Macaulay, his *Autobiography*, which contains one of the best childhoods in literature, stands in implicit defiance of *The Way of All Flesh*. He lacked entirely that modern habit of mind, probably traceable to Rousseau, that regards all that has existed and all that now exists in society as the enemy of some putative unconditioned freedom, in the name of which it is to be decried and destroyed. Chesterton thought of the past as being as complex as the present and as possessing its particular virtue and charm. He knew that "no one can understand tradition, or even history, who has not some tenderness for anachronism." He thought that in Macaulay, as in Scott, "some of the best things . . . are the surnames that he did not make."

One reason he lacked the modern hatred of the past, as John Cuddihy, a devoted Chestertonian, has pointed out in an unpublished paper, is that he liked his own past, his own family, and particularly his father. He had no *resentiment*, no contempt for his own class or desire to leave it, either by rising socially or claiming the classlessness of the artist and intellectual. "It may be taken generally," he wrote in one of his earliest essays, "that a man loves his own stock and environment, and that he will find something to praise in it." This assumption, alas, sounds rather old-fashioned now; it cannot, any longer, be "taken generally."

His father, Edward Chesterton, a businessman of the older sort, ran a house agency business. He was a Unitarian and, in politics, a Liberal, though he knew that even these commitments, as he understood them were becoming old-fashioned. "I was brought up," his son recalled, "among people who were Unitarians and Universalists, but who were well aware that a great many people around them were becoming agnostics or even atheists." The extraordinary variety of his father's hobbies may have had much to do with his son's sense of the richness of domestic possibility. "His den or study was piled high with the stratified layers of about ten or twelve creative amusements; water-colour painting and modelling and photography and stained glass and fretwork and magic lanterns and medieval illumination." Characteristically, he had written a book about old Dutch architecture but never bothered to publish it.

In his father, Chesterton found something that was to be central to his own character: a resistance to the demands of ambition, a refusal to allow ambition to absorb the energies of the private self. It is suggestive of Chesterton's evaluation of one of the main impulses of modernity that he defined this refusal by saying that his father declined to be what virtually everyone now seems secretly to wish to be, that modern priest-hero, the artist. "On the whole," he wrote, "I am glad that he was never an artist. It might have stood in his way in becoming an amateur. It might have spoilt his career; his private career. He could never have made a vulgar success of all the things he did so successfully." From his father, then, Chesterton learned that high valuation of limits, that love of property on a small scale, which he connected with self-respect and which was so characteristic of his moral temper.

In one of his best short essays, written after her death in 1901, Chesterton viewed Queen Victoria as representative of that older England he associated with his parents and their class, which even then he felt was giving way before the self-assertion and egotism he was aware of all about him. "That Queen Victoria," he wrote,

was a model of political unselfishness is well known; it is less often remarked that few modern people have an unselfishness so completely free from morbidity.... No eminent person of our time has been so utterly devoid of that disease of self-assertion which is so often rampant among the unselfish.... Amid ... all this hedonistic desire to make the most of everything there is something altogether quiet and splendid about the sober disdain with which this simple and courteous lady in a black dress left idle beside her the scepter of a hundred tyrants. The heart of the whole nation warmed as it had never warmed for centuries at the thought of having in their midst a woman who cared nothing for her rights, and nothing for those fantastic duties which are more egotistical than rights themselves.

Chesterton knew what makes a person who is insisting, even justifiably, on his "rights" so oddly unattractive: the assertion of rights, he saw, might be only or in large part a mode of self-assertion, and an especially corrupting mode in that the egotism is masked by "virtue." He sensed in the self-restraint of the older middle class, as represented by his father and by Victoria, a kind of reminiscence of the Christian virtue of humility.

Because Chesterton had this quality himself, he possessed a kind of security in relation to the question of social class that has since entirely disappeared. He was, he said flatly, entirely bourgeois. His acceptance of that fact constituted a kind of security. Knowing quite easily and naturally who and what he was, he did not, in the familiar modern way, derive his identity from *ideas*. One senses in reading through his works that because of his acceptance of the given and his consequent liberation from the need for self-assertion, he was capable of peculiarly acute perception. He was able to see things clearly because he had a genuine disinterestedness in relation to them: he could relax any will to improve and to use. Innocence, as Milton knew, is corrupted by ambition, and it was Chesterton's freedom from a certain kind of ambition that allowed him so often to see the object innocently, as it really was.

ii

Some discussion has gone on among Chestertonians as to whether he was a liberal or a conservative, and it is an important point because his thought was, perhaps, essentially political. Even his religious beliefs, as he shows in *Orthodoxy*, had their origin in his experience of how men behave in society, though he moved, and it is not generally recognized how slowly he moved, toward the formulation of this experience in metaphysical terms. He agreed with Aristotle on the primacy of politics, and he asserted that primacy, although his own culture was more and more disposed to consider art the most important of man's pursuits. Thus, in considering Savonarola's attempt to establish decent government in Florence, he was able to deplore the fact that there "are some at the present day who have so strange a respect for art and letters, and for mere men of genius, that they conceive the reign of the Medici to be an improvement on that of the great Florentine republican."

His father, "a Liberal of the school that had existed before the rise of Socialism," had assumed as a matter of course "that all sane people believed in private property." Chesterton himself began as a partisan of the Liberal Party and campaigned for it in the election of 1906, but he soon became disillusioned with the policies of the party. Even more, he began to sense that there was something sinister, something inhuman, about the progressives and reformers he met, "high-minded, hatchet-faced, hard humanitarian idealists." For his father's generation, a liberal had been someone who favored the extension of liberty—religious and intellectual freedom, more humane economic institutions, privacy of all kinds, the "popular" cause, generally speaking, against kings and oligarchs. But by the time Chesterton became involved with politics, "liberal" had come to mean someone who favored the extension of government in the interest of efficiency, hygiene, and morality rather narrowly interpreted. Freedom, Chesterton saw, was something the newer liberals no longer believed in. The growing use of the term "progressive" was disturbingly symptomatic: "liberal" had, at least, implied values of some sort, but "progressive" implied only movement. Still, Chesterton could scarcely have called himself a conservative. He had even less in common with the party of Balfour, Bonar Law, and the absurd "King" Carson than he had with the Liberals. He became, accordingly, a political maverick. Nevertheless, I think it is fair to say that his instincts, in a general way, were what we today would call conservative.

He was a populist in the manner of Cobbett, and he agreed with Cobbett's interpretation of English history. What he liked about the populace, though, were its conservative instincts, its resistance, based on experience, to cant and intellectual fashion. Like them, he deeply distrusted novel theories of human nature; nor would it have surprised him to find that today the ordinary man is likely to have a surer sense of the political significance of, say, the Berlin Wall than the *New Statesman* essayist. Chesterton spoke of tradition in words Burke would have approved:

Tradition may be explained as an extension of the franchise. Tradition means giving the vote to the most obscure of all classes, our ancestors. It is the democracy of the dead. Tradition refuses to submit to the small and arrogant oligarchy of those who merely happen to be walking about.

Chesterton's attacks upon the progressives have much in common with those later made by George Orwell, another admirer of Cobbett. In *The Road to Wigan Pier,* Orwell argues that there is something less than human about those who are attracted to progressive movements, that such movements attract "every fruit-juice drinker, nudist, sandal-wearer, sex maniac, Quaker, 'Nature-Cure' Quack, pacifist and feminist in England." In a similar vein, Chesterton, recalling that early in his career he met "an ethereal little lady with pale blue eyes and pale green garments" who was the vegetarian wife of an antiwar journalist, remarked that "her type of thinking has run through all my life and times like a thread of pale green and blue." Like Orwell, he was convinced that people of this sort, who had rejected some qualities of normal humanity, would, if given power, do violence to the instincts of normal human beings.

Living in an era of utopianism—the names of Wells and Shaw suggest one of its dominant moods—Chesterton noted that the future the progressives invoked had very little actual content; it was merely to be quite different from anything that had as yet existed. This future, indeed, seemed merely a missile aimed at what was familiar:

Disapproving of all soldiers, of all priests, of most merchants and especially merchant adventurers, of all kings and princes and a great many other rulers as well, feeling only irritation against squires or gentry, sneering by habit at the bourgeoisie or respectable middle class, having been always taught that peasants are stagnant or superstitious . . . having successfully rejected all these different human traditions, as falling below some one or other of the new notions of progress, they are left with a humanity in which they can love in the abstract but hardly in the concrete. There is not much of humanity left when you take away all the people whom they regard as obstacles to the progress of humanity. Therefore, any outline they trace of a world without war is a curiously hard and blank outline.

He saw that the progressives—he called them the "new Puritans, who have purified themselves even of religion"—had inherited the historic role of the aristocrats and the oligarchs. When they got control of the machinery of the modern state, they would grind ordinary men just as their predecessors had done, only in a subtler and fiercer way since it would be carried on in the name of virtue rather than for material profit.

Chesterton battled the new humanitarian oppressors in characteristically vigorous fashion. In his paper the *New Witness*, for example, he campaigned against the schemes of the hygienists—against the bill that would permit the removal of "retarded" children from their parents in order to place them in institutions; against the Health Visitors Bill, which empowered inspectors to enter the homes of the poor to see that the children were kept clean; against the forcible sterilization of those deemed "mentally unfit." In each case, Chesterton was defending a particular kind of freedom against the virtuous oppression of the new "liberals."

His sister-in-law, Mrs. Cecil Chesterton, writes of an incident that shows what he was driving at. One day a father whose son was to be taken away and placed in a mental hospital came to the Chestertons for help. "You see," he explained, "Jim doesn't speak much yet, but he understands all we say and is very bright at his lessons. He loves sums, but they tell us he is so backward in his speech that he has to go away." *He loves sums:* it is a memorable phrase. Nothing could be added; one could only act. The Chestertons, hiding Jim away with his grandmother in the country, enlisted the aid of a private mental specialist and fought the Board of Education in the courts. In the end they won. But it is far from certain that the things they were fighting for will win in the end. "From the very beginning," wrote Chesterton in 1936 as he looked back over his life,

my instinct about justice, about liberty and equality, was somewhat different from that current in our age; and from all the tendencies toward concentration and generalization. It was my instinct to defend liberty in small nations and poor families; that is, to defend the rights of man as including the rights of property; especially the property of the poor.

He hoped "by guilds and small independent groups gradually to restore the property of the poor and the personal freedom of the family." One of the things he most disliked about Germany was that it had, even before the First World War, developed to a high degree the sort of state control that "everywhere involved an external power having a finger in the family pie."

He was, of course, far from supposing that the complexity of modern life could be abolished. He was not against the machine as such; he supported the early efforts to organize workers into labor unions. But he did think, as Gary Wills says in his excellent book on Chesterton, that "man's need for a decentralization of modern society was going to become more drastic as the twentieth century wore on." In this he was surely right. Nor did his hope for the future resemble in any way that "curiously hard and blank outline" of the progressives. It was based on the privacy, personal freedom, and self-respect he had known in the Victorian family he had grown up in, and it was informed by traditions as old as the West.

Homage to
C. S. Lewis

To most university students and their professors, C. S. Lewis is well known as a scholar and literary critic. His two books on medieval literature, his books on Milton and on sixteenth-century literature, and his widely ranging essays have firmly established his authority in the academy. Such scholarly and critical work has its independent importance, of course, quite apart from his other writing, and indeed, those students and professors who admire him in this aspect are very likely to be only marginally aware of him as he appears to the broad reading public: a phenomenally popular writer on religious subjects. As a scholar, Lewis simply knew too much to remain a prisoner to the Spirit of the Age, to succumb to the appeal of the merely fashionable. He was completely liberated from chronological snobbery. He did not suppose a statement true just because it had been made recently or because people around him seemed to accept it. "I take a very low view of 'climates of opinion,' " he wrote. "In his own subject every man knows that all discoveries are made and all errors corrected by those who ignore the 'climate of opinion.' " And beyond this, Lewis learned, by studying earlier periods and examining their assumptions, to become aware of what Whitehead calls the "of courses" of culture—the things everyone assumes to have been proved or to be self-evidently true and therefore leaves unexamined. Lewis condemned

the uncritical acceptance of the intellectual climate common to our own age and the assumption that whatever has gone out of date is on that account discredited. You must find why it went out of date. Was it ever refuted (and if so by whom, where, and how conclusively) or did it merely die away as fashions do? If the latter, this tells us nothing about its truth or falsehood. From seeing this, one passes to the realization that our own age is also a "period" and certainly has, like all periods, its own characteristic illusions. They are likely to lurk in those widespread assumptions that are so ingrained in the age that no one dares to attack or feels it necessary to defend them.

Surely such liberation from present-mindedness is one of the main reasons—perhaps even *the* main reason—for studying history or literature. In Lewis' last book, *The Discarded Image*, the liberating effect of historical study is demonstrated with particular clarity. This book, published posthumously, consists of a series of lectures he delivered several times in his course at Cambridge, and it deals with the medieval conception, or "image" as the title specifies it, of the universe. This model is fairly familiar in its outlines. At the center is the earth—spherical, of course (the idea that the Middle Ages thought the earth flat is entirely false)—and the earth is surrounded by a series or transparent globes, one above the other. Fixed in each of those spheres is a luminous body, a planet. Farther out comes the *stellatum,* the sphere of the stars, and finally the *Primum Mobile* or First Mover, itself invisible but, moved by its love of God, imparting movement to all the inner spheres. Beyond the *Primum Mobile* we move outside space and time altogether into a realm of pure intellectual light—Heaven.

ii

Medieval space, unlike ours, was neither dark nor silent. "The sun illuminates the whole universe; night is merely the conical shadow cast by the earth, and it turns through the brilliantly lighted universe like the hand of a clock." Beyond that, the spheres as they turn produce harmonious music.

How did it feel to inhabit such a universe? To "look out on the night sky with modern eyes is like looking out over a sea that fades away in the mist.... To look up at the towering medieval universe is more like looking up at a great building." Our "universe is romantic and theirs was classical." Or again: in "modern, that is, in evolutionary thought Man stands at the top of a stair whose foot is lost in obscurity; in this, he stands at the bottom of a stair whose top is invisible with light."

Lewis knew and could communicate what it felt like to live inside the model, but he knew other things as well. He knew that in many respects medieval thought was highly sophisticated. No more than a modern theologian does, for example, did St. Jerome hold every sentence of the Old Testament to be scientific or historical truth. He said that Moses described Creation "after the manner of a popular poet" or, as we would say, "mythically." Lewis knew that symbolism and a subtle sense of the relations between symbols and facts are not things we have discovered recently. The Middle Ages, for example, believed in the existence of three hierarchies of angels, each hierarchy consisting of three different kinds. The scheme derived from a writer known as the pseudo-Dionysus. A modern writer, with a good deal of bad nineteenth-century art in mind, would consider the entire system clear proof of medieval fatuity. But Lewis points out that these angels, of course, were *celestial* beings and that "educated people in the Middle Ages never believed the winged men who represent angels in painting and sculpture to be more than symbols." Even the vast intricate model of the universe itself, he points out, had a symbolic quality. "The great masters do not take any model quite so seriously as the rest of us. They know that it is, after all, only a model, possibly replaceable."

In that last sentence, Lewis' phrase "the rest of us" can be only a lecturer's courtesy, for the point he is making is in fact the main one to emerge from *The Discarded Image.* Our mental models of reality, he argues, are metaphors and not reality itself; even more, they are cultural productions, as much the constructions of imagination as a poem or a sonata. Models of the universe change because "nature gives most of her evidence in response to the questions we ask her"; or, elsewhere, "What we learn from experience depends on the kind of philosophy we bring to experience."

As he points out, it is possible to trace the human demand for a developing, or "modern," universe back into the eighteenth century. When the demand "is full grown, the scientists go to work and discover the evidence on which our belief in that sort of universe would now be held to rest. . . . Nature has all sorts of phenomena in stock and can suit many different tastes." Lewis' contention is not, of course, that the universe does not develop. It does. But our stress on that fact is cultural. A hierarchical arrangement of the evidence is also perfectly conceivable. Even the old cosmology accommodated the facts and might actually still do so:

The "old" astronomy was not in any sense "refuted" by the telescope. The scarred surface of the Moon and the satellites of Jupiter can, if one wants, be fitted into a geocentric scheme. Even the enormous, and enormously different distances of the stars can be accommodated if you are prepared to make their sphere, the *stellatum,* of a vast thickness.

As we come to the end of these lectures, we realize that we have witnessed a breathtaking piece of intellectual virtuosity. Lewis' point, of course, is not that we should attempt to will the medieval cosmology back into being. For some reason, any writer who deals with the Middle Ages runs the risk of being charged with a desire to "turn the clock back," and indeed, Miss Kathleen Nott, an English critic of leftist and anti-Christian bent, has wooden-headedly accused Lewis of just such an intention. But Lewis' imaginative sympathy is not to be construed in any such fashion. Did not Tawney observe that sympathy is a catalyst of knowledge? Still less does Lewis mean to argue that Christianity is bound up with the old model. He even points out ways in which the model and the spirit of Christianity are in tension, if not outright conflict. He means, rather, to demonstrate—by describing the model and then stepping outside it—how rooted in assumption *any* model is and, finally, how rooted in assumption are many attitudes that pass as established truth.

This is a theme that recurs again and again in his books. "The moment rational thought ceases," he writes in *Miracles,* "imagination, mental habit, and the 'spirit of the age' take charge of you again. New thoughts until they have themselves become habitual, will affect your consciousness as a whole only while you are actually thinking them. Reason has but to nod at his post, and instantly Nature's patrols are infiltrating. Therefore ... the mere gravitation of the mind back to its habitual outlook must be discounted" when we are considering whether a statement is true or false. By inhabiting the medieval consciousness and then stepping outside it, we practice, so to speak, performing the same operation with regard to the presuppositions of our own period. Far from being antimodern, as Miss Nott would have him, Lewis, in his rationalism, in his distrust of habit and established attitude, is (compare him with Burke) almost frighteningly modern. And paradoxically, it is this radical skepticism about assumptions, this distrust of received opinion, that gives to his religious writing its special kind of power.

iii

The point is that, as far as religion is concerned, the current climate of opinion is hostile. As Lewis says in *Miracles,* "We all have Naturalism in our bones. . . . Naturalistic assumptions, beggings of the questions . . . will meet you on every side—even from the pens of clergymen. You must develop a nose like a bloodhound for those steps in the argument which depend not on historical or linguistic knowledge" but on concealed assumptions, and "this means that you must really re-educate yourself: must work hard and consistently to eradicate from your mind the whole type of thought in which we have been brought up." This is certainly a large undertaking, but the intention to re-educate, to combat rooted assumption, is central to Lewis' work.

Mr. Edmund Wilson blandly informs us that religious belief is an impossibility for any intelligent modern person and, further, that no intelligent person can now suppose Jesus to have been divine. Wilson himself is intelligent and well-read; his ratiocinative powers are far from contemptible; he would have known at once that both of his statements are completely untrue, if he had paused to examine them. Whether or not religious propositions are true or not, it is simply a matter of fact that men who are both intelligent and modern affirm that they are true. Eliot, Lewis, Maritain, Tate, Auden, Gilson, Waugh, Claudel—all believe precisely those propositions that, Wilson asserted, no intelligent modern person can believe. They are intelligent. They are modern. And Wilson himself knows no pertinent fact they are unaware of.

When he made those statements, Wilson was acting as a spokesman for the Spirit of the Age. He supposed that the assault upon Christianity has been intellectually conclusive merely because it has been, in many places, historically successful. Most intellectual solecisms have moral roots; Wilson's proceeded from a form of success worship. At one time, as the elderly devil Screwtape writes to his nephew Wormwood in *The Screwtape Letters,* men "knew pretty well when a thing was proved and when it was not; and if it was proved they really believed it." But "with the weekly press and other such weapons we have largely altered that." They now do not "think of doctrines as primarily 'true' or 'false,' but as 'academic' or 'practical,' 'outworn' or 'contemporary,' 'conventional' or 'ruthless.' "

If the average intellectual during the Middle Ages did not really entertain the idea that Christianity might be false, the average intellectual today does not really entertain the idea that it might be true. He does not ask those essential question, so insisted upon by Lewis: "Was it ever refuted (and if so by whom, where, and how conclusively) or did it merely die away as fashions do? If the latter, this tells us nothing about its truth or falsehood." Of course, it takes a remarkable man, and a remarkably free one, to insist upon those questions.

The explanation of how a climate of opinion hostile or indifferent to Christianity came to be established cannot be attempted here. It is no doubt symptomatic that we lack a genuine history (and I do not mean a self-congratulatory account of the advance of the Light) of the emergence of naturalism—a history that investigates it in its significant sociological, psychological, political, and economic aspects. In a recent book, John Courtney Murray made a distinction between "the aristocratic atheism of the seventeenth and eighteenth centuries" and "the bourgeois atheism of the nineteenth century." The first was an attempt to understand the world, the second, to make money in it. Both were deeply involved with politics.

The aristocratic atheism of the French Enlightenment . . . embodied a political will. The attack on religion—more exactly on the Catholic faith and on the status of the Church in public life—had as one of its important purposes to undermine the status of the king, to clear the way for a direct attack upon the absolute monarchy, which was supported by the power of the Church. Similarly, a political will lay behind the bourgeois atheism of the nineteenth century. Across its hostility to religion ran the intention of eradicating the remnants of feudalism—the power of the Restoration monarchies, the privileges of the nobility, the wealth of the great landowners—which, again, stood in close relationship to the ecclesiastical order. In the seventeenth and eighteenth and even in the nineteenth centuries, you could not touch religion without touching politics—and vice versa.

The emergence of antireligious thought was thus in resonance with powerful political and economic tendencies, in harmony with the Spirit of the Age. And when an argument is thus in resonance with powerful historical tendencies, it receives a great deal of unearned power.

iv

When we examine as closely as we can the process by which the "climate of opinion" actually became established, some remarkable things emerge. The closeness of the examination is important, because it is *specialized* knowledge that seems to be the most effective weapon against assumption and erroneous if widespread opinion. In the study of history, for example, intensive research on limited areas has exploded most of the assumptions reflected in nineteenth-century history books or in such broad popular surveys as H. G. Wells' *Outline of History.* But though such specialized knowledge does, I suppose, diffuse itself throughout society, the process is at best a slow one. How many of us actually know, with any degree of certainty, the state of knowledge on matters outside our immediate field—even on matters of great importance? How many people actually know very much about the state of knowledge on the question of the historical reliability of the synoptic Gospels? Are they, in the view of sober scholars today, mostly myth? Works of fiction? Is Christ a corn god?

We recall that Arnold spoke of "all the science of Tübingen," meaning the most important and influential school of German Biblical criticism, and that he considered it a model of scientific method. But what, in fact, has been the fate of its scholarship? The best modern scholarship now asserts that vital parts of the German criticism rested "on no evidence whatsoever, and belongs purely to the realm of fancy." It is now clear that Ferdinand Bauer, the greatest of the Tübingen scholars, as well as his followers, was fatally in error about the dating of the New Testament, and, supposing large parts of it of late origin (sometime in the second century), he spun out fanciful theories about the "development" of the text we possess. But as Stephen Neill points out, "Every serious scholar now agrees that the books were written not later than 100 A. D., that is, within seventy years of the death of Jesus Christ, and in the lifetime of at least some believers who had seem Him in the flesh." Most importantly, the Gospel of Mark "was written not more than forty years after the death of Christ" and "may have been written considerably earlier." This dating is of immense importance. The Tübingen school held that the gospel narrative evolved out of the life of the early Church and reflected not history but disputes within the early community (and so "would have allowed us no more than the echoes of early conflicts and tendencies in the primitive Church, from which we could pick up faint gleams and shadows of a real Jesus of Nazareth"). The earlier dating, however, rules out such an evolution. What disputes did occur took place after the narrative was established.

Not only are the key documents now accorded an early date, but it is known that they were written *as history* by writers who knew what a historical fact is, and by individuals to whom history was of supreme importance. According to Stephen Neill's *Interpretation of the New Testament, 1861–1961* (1964), it "was of immense importance to the Christian that the later acts of God, like the earlier in the Old Testament, were acts of God in history." Or again: "When the historian approaches the Gospels, the first thing that strikes him is the extraordinary fidelity with which they reproduced, not the conditions of their own time, but he conditions of Palestine in the time and during the ministry of Christ."

Thus, though the older theory held that the Gospels had evolved over an extended period and that they were in large part myths or fictions designed for the edification of the early Christian community, we now know that they were of very early date, that the incidents they describe were well known before they were written down, that in the ethos of the community history was crucially important, and that a scrupulous regard was held for protecting the narrative from accretion or distortion. Finally, we know that the narrative was written down because the community was turning outward to the world, and it was intended for people who did not know the living local tradition.

As for the Resurrection story itself—which is absolutely decisive for Christianity and for which the so-called biographies of Strauss, Renan, and others had offered purely naturalistic explanations (thus moving, said Arnold, in the right direction)—one of the best modern studies is by Hans Freiherr von Campenhausen of the University of Heidelberg. In his *Tradition und Leben: Krafte der Kirchenge-schichte* (1960), he includes a lengthy study of the Resurrection narratives. He attaches great weight to the historical evidence of I Corinthians 15, pointing out that the epistle was probably written in A. D. 56, less than thirty years after the Crucifixion, and that Paul, in touch with the leaders of the Church in Jerusalem, would hardly have confined his conversations with them to the issue of whether Gentiles should be taken into the Church. Von Campenhausen concludes that probably no more than ten years passed between the Resurrection itself and the day on which Paul received first-hand information concerning the events of Christ's life from those who had direct knowledge of them. It is this knowledge that he claims to have transmitted to the Corinthians when he led them to Christ.*

---

*Here is the relevant passage in Ronald Knox's translation of *I Corinthians 15*: "The chief message I handed on to you, as it was handed on to me, was that Christ, as the scriptures foretold, died for our sins; that he was buried, and then, as the scriptures foretold, rose again on the third day. That he was seen by Cephas, then by the eleven apostles, and afterward by more than five hundred of the brethren at once, most of whom are alive at this day, though some have gone . . . and if Christ has not risen, then our preaching is groundless. Worse still, we are convicted of giving false testimony about God."

"It is only rarely," observes Stephen Neill, "that we have such good historical evidence for anything in the ancient world."

Plainly, this evidence cannot establish with finality the truth of the Resurrection story. But it is also fair at this point to ask the following question: Supposing for a moment that the story *is* true, what *other* evidence than what we have might reasonably be expected?

We are driven to the conclusion, then, that the Gospels are historical in intention. This is not to say, of course, that they could not be mistaken or even deceitful—the question on which the whole issue turns. Whether or not they are inaccurate (through delusion or conspiracy) is precisely what each individual judgment must face, asking the questions normally applied to any testimony: number of witnesses, their agreement or lack of it, their character and credibility (i. e., Are they reliable on other matters?), and so on; and we will see how C. S. Lewis' judgment operated here. But the Gospels are not myth, and they are not mainly a reflection of Church history. In this sense, sober modern scholarship has lead to an attitude toward the Gospels that, oddly enough, is closer to the traditional view of them—to the view, say, of Dr. Johnson or Newman—than to that of Strauss or Renan or Arnold.*

I do not for a moment mean to say, of course, that the great critical effort of the nineteenth century—all the science of Tübingen—was in vain. It possessed, to be sure, perhaps more than its share of the pathos that so often surrounds our enterprises. One thinks back on Ferdinand Bauer (1792–1860), a heroic figure, tireless, at his desk by four o'clock every morning, turning out in his mature years sixteen thousand pages of scholarly prose—the equivalent of a four hundredpage book every year for forty years—yet led by false assumptions "into error on every principal point of New Testament criticism." And, because that scholarly error, eloquently diffused by *literati,* helped to create a climate of opinion dismissive on mistaken

---

*One would not guess from their paperback sales that the more recent antihistorical approaches to the Gospels, those of Barth and Bultmann, as well as of the so-called Form Critics, have been dealt with devastatingly. See the relevant chapters in Neill, as well as *The Study of the Synoptic Gospels* by Augustin Cardinal Bea (London, 1965). The attitude of both Barth and Bultmann has been conditioned by the tactics of preaching: Bultmann wishes to give the narrative an existentialist meaning, and Barth deliberately turns away from the historical question in order to purify and heighten the act of "faith." As for the Form Critics, some of their basic axioms, upon which their whole approach depends, have simply been shown to be false.

grounds of Christian claims, the critical movement must also be said to have had tragic effects. Throughout the nineteenth century, indeed, the whole enterprise appeared baneful not only to the benighted but to men of sensitive conscience as well. Still, despite the fact that it made egregious mistakes and often created a misleading impression, we can see that, through raising key questions, the critical movement transformed the study of the Bible. Today we know more about the text, about the date and mode of its composition, about the meaning of key words and passages, and about the life of the early Church than would have been possible without the critical movement. If it has thus resulted not in the destruction or de-mythologization of the Bible but rather in a strengthened sense of its value as historical evidence, then that result is simply another of those ironies of which history is so fertile.

But this conclusion remains as, I think it is fair to say, "specialized knowledge." It would not be known to the average professor of sociology or of English, let alone in the marketplace. It was not known to Mr. Edmund Wilson. Given this situation, C. S. Lewis, and before him, G. K. Chesterton, had a vital and indeed unprecedented function to perform. They are, so to speak, *substitutes* for tradition. Until modern times, the majority of people received their knowledge of religious matters by a kind of cultural osmosis. Philosophical conclusions and doctrinal significance reached them through ceremony and sermon, custom and observance. They did not have to be scholars or reasoners to stand in some kind of relationship to specialized knowledge and to the insights of genius. But this condition no longer obtains. Not only does the life of the community no longer incorporate religious knowledge, but the churches themselves, in consequence of the cultural situation, too often have little intellectual vitality. I myself have heard only half a dozen sermons that were not outright insults to the intelligences of those who heard them.

Indeed, a kind of historical reversal has taken place. At the beginning of the nineteenth century, the majority of people were Christians and were in a vital relationship with a continuous tradition. They actually knew a great deal about religious doctrine. If they did not always understand, they nevertheless read the Bible. At the same time, a few advanced thinkers were skeptics. Today the masses, especially in the great cities, are quite cut off from tradition and know very little about Christianity, even when they profess it. A great many are indifferent. The clergy seem more and more driven to making fantastic statements in order to attract attention, or perhaps through simple ignorance on their own part. Yet today a number of advanced thinkers are Christians. The Victorian situation has been reversed. These circumstances define Lewis' role. "In the conditions produced by a century or so of Naturalism . . . we must get the truth ourselves or go without it."

A moment ago, I spoke of the "surprises" that constantly emerge out of Lewis' writing. But I was far from meaning that he invents things or that he introduces doctrinal novelty. No one could be less like a modish bishop. In *The Screwtape Letters,* he notes the Vicar, "who has been so long engaged in watering down the faith to make it easier for a hard-headed congregation that it is now he who shocks his parishioners with his unbelief, not vice versa." The point is worth stressing. Some years ago, I happened to attend a course of lectures on modern literature at a university in Boston. The lecturer was extremely good. He was devoted to modern literature, he was an atheist, and—not necessarily in consequence—he was far to the Left politically. As the weeks went by, he found himself increasingly embarrassed by the *Christianity* of so many of the writers he had to deal with and whose works he loved. At long last he broke off the lecture and addressed the class personally and angrily. The class was made up of college students, for the most part, Irish Roman Catholics from the Boston area. It was clear that he knew the writers in question better than anyone who was listening to him. "See here," he said. "these men, Eliot and Lewis and Tate and the others, *they* don't believe what *you* believe: Heaven, Hell, the Virgin Birth, the Resurrection, and all that. For *them* it's only a system of symbolism, a way of disciplining *feeling.*"

No, it is not. Doctrinal differences aside—Lewis was an Anglican—and taking into account differences in erudition and intellectual power, Lewis believed precisely what those students believed and in the same literal way. He knew what symbolism is, and he knew when symbolic language is being used, and he knew that men in the past had known this too. But he did not consider as symbolic the supernatural events of the Gospels or the doctrines of the Virgin Birth and the Incarnation, and he did not think the doctrine of the afterlife a myth. A modish bishop once announced smilingly that he had "given up" belief in the Virgin Birth. But Lewis, in his clear-minded way, knew what the issue really is, and he knew that the advance of science does not affect it one way or the other. We do know more about biology than St. Joseph did, but on the point in question, he knew as well as we do the way in which infants ordinarily are conceived. He did not consider that what had happened was anything other than extraordinary.

The real question at issue here is of presuppositions—that is, Is the universe the kind of place in which miracles can occur? The Spirit of the Age answers no, and many liberal clergymen tacitly agree, even though, as Lewis says, then "the claim which Christianity has been making for the last two thousand years is simply false." But in his very convincing book on the subject of miracles, Lewis faces the philosophical issue squarely and answers yes, on the evidence, the universe is that kind of place. Reflection can liberate one from a thoroughgoing naturalism. And although Lewis thought that "it is easier to argue, on historical grounds, that the Incarnation actually occurred than to show, on philosophical grounds, the probability of its occurrence," he also saw that:

the "historical difficulty of giving for the life, sayings, and influence of Jesus any explanation that is not harder than the Christian, is very great. The discrepancy between the depth and sanity and (let me add) *shrewdness* of His moral teaching and the rampant megalomania which must lie behind His theological teaching unless He is God, has never been satisfactorily got over. Hence the non-Christian hypotheses succeed one another with the restless fertility of bewilderment.

As for the Resurrection, Lewis believed that, far from being a myth, it had occurred in history in the same sense as, say, the Battle of Waterloo had.

For Whom
the Bell Tolled

It was fifty years ago now, the "wound in the heart." Rightist uprisings against the republican government occurred throughout Spain and succeeded in Seville, Galicia, and Badajoz. Government forces held in Madrid, Valencia, and Barcelona. In an azure dawn, General Francisco Franco, commander of the Spanish forces in the Canary Islands, arrived in Morocco in a Dragon Rapide biplane rented in London by a journalist to take command of the Spanish Foreign Legion. The war in Spain became a political obsession in the West.

That same summer, Hitler and Mussolini loomed over the Continent. It seemed to many that the Axis powers were on the march against democracy in Spain and that Franco and the Nationalists were their chosen instruments. Looking back on the Spanish Civil War today, however, one concludes that it was not very well understood. Franco was no Hitler or even Mussolini, and in victory he refused to cooperate in Hitler's projected seizure of Gibraltar. Spain was different.

And so it remains. Some years age, I was hitchhiking along the beach road north of Barcelona, the sun so bright that it hurt my eyes, the landscape utterly parched. A pickup truck pulled up, and I climbed in. A young Spaniard was driving, dark eyes and all smiles. I tried not to notice that on the floor by my feet was a small, sophisticated-looking submachine gun. On the floor also was a stack of political literature. His organization appeared to be something called Warriors of Christ the King. We chatted about the upcoming bullfights in Gerona, a provincial capital. At length, I acknowledged the presence of the machine gun with a weak joke: "Going to do

This article originally appeared in *Commentary,* December 1986. Reprinted with permission. The review of Kenneth Lynn's *Hemmingway* first appeared in *Commentary,* October 1987 and is reprinted with permission.

some hunting?" "No, Señor. But you just don't know what can come up." Basque terrorists? Catalonian separatists? Communists? A rival faction? Who knows.

My point is that this was Spain and not England or the United States. Would that, fifty years ago when the Spanish Civil War broke out , this distinction had been more clear. The fact is, the republican government in Madrid in 1936 could not govern the country. Perhaps no government could. Politics were wild: partisan *pistoleros* roamed the streets, parliamentarians were murdered, the Communist deputy known as La Pasionaria made blood-curdling speeches in the Cortes, churches were put to the torch. This hot and tawny peninsula, this piece of Africa attached to Europe, became a killing field.

Different or not, however, the mentality of the democratic West became intensely involved in Spanish matters, and on the evidence of the recent bout of nostalgia aroused by the fiftieth anniversary of the war, it remains involved to this day. The literary critic Alfred Kazin recently lectured in Spain, and there is fire in his ashes. The Spain of today is "not my country," he has written in the *New Republic.* "The Spanish Civil War, like what followed, was *my* war. In the course of it, I lost friends. . . . The destroyers of the Spanish Republic would always be my enemies." Kazin acknowledges that today his "Spanish colleagues and friends smiled gravely at this. Since they and their families, the Spanish people, had borne the brunt of the war, they now seemed disposed to let well enough alone." Spain now has a moderate democratic government. It has joined the Common Market. The Spanish Communist Party is a fossil, and Spanish conservatives consider pornography a greater threat than communism. For most Spaniards, then, the war is over. But not for Kazin. The "destroyers of the Spanish Republic" will "always" be his enemies.

ii

In 1936, a young Communist, Josip Broz, who would be known to history as Tito and who could not then live in his native Yugoslavia, ran an operation in Paris. He funneled volunteers down the road to Spain to fight for the Republic. George Orwell, seething with resentment at the British class system, experienced Spain (very temporarily) as a deliverance. In a revolutionized Barcelona, he had a kind of social orgasm, seeing at first hand *real* egalitarianism.

Barcelona was the antithesis of Eton. You could get shot for wearing
a necktie. "Sitting in the lobby, "Orwell wrote, "it came to me that
in the most real sense my vital life did indeed end with Spain.
Nothing so vital, either in my personal life or the life of the world,
has ever come again." At the front, Orwell got a bullet through his
neck and went home. John Cornford, the brilliant young Cambridge
Communist, died fighting in Madrid. W. H. Auden went briefly to
Spain and wrote a great poem about it. He was appalled by the
carnage, but the poem remains a strong expression of the passions
involved. Auden's theme was that the past was dead, the future a
possibility, but today we face the harsh struggle:

> Tomorrow, for the young, the
>   poets exploding like bombs,
> The walks by the lake, the
>   winter of perfect communion;
>   Tomorrow the bicycle races
> Through the suburbs on summer evenings;
>   but today the struggle.
>   . . .
> Today the inevitable increase
>   in the chances of death;
> The conscious acceptance of
>   guilt in the fact of murder;
>   Today the expending of powers
> On the flat ephemeral pamphlet
>   and the boring meeting.
>   . . .
> The stars are dead; the animals
>   will not look;
> We are left alone with our day,
>   and the time is short and
>   History to the defeated
> May say Alas but cannot help or
>   pardon.

Auden later excluded this work from his collected poems because
of embarrassment over the ruthless emotions it documents and over
the personification of "History." From the perspective of the present,
indeed, its apocalyptic language about the war in Spain does seem
rather absurd. But the poem perfectly expresses an important aspect
of the spirit of the time. Emotionally, just about everyone in the
world of arts and letters went to Spain, from Auden's friend and

fellow poet, young Stephen Spender, to novelists like Ernest Hemingway, John Dos Passos, and Andre Malraux. No wonder Kazin is still so possessive.

iii

The exact nature of the Spanish Civil War, imperfectly understood at the time, can be crystallized in retrospect. At least three wars were going on there. First, many people saw the conflict as an early version, a rehearsal, of the coming war against Hitler and Mussolini—indeed, some thought the defeat of the Spanish fascists might forestall that war. For their part, Mussolini and Hitler, the former eagerly and the latter reluctantly, supported the insurgent Nationalist side represented by Franco. From this perspective, Spain was a struggle between national powers, actually not so dissimilar to an old-fashioned war.

Within Spain, however, the conflict had roots that went back at least a century, involving monarchists and republicans, anticlericals and the Church, landowners and labor unions, Basque and Catalonian separatists and Madrid centralizers, Communists, anarchists, and the fascist Falange. The permutations were often peculiar. The Basques, for example, though intensely Catholic, fought with the Republicans because they offered them great local autonomy.

From another perspective, the Spanish war prefigured not so much World War II as it did the ideological battles of our own time. It was an internationalized civil war. As the historian Vincent Brome has written, "The civil war in Spain represented a cleavage in European thought too deep and universal to remain confined to the Iberian peninsula." Indicative enough is the fact that the authoritative bibliography of the conflict by Juan Garcia Duran, published in 1964, provides a scholarly apparatus in three languages—Spanish, French, and English. Because opinion in the Western democracies was so deeply engaged, the Spanish Civil War in this perspective resembles the internationalized postwar conflicts in Greece, Korea, Vietnam, and now Nicaragua.

About forty thousand non-Spanish volunteers fought in the Communist-led International Brigades; among them were the Americans gathered in the Abraham Lincoln Battalion. Some 75 percent of these soldiers were members of the Communist Party. The Soviet OGPU, predecessor of the KGB, investigated every volunteer to insure political orthodoxy. The German Communist Willi Munzenberg, until murdered for obscure reasons at Stalin's orders, set up a vast array of "front groups" focused on Spain and was a master at manipulating the media; the Soviet agent Kim Philby, for example, went to Spain as a British journalist.

At a camp in Albacete run by French Communist Andre Marty, the volunteers received perfunctory military training and then got a quick trip to the front, where they would come up against Franco's professionals. Every unit in the International Brigades had a Communist political commissar. The only non-Communist battalion commander was an English professional soldier named Wilfred Macartney; but not for long: the unfortunate Macartney was summoned to headquarters by car, accompanied by the political commissar of the British battalion. On the brief trip, a gun somehow went off, and Macartney was wounded. Tom Wintringham, a party member, took command of the battalion.

All of the International Brigades marched behind red banners. The German contingent, the Thaelmann Colonna, took its name from a German Communist, Ernst Thaelmann, who had been murdered by Hitler. Its marching song. *"Freiheit,"* was written by Gerhardt Eisler, later a Soviet spy.

Stephen Spender visited the front a few months after the November 1936 battle of Madrid, in which a suicidal charge by two thousand men of the Eleventh International Brigade broke the back of the attacking Nationalist forces. There he met a young Englishman who had left school to fight in Spain because he identified with the struggle with liberalism. When the boy discovered that the International brigades were run entirely by Communists, he was severely disillusioned. Spender told him that, nevertheless, this was a liberal cause. "I don't know about that," the boy said. "All I see are the Communist bosses of the brigade." A couple of weeks later, the boy was killed.

iv

Spain was, altogether, a place to die, and Hemingway, with his unerring nose for death, understood this perfectly. Like so many others who went to Spain, Hemingway used the war to work out and express personal problems. The result was his 1940 novel. *For Whom the Bell Tolls.*

The "daylight" narrative of *For Whom the Bell Tolls* goes something like this. Robert Jordan, a university instructor in Spanish, joins the government (Loyalist) side in Spain because he wants to fight fascism. He accepts Communist discipline because at that time and in that place the Communists seem to be offering the most practical military program and the best military discipline, especially when compared with the Anarchists. Jordan believes in the idea of a Spanish republic. He falls ecstatically in love with Maria, the daughter of a republican mayor, who has seen her parents killed and is herself the victim of a rape by Falangists. He dies in a military operation designed to support an important government offensive. As Jordan dies, he thinks, "If we win here, we will win everywhere."

But a dark mass of knowledge in the book presses in on the reader from a contrary direction. The central movement of *For Whom the Bell Tolls* is via an awful rowing toward death, and the boat moves faster as Robert Jordan's cynicism about his political cause deepens. That deepening cynicism and the growing perception within the narrative of the corruption, disarray, and incompetence of the government side are indeed why this novel was received with such hostility by many "progressives" when it appeared.

Robert Jordan's relationship to his own immediate past is one of disgust: his father was a sentimental and religious weakling who committed suicide. The man Jordan most admires back in America is his Grandfather, a Civil War hero and Indian fighter, who is dead. In a powerful scene, Jordan recalls throwing his father's suicide weapon, the grandfather's Civil War pistol, into a lake: "and then he dropped it, holding it by the muzzle, and saw it go down making bubbles until it was just as big as a watch charm in that clear water, and then it was out of sight." But Robert Jordan is more closely involved with his father than this act of exorcism might suggest. Indeed, he possesses a sharp awareness of the reasons for his father's suicide, as the following ironic exchange with Maria indicates:

"My father was a republican all his life," Maria said. "It was for that they shot him. . . ."
"My grandfather was on the Republican national committee," Robert Jordan said. That impressed even Maria.
"And is thy father still active in the Republic?" Pilar asked.
"No. He is dead."
"Can one ask how he died?"
"He shot himself."
"To avoid being tortured?" the woman asked.
"Yes," Robert Jordan said, "to avoid being tortured."
Maria looked at him with tears in her eyes. "My father," she said "could

not obtain a weapon. Oh, I am very glad that your father had the good fortune to obtain a weapon."

"Yes. It was pretty lucky," Robert Jordan said.

"To avoid being tortured." Like his father, Jordan avoids thought, immerses himself in his professional task, and relies on absinthe because of the many things he cannot stand. What he cannot stand is the truth about existence as it is unfolded in the novel.

For Whom the Bell Tolls contains a series of set-piece narratives within the larger narrative that in their revelatory intensity resemble the italicized "chapters" of Hemingway's early collection of stories, *In Our Time.* They include a description by Pilar, the powerful female whose spirit dominates the novel, of the slaughter of some "fascist" villagers and her discourse on the odor of death. These are some of the things revelatory of existence that Jordan cannot stand.

What might be thought to justify such inevitable horrors is the "cause"—the cause of the Republic, of antifascism, of the socialist future. But the novel relentlessly strips away the possibility of such a political justification. Pilar, a true believer, puts her trust in the Republic "with a fervor as those who have religious faith believe in the mysteries." Pilar asks Jordan if he too believes:

> "And you have this same faith?"
> "In the Republic?"
> "Yes."
> "Yes," he said, hoping it was true.

At other times, his fundamental skepticism comes to the fore. "You're not a real Marxist and you know it," he tells himself. "What were his politics then? he had asked himself. He had none he told himself. But do not tell anyone else that, he thought. Don't ever admit that."

For Jordan, the ostensible cause represents a kind of fiction that permits him to function without thinking about the inexorable doom he faces or about those things that constitute the dark truth about existence. Only by completely absorbing himself in his major task, blowing up the bridge over an obscure river in the Guardarama, can he choke off his dark consciousness, but as the cause itself wears thinner, this becomes increasingly difficult to do. By the denouement, Jordan knows how it will turn out. As he spends his last night with Maria, she tells him, "The Pilar told me that we would all die tomorrow and that you know it as well as she does and that you give it no importance." Later Jordan whispers to Maria as she sleeps, "You have not known about it. We'll all be killed but we'll blow the bridge." Jordan heads for self-destruction like his father, though in the military mode of his grandfather:

Oh, let them come, he said. I don't want to do that business that my father did. I will do it all right but I'd much prefer not to have to. I'm against that. Don't think about that. Don't think at all. I wish the bastards would come, he said. I wish so very much they'd come.

This is the point toward which the novel has been driving with all of its energies from the very beginning.

V

As the case of Robert Jordan suggests, and probably that of Hemingway too, those who went to Spain fifty years ago did so for all sorts of private and personal reasons. They told themselves they were fighting fascists, and so in part they were—but to what end? They could not know that Franco quickly would purge virtually all fascists from key positions or would later block Hitler's projected march on Gibraltar, an act that undoubtedly saved the vital Mediterranean for the Allies. Recent studies have demonstrated that Franco's Spain had a better record in its policy toward Jewish refugees from the Nazis than most other countries in Catholic Europe. And as for Stalin, whose purposes the International Brigades were mainly serving, he clearly did not want victory in Spain enough to intervene in sufficient force to achieve it; perhaps what he wanted was the Spanish gold reserves, which were shipped to Russia before the final defeat of the Left. Not long after that defeat, in any event, Stalin signed a pact with Hitler.

Yet thousands of non-Spaniards waded into this mess, among them Robert Jordan and his creator, with their pathological tug toward death. George Orwell went to Spain seeking a classless society, just as, seething with guilt and class resentment, he had earlier gone "down and out" in Paris. The classless utopia Orwell thought he saw briefly in Barcelona was crushed by the Stalinists, and he got shot through the throat for his trouble and then abused by his old comrades on the Left for telling the truth about Spain—something his friend Spender deliberately refrained from doing.* No doubt simi-

---

*See "Spain and the Intellectuals," by Ronald Radosh in the *New Criterion,* October 1986.

larly powerful private emotions could be demonstrated for the journey to Spain by Spender, Malraux, Cornford, and the rest. Alfred Kazin went to Spain only in his imagination, and for him it still seems to be 1937, though, as he admits, the Spanish themselves have mostly packed it in. At least Auden had the sense to know that he was in over his head and got out fast.

vi

Ernest Hemingway began as a miniaturist, writing highly concentrated vignettes and very short stories, all of them full of multiple shaded meanings. During the 1920s, literary critics like Edmund Wilson regarded him, rightly, as a hero of art. His discipline was taut, his prose concentrated to an unprecedented degree. After 1930, however, the "sportsman" supervened, with tedious accounts of safaris and game fishing appearing regularly in the pages of *Esquire*. Wilson wrote then that Hemingway had developed an ominous resemblance to Clark Gable and was his own worst invented character. In "The Snows of Kilimanjaro" (1936) he made a sensational recovery, even though the story was in fact about his own artistic disintegration, a process confirmed in *To Have and Have Not* (1937). With the huge best-seller *For Whom the Bell Tolls* (1940), contemporary opinion diverged, but the public believed, and some critics as well, that Hemingway had written his masterpiece.

Then came the war. Hemingway covered D-day and Normandy and preceded the French general LeClerc into Paris, where he allegedly liberated the Ritz bar. During the postwar years, his "big book," eagerly awaited, never arrived. *Across the River and Into the Trees* (1950) was a disaster, somewhat recouped in 1952 by *The Old Man and the Sea* and the Nobel Prize for Literature. But as we now know from his recent biographers and from those who have seen the unpublished manuscripts at the Kennedy Library in Boston, the true story of Ernest Hemingway in the years after World War II and leading up to his suicide in 1961 was one of catastrophic moral and mental decline.

Kenneth S. Lynn's new biography of Hemingway—a book spectacular in the thoroughness of its research, in its analytical energy, and in its intellectual love of its subject—marks the culmination of a change in our biographical-critical understanding of who Hemingway was and what he achieved as an artist. The first major attempt at a definitive Hemingway biography was published by the late Carlos Baker in 1969. It remains indispensable, yet it conceals, except here and there between the lines, Hemingway's Jekyll-and-Hyde viciousness to virtually everyone around him, a viciousness in which the Hyde predominated to a terrifying degree as time went on. Carlos Baker probably had to suppress this material, which certainly was available to him from the people he interviewed, in order to retain the necessary cooperation of Hemingway's widow Mary, who knew all the horrors but who also controlled the papers and wished to preserve what was left of the facade of her relationship with her late husband.

In his 1985 biography, Jeffrey Meyers let all the horror spill out: the mounting daily cruelty, physical violence, gun threats, threats of suicide, prodigious alcoholism, public insults, continuous drunken infidelity. Kenneth Lynn records even more horrors than Meyers turned up, and others could add still more. And yet, knowing the full story, Lynn still has the charity to conclude that "while Hemingway's faults were terrible, he was also a more truly heroic figure than even the gaudiest version of his myth would grant him." Lynn means that by his art Hemingway held his powerful psychological demons at bay, at least for a while.

Lynn's book has a clear and controversial central thesis concerning the biographical source for the notorious sense of dread and nightmare that lurks beneath the surface of Hemingway's prose. Contrary to a host of critics—Malcolm Cowley, Edmund Wilson, Philip Young, and others—he holds that it derives not from a famous wound Hemingway sustained at Fossalta di Piave while serving as an ambulance driver in World War I but from a much more comprehensive wound delivered to him in early childhood by his parents, Clarence and Grace Hemingway. "Hemingway's hurt began in childhood and expanded until his death. . . . Uncertain to the point of fear about himself, he was compelled to write stories in which he endeavored to cope with the disorder of his inner world by creating fictional equivalents for it." Before he was shot down by the Austrian *Minenwarfer* (mine-thrower), Hemingway was shot down in Oak Park, Illinois, a place he ever after "hated."

His mother was imperious and sexually ambiguous and bullied his father, who was (ironically) an obstetrician. The child Ernest was dressed as a girl and treated as the "twin" of his slightly older sister Marcelline. Grace kept the male child in her own bed. Yet she encouraged his efforts at masculinity, praising him when he would pipe up that he was "'fraid a nothing." Caught up in the contradictory emotions imposed by a powerful female personality, the child developed huge fears. At the same time, his father was a weakling. Dominated by Grace—you can enjoy the pun if you want to—he taught his son to hunt and fish but also submitted to henpecking, and later he committed suicide. The mixture was potent. All his life Hemingway hated and also wanted to be loved by his mother, at the same time wanting to prove himself better than his father, whom he despised but in so many ways emulated.

Lynn is persuasive in assembling these biographical data, and he is highly illuminating as he pursues his biographical approach through the stories and novels. Again and again he makes connections between the life and the art in close rereadings of such stories as "Now I Lay Me," "Indian Camp," and the crucial "The Doctor and the Doctor's Wife." If I differ somewhat with him on the relative weights of the two "wounds," it is not because I think him wrong about the nature of Hemingway's childhood trauma, but only that I believe the war wound should not be minimized out of existence.

Lynn argues that Hemingway exaggerated the seriousness of the 1918 wound, perhaps to cover up the "real" wound, and that countless critics foolishly took him at his word. He convincingly shows on ballistic evidence that Hemingway could not have been hit by a machine-gun bullet, as he claimed. But he is less convincing when he argues that the multiple shrapnel wounds Hemingway undoubtedly did receive must therefore have been psychologically minor. Whatever Grace and Clarence did to imbue their son with his sense of mortal dread—and Lynn shows they did plenty—they are not the only ones present in the shadows of *In Our Time* (1925), the collection of stories and vignettes revolving around the Hemingway surrogate Nick Adams in which that sense of dread figures almost as a protagonist. The war, or war itself, is pervasive too. Indeed, what *In Our Time* does is seek to break down the conventional distinction between war and peace. Everyone in the book is at war, even during peacetime. Psychological bullets fly in these stories, but real bullets fly too.

vii

There are so many things in Lynn's rich study that only a sampling is possible here. Lynn informs us, or at least me, that Hemingway identified himself from childhood with Theodore Roosevelt, the Rough Rider, big-game hunter, and of course masculine hero. At the Chicago Museum of Natural History, Hemingway as a child haunted the Hall of African Mammals. He wore khakis and imagined that he was Teddy Roosevelt on safari. When he finally earned enough money to go on his own safaris, his guide was the hunter Philip Percival, who a generation earlier had actually guided Roosevelt. The brush mustache, wide grin, and restless energy that typified Hemingway owed a good deal, it seems, to a deliberate emulation of that Rough Rider.

Yet, beneath the ebullience and bonhomie, as we have learned, there existed a feral, sick viciousness, and it was directed not least at Hemingway's fellow writers. From his early attack on his mentor, Sherwood Anderson, to his attack—full of lies—on F. Scott Fitzgerald in the posthumously published *A Moveable Feast* (1964), he tried to vilify and denigrate virtually everyone in his fraternity. Both Anderson and Fitzgerald had befriended him, and before anyone had heard of him, they had promoted him as a writer. Yet Hemingway subjected both to calumny. He was also indebted, thematically and technically, to T. S. Eliot, yet he said in print that he would like to grind Eliot into powder.

Even by the loose standards of his own generation, Hemingway was a far-out anti-Semite. The character Robert Cohn of Princeton in *The Sun Also Rises* is a billiard-shot off Scott Fitzgerald, a Catholic Princetonian; Hemingway is intimating that Fitzgerald is the social equivalent of a Jew—that is, a pariah. The word "kike" flows steadily through his correspondence and conversation. The publisher Horace Liveright saw the greatness of *In Our Time* and published it in 1925, but when Hemingway wanted to break his contract with Liveright in favor of Scribner's, Liveright became a "Jew publisher." The story "Fifty Grand" contains an anti-Semitic rage disguised as a drunken tirade, with a shot at Gertrude Stein as "Steinfelt." As Lynn puts it, gently enough, Hemingway was "a much more self-controlled bigot than his friend Ezra Pound," but the fact of the matter is that here, as elsewhere, he was a ghastly bully, the obverse side of his deep insecurity.

Lynn is the first Hemingway biographer of importance to be straightforward about Hemingway's 1936–1939 Communist phase. He never joined the party, but he was a Stalinist, and out of ignorance and opportunism, he worked hand in glove with the Comintern as a willing propagandist and apologist. He removed his name from the masthead of an independent leftist magazine because it had published an anti-Stalinist cartoon. He broke with his friend, the novelist John Dos Passos, when Dos Passos protested the Stalinists' murder during the Spanish Civil War of Jose Robles, a mutual friend. On the whole subject of Spain, until 1939, when it dawned on him how he was being taken in, Hemingway was a "Republican" only in the Communists' sense of the word. There are many other discoveries and sharp insights in Lynn's *Hemingway,* illuminating to both the general reader and the specialist alike, and they are hardly all detrimental to his subject's reputation. Indeed, the greatest virtue of this biography is that it vividly reminds us how, despite everything—the vanity, the cruelty, the alcoholism, the physical disasters, and even the catastrophic loss of his powers as a writer that intensified unstoppably after World War II—Hemingway yet commanded a special music that still holds the power to thrill and delight.

Those Cypresses

About halfway between the French border and the great industrial city of Barcelona lies the provincial capital of Gerona, with its spires and arches and white-walled buildings rising among the low hills and the ochre and green farmlands of Catalonia. Foreigners and tourists know Gerona mainly as the last, good-sized town on the way to the seaside resorts of the Costa Brava. Half the year its principal thoroughfares cough and roar with Isettas, Citroens, and Mercedes Benzes. Its features are those of most small Spanish cities: the bullring, the barracks, several cafés, each with a distinctive clientele, the bank, the ramblas. Gerona is also distinctive, a city of particular charm, an ancient city, and for those who know it, its rich historical memories are very much a part of its present.

Its 1,700-year Christian past lives on and flourishes in its shrines, festivals, and processions and in its famous churches—the medieval cathedral, with its baroque facade, and the two churches of San Pedro and San Felix. San Felix dated from the fifth century, when it was built in honor of Gerona's patron, San Narciso, martyred on that spot during Diocletian's persecution. Gerona's location is strategic, and its history had been warlike. Charlemagne's armies took the city from the Moors. It figured in the Carlist wars. Napoleon's forces captured it, only to be thrown out by the inhabitants after a week of ferocious fighting. In Jose Maria Gironella's great novel about the prelude to the Spanish Civil War, this past, in all of its violence, devotion, and beauty, can be seen as continuous with the Gerona of our own century.

Though Gironella himself fought on the Nationalist side, his book is anything but slanted in favor of the Nationalists. It tells us that base motives existed on both—or, more accurately, on all—sides of the conflict but that at its deepest level the conflict flowed from men's best motives rather than from their worst, from their valid and admirable but, in these circumstances, irreconcilable ideals. On the one hand, justice, progress, reason, and freedom; on the other,

tradition, order, nation, God. *The Cypresses Believe in God,* moreover, can stand alone as one of the very greatest of modern novels.
It possesses the imaginative authority of Joyce or Conrad or Mann.

The canvas is a large one. Some eighty characters populate Giro-
nella's thousand pages. His subject is equally vast: nothing less than
Spanish society as shaped by history and the deep causes of the Civil
War and, even beyond that—because Spain is part of Europe—the
deep fissure in the soul of the West that is the tragic legacy of the
European Enlightenment.

"In Spain," Gironella comments in a prefatory note to his book,
"the reaction to this novel has been that it is 'implacable.' Nothing
could satisfy me more." Understandably is he pleased—for the novel
achieves that implacable quality that is the defining characteristic
of the highest art. A great musical composition is implacable. It *had*
to be that way and no other. The tragedy of Sophocles or Shakespeare
is implacable. Take these conflicting elements, such works say to us:
this conflict cannot be resolved or avoided. There is nothing to be
"done." There is no road around it, and nothing is negotiable. The
thing must simply be faced and, as the knot grows tighter, endured.
This is the effect of *The Cypresses Believe in God.* It proceeds as
inexorably as *Lear* to the engulfing catastrophe. And, as in great
tragedy, it is only the point of view, the consciousness informing
the whole, that triumphs; we are sustained only by the knowledge
that the human imagination *can* look so steadily at the inexorable,
never submitting to the desire to cheat on the vision, never turning
aside. The implacability of the art is a triumph of the human spirit.

ii

Though Gironella has unquestionably produced in *The Cypresses
Believe in God* one of the major novels of the twentieth century—
a novel in no respect inferior to the best work of the great twentieth-
century novelists—he himself remains virtually an invisible presence outside of Spain. No doubt this invisibility is partially due to
the fact that he is a Spaniard. An odd sort of wall seems to exist
between contemporary Spanish intellectual culture and the rest of
the Western world. The work of Xavier Zubiri, for example—a
philosopher comparable to Heidegger or Tillich—is untranslated
and virtually unknown outside of Spain.

But in the case of Gironella, this international invisibility has
much to do with the man himself. He has steadfastly refused to

merchandise his personality in the customary way: he has not toured abroad or put in campus appearances; he did not, like Saint Genet, present himself outside the 1968 Democratic convention. He lives quietly in Barcelona, deeply involved with the sequence of novels of which *The Cypresses Believe in God* is the earliest. He has not become a celebrity; he is content to allow his art to speak for itself.

In many respects, Gironella's life resembles that of his protagonist, Ignacio Alvear. He was born in Gerona in 1917, went to primary school in Gerona, and, like Ignacio, spent a short period in the seminary; again like Ignacio, he left the seminary and went to work. Here they diverge, for though Ignacio goes on to the study of law, Gironella had no formal education after the age of thirteen. For the two years prior to the outbreak of the Civil War, he worked in a bank. After the war, he held a variety of miscellaneous jobs while devoting himself to his craft as a writer. In 1944 he published a long poem entitled "Winter Has Come and You Are Not Here"; his first novel, *Un Hombre,* appeared in 1946 and received the Nadal Prize, the Spanish equivalent of the Prix Goncourt. For a time, Gironella lived in Paris—he supported himself by driving a sand truck and by giving chess lessons to American tourists. His second novel, *La Mares,* was published in 1948.

With regard to the central and traumatic event of modern Spanish history, Gironella is strategically situated. Intellectually a part of the Catholic humanist tradition, his mind characteristically moves first to understand, to see; though he does not disavow judgment, it is the act of understanding that is always in the foreground. Gironella was nineteen when the Spanish Civil War broke out. He survived the war as a member of a generation still young, and for that generation he remains very much a representative figure. Spain had been shattered by the war, not only politically but morally and intellectually as well; things had fallen apart, and the center not only had failed to hold but had disintegrated. The very scope of Gironella's novel suggests his intention: with intelligence and imagination he will reach out and encompass the whole of Spain, piecing the scattered parts together. He conceives of his vocation as an artist in heroic terms: through the shaping intelligence of the novelist, reaching back, understanding, finding appropriate forms, the fragmented consciousness of modern Spain will be given shape and meaning.

iii

The narrative of *The Cypresses Believe in God* covers five years, from the birth of the Republic in April 1931 to the outbreak of the rebellion in July 1936. At the center of the story is the middle-class Alvear family of Gerona, a family possessing great solidarity yet suggesting, because of the differences among its members, the forces that will tear Spain apart.

Matias Alvear, the father, a telegrapher, is like a steel engraving— all greys and whites and distinctive lines. He is warm-hearted, ironic, and gifted with a splendid common sense. He "avoided fanatics as much as he could." He "was neat, and preferred grey clothes and sober ties except on his children's birthdays. He liked dominoes because he said it was a clean game and the pieces were clean and pleasant to touch." Appropriately enough, though "he was a wizard at dominoes," as "a fisherman he rated zero." He is a man of the city, and of reason, rather than of the countryside. He delights in the tiny fish he occasionally catches while fishing in the Onar from his apartment balcony, but "once he caught such a big one it almost frightened him." Matias has all the genuine virtues of common sense as well as, admirable as he is, its limitations. He is destined to be surprised by events, for he will not be able to avoid fanatics, or even understand them. Like the rest of his family back in Madrid, Matias is a liberal and a Republican, but his anticlericalism has been modified by the powerful influence of his wife.

Carmen Elgazu is a Basque and a devout Catholic, an emotional, instinctive, maternal, vivid woman. Gironella seems to be suggesting that, for Spain, salvation must lie in some such marriage of opposites—that such a marriage is not only possible but, as the Alvears show, productive of enormous good. In contrast to the greys and whites and fine lines of the telegrapher, Carmen Elgazu is all color. Her family was

Basque, conservative, Catholic to the marrow of their bones. Her father had died clasping a crucifix, and his last words to his children were: "Don't marry anyone who doesn't believe in God." The mother was still living in a village in the Basque provinces, unbowed for all her eighty-odd years, bombarding her eight children with letters written in violet ink and an incredibly firm handwriting that belied her age. They were apostolic letters that only Carmen Elgazu read all the way through, but that none of the children ventured to throw away or burn.

Physically, too, Carmen is opposite to Matias. She "was of medium height, with intensely black hair drawn back in a knot, and a head firmly set on her shoulders. . . . Lean Matias Alvear had greater distinction, but made less of an impression."

Besides a daughter, Pilar, there are two sons, Ignacio and Cesar, who embody different possibilities of the family tradition and, indeed, of Spanish history. Ignacio is a seeker, both skeptical and religious, more like his father than Carmen Elgazu, yet more emotional than Matias. He is moved by the claims of different points of view. He tries to see things as they are, in all their complexity, and finds it difficult to arrive at conclusions. Under his mother's influence, he enters a seminary but finds that he has no vocation and studies law instead. Disturbed by the plight of the poor, he is drawn to socialism but withholds full commitment because of its anticlericalism. "The truth is that he was too sensitive to slough off a world that had been his. Many ex-seminarians did it and could hardly wait to avenge themselves on God. Ignacio did not know. At the moment what he felt was infinite curiosity."

Ignacio's story is in the tradition of the *Bildungsroman:* his curiosity, his testing of different theories, his youthful loves, his intellectual and moral development. He is not only sensitive but convincingly intelligent and an acute observer of his milieu. He notices the deeper, subsurface changes in Gerona. He notices that the most violent temperaments among the political figures are those, often, who have the fewest family ties; their emotion is concentrated in a cause rather than attached to actual people. Many of the details in his life resemble those of Gironella's. Of all the characters in the book, he probably is the one most like the author.

Ignacio is the protagonist, central to the narrative, but his younger brother Cesar is the haunting presence in the novel. In Cesar, Gironella provides the only plausible portrait of a saint that I am aware of in contemporary literature. We have to go back to Dostoyevsky's Alyosha to find anything comparable. To compare Gironella with Dostoyevsky in this respect is suggestive, for it reminds us of some of the ways in which Dostoyevsky's Russia and Gironella's Spain are alike—to a large degree preindustrial and traditional societies for which the Enlightenment is an uneasy and incompletely absorbed inheritance. Both countries have all the spiritual advantages of being far from Paris.

Cesar was eight when the Alvears came to Gerona, and "he was much shyer than Ignacio." His "huge ears and his big feet . . . gave him a kind of shuffling gait as he walked." His physical awkwardness is an accurate reflection of his worldly incapacity, of the fact that his presence in the world is a temporary thing and that he really belongs to eternity. In contrast to the outgoing Ignacio, Cesar is a natural contemplative who

> would stop, and in every stone, every blade of grass or mineral vein in a rock, would see what he always saw: a miracle. . . . Cesar wanted to turn the miracle over in his mind, meditate upon it. In this way the afternoon was gone before they knew it, and they had to come home without Ignacio's having seen half or a quarter of the things he had planned.

Even as a boy, Cesar is on friendly terms with death, instinctively viewing it as the gateway to eternity. Cesar is so convincingly drawn by Gironella that even his daily visits to the cemetery do not strike us as bizarre:

> Cesar always trod lightly when he entered the abode of the dead, but his father would have been wrong if he had thought him morbid. It was just that his attitude toward death was one of familiarity; he felt himself surrounded by brothers. He looked at the crosses rising above the ground and they did not seem daggers to him. Of the photographs in the niches, those which made the deepest impression on him were the men dressed in the uniform of the African war, and one of a child wearing a white sailor suit and holding a celluloid duck. Cesar went there to pray. The cemetery was enormous, but seen from Pederas it was a tiny rectangle that gave a sense of the pitiful fragility of the skeletons huddled within it.

For all his strangeness, Cesar represents something both necessary and true. He is a valid possibility of the spirit, its impulse beyond the world, and it is Ignacio's unformulated awareness of this that prevents him from joining wholeheartedly the antireligious Left. Cesar replaces Ignacio as a seminarian, and his instinctive spirituality becomes disciplined and focused.

> He imitated St. Francis in many things, but especially in courtesy. He was polite to everyone, beginning with inanimate objects. It goes without saying that he was especially so toward Latin. Latin, the language of the Popes. For a long time he had believed that Jesus Christ talked Latin, and for that reason the declensions gave him a feeling of approach to the divine person.

As he matures, he develops that striking combination of toughness and tenderness that so often seems characteristic of the saintly and mystical temperament. He spends entire nights in prayer without feeling tired. He wears a penitent's belt. He has visionary experiences. A priest asks him what happens when he prays.

Cesar shrugged his shoulders, somewhat confused. "Why—nothing happens to me. I try to bring the image of Jesus before me, that is all."

Mosen Francisco nodded his head. "And do you achieve it?"

"Sometimes it seems to me I do."

"How do you see Jesus? Under what circumstances?"

Cesar thought for a moment. "It's nearly always at the moment of the Transfiguration."

"Robed in white?"

"Always."

Mosen Francisco looked hard at Cesar, struck by the concentration the seminarian's countenance revealed. "Tell me one thing. Does the body of Jesus emit rays of gold?"

"No," answered Cesar with assurance, "rays of white."

"Is Jesus carrying anything in his hand?"

"No, nothing at all." Mosen Francisco marked a pause. "Do you see Him on the peak of a mountain?"

"Yes. On the peak of a mountain."

"And where do the rays come from?"

"From his heart."

Mosen Francisco nodded his head again. "Don't you realize? All this is very great, Cesar." The seminarian said nothing. Mosen Francisco added: "But tell me in more detail what it is you do. What do you feel, or what do you say?"

"Feel—I don't know," Cesar answered. "At times a great peace. At times it seems to me I don't feel anything."

"And what do you say?"

"I say: O Lord, my God. Or at times I sing the Magnificat."

Though Cesar spends most of the year at the seminary, visiting Gerona only during summer vacations, he is a powerful presence in the novel. He embodies in an intense and purified way qualities the other characters can only intermittently approach. Ignacio, for example, though so much a part of the world, finds during a period of adolescent moral confusion that the contemplative characteristics of silence and attention can help restore balance to the spirit. He discovers in his own way a realm that Cesar habitually lives in.

iv

Gradually the public world of politics and social upheaval intrudes upon the domestic life of the Alvears, and as it does, the focus of the narrative turns outward, away from the household, from summer vacations at the seaside and domino games in the cafe, from the inner life, from the reassuring annual rhythm of festival and holy day. Instead, we turn to the world of political fermentation, election campaign, civil breakdown, revolutionary politics, and war.

Throughout the novel, Gironella's technique is naturalistic, but beneath the detail of the narrative there is a strong undercurrent of poetic suggestion. The opening paragraphs of the novel, for example, which establish the Alvear family and put them into their environment with marvelous concreteness, also foreshadow through the imagery they employ the future course of the story—its movement from domesticity and tranquility to public catastrophe. First, the Alvear apartment—old, intimate, secure, and full of odd and intricately interesting things:

> On the second floor of one of the oldest houses on the right bank of the river lived the Alvears. The front balconies looked out on the Rambla, opposite the Cafe Neutral, located in the middle of the pleasantest arcade of the city; the rear window and balcony overhung the river, the Onar.
> The house, therefore, led a double life, like all the others along the Rambla. As a result, the inner life of the flat was gay, and all the doors had to be closed to create an atmosphere of intimacy. If one of them was carelessly left open, all the clocks of the city would be heard; nevertheless, the Alvears knew that in a fistful of space they could create an intimate and impregnable world of their own.

In these opening paragraphs, the dominant motif is security, privacy, apparent impregnability; yet, there are discordant minor notes: a door might be carelessly left open, and all those clocks of the city suggest that the felicity found here cannot be immune to the exigencies of time.

In the next few paragraphs, more ominous suggestions become dominant. It is a fine thing to have a balcony overlooking the Onar, but sometimes the river gives off unhealthy odors, and a few hundred yards away there are "marshy backwaters." The people on the first floor

> were out of luck when the Onar rose. The Ter could not absorb its volume of water, and then the little river rose and seeped through all the cracks and openings in the house, rushing furiously through the kitchen, dining room, and hall and cascading out the front door, pouring a thousand household secrets into the Rambla, right in front of the Cafe Neutral.

The potentialities of this imagery are fulfilled later on when the flood of revolution and civil war rushes through the households of Gerona, destroying some families, scattering and transforming others. At the very beginning of the narrative, the process is set in motion with religious persecution. "Spain has ceased to be Catholic," announces Azana, the prime minister, and the measures taken against the Church constitute a declaration of war on half of Spain.

In Gerona at this time, party commitment intensified all along the political spectrum, from the anarchist CNT and the nascent Communist Party through the socialist UGT, the monarchists and masons, the rightist CEDA, and the Catlan separatist parties. None of this action remains abstract or schematic in Gironella. His party leaders and political personalities are fully human—the anarchist leader, El Responsable, with his background of grinding poverty and his wife in the asylum; the landowner Don Jorge, with his responsible and productive sense of the land, admirable, yet not imaginative enough to grasp the condition of the peasant; the progressive industrialist Costa brothers; the abrasive right-wing journalist Warning Voice; the complex aesthetic priest Mosen Alberto. Ominously, their goals are so different and so opposed that violence is virtually inevitable. El Responsable and Estrada of the CEDA have nothing in common; the Catalan separatists can hardly be expected to coexist with an army fiercely attached to the unity of Spain; Catholics cannot come to terms with atheists, who regard the Church as an infamy to be destroyed.

And beyond these overt conflicts, the social fabric itself shows signs of transformation. An excessive admiration for "youth" reflects a disenchantment with tradition; uninformed admiration for foreign achievement spreads; the language of politics becomes heated and violent. Gironella's grasp of the social process, with its significant details, inner logic, and effect upon character, is reminiscent of Conrad's in *Nostromo.*

v

The process is inexorable. The Republic fails to maintain order, and a conservative coalition wins a landslide victory in the election of 1933. But the conservatives prove complacent and inept.

The winner of the election showed no sense of urgency. Portfolio deals, displays of strength, banquets. And meanwhile growing unemployment, famine areas in the country, plans for education reform at a standstill, and the trains limping along. All the plans outlined by the previous government had been discarded as unsuitable, but nothing viable was offered in their stead.

Financial scandals beset the government, and the Left benefits from popular indignation over Mussolini's Abyssinian adventure. In the elections of 1936, the Popular Front scores a narrow victory, and the country slides toward chaos. The election itself is marked by violence—looting, church burning, assassination are daily occurrences. Communist strength grows, and Russian Communists become prominent in the affairs of the Left.

As order breaks down, impressive and fanatical leaders move into the foreground. Cosme Vila, a former bank clerk, consolidates his position as chairman of the Gerona Communist Party and becomes a formidable force through his adept tactics. Vila's devotion is as great as Cesar's: Gironella shows him to possess a kind of religious selflessness in his passion to bring about the "scientific" future. His counterpart in political fervor is Mateo Santos, an intense young law student from Madrid who organizes the first cell of the Falange in Gerona. Mateo is as pure and fanatical as Cosme Vila, and he has hold of an essential truth that eludes the bourgeois parties of both the Left and center. He sees that

in practice the theory that all that was needed was maternity clinics, good schools, work for all, and security for old age had many pitfalls. For the moments move slowly in the heart of man, and they must be lived one by one. He had told Ignacio before that all that was not enough, and if man was not offered a patriotic or religious ideal, he would go looking for other things, because the spirit has its needs.

Mateo believes that "every Spaniard should be half monk, half soldier." His Falangist group is small and written off as a joke by everyone except Cosme Vila, who possesses a comparable political penetration.

Out of Gironella's portrayal of these two figures an important theoretical point emerges. We are accustomed to thinking of political positions as abiding on a line running from the Left to the Right, the extremes of both positions being, by definition, the most violent. But with Cosme Vila and Mateo, their violent posture belies their relatively moderate political views. Mateo, for example, does not believe substantively in anything other than what many other middle-class and patriotic Spaniards believe in. The content, similarly, of Cosme Vila's politics is shared by many: a scientific and humanitarian future. What separates them from others who have similar substantive positions on the "Left" to "Right" continuum is an impulse toward direct action, toward violence. Mateo's fascism is not "further right" than the political beliefs of many. His difference is his willingness to move directly to confrontation and force.

The July 18 military uprising succeeds temporarily in Gerona but is bungled in Barcelona and Valencia, and soon eastern Spain is entirely under the control of the Left. In Gerona, as elsewhere, the Anti-Fascist Revolutionary Committee goes about the business of wiping out its class enemies. Cesar is shot by the militia. For the time being, the Alvears try to go about their normal affairs, remaining inconspicuous. Others, like Mateo, escape to nationalist Spain, where a similar "clean up" is underway. The radio brings bewildering reports of fighting throughout the west and south of the century.

vi

Driving down into Spain from the north, you become aware, visually, that you are in a very distinctive place. In France, those lines of poplars, those carefully cultivated fields, and that soft and silvery light produces an Impressionist landscape. But in the south things sharpen. The moisture of the northern air no longer blurs the outlines. The sky is hard and blue, and the white edges of the buildings are sharp against it. In the streets, the shadows cast by those edges are as sharp as a draftsman's ruled line. Visually speaking, the great modern feeling of ambiguity has no place in the landscape of the south. The outlines of things are clear, and there is no shading of one thing into another. Things are what they are.

The clarity of the Spanish landscape may be taken as a kind of analogue to the role Spain has played in the history of our time. In that history, too, there is no ambiguity; one side does not melt into another. Today, the lines are drawn in writing about Spain just as clearly as they were drawn on the Ebro or at Madrid, and because the war that was fought in Spain is not over but goes on and on in other places, the Spanish war retains its fascination. Books about it tumble from the presses.

In warfare, as in architecture or poetry, each period has a dominant style. The elaborate encircling sieges of Louis XIV went forward with all the decorous precision of a minuet; the king himself usually turned up for the denouement, attended by his mistress and his Epic Poet. More recently, the campaigns of Grant and Eisenhower were quite clearly continuous with the culture of the factory and the assembly line. The importance of the Spanish Civil War lies in the fact that it was the prototype of a new style. Despite frequent claims to the contrary, the Spanish War did not foreshadow World War II, which was (at least in the West and in spite of stirring revolutionary currents) really a replay of World War I. The Spanish Civil War established a new pattern of our international civil war, and that is why it continues to be the subject of fascinated examination—indeed, of ideological rancor.

The two world wars were fought between nations and were thus an old model industrialized. The Spanish Civil War was international in quite another sense. Opinion outside Spain became deeply engaged, and all Western nations were divided within themselves. As one writer observes, "The civil war in Spain represented a cleavage in European thought too deep and universal to remain confined to the Iberian peninsula." Significantly enough, the authoritative bibliography of the conflict by Juan Garcia Duran (1964) provided a scholarly apparatus in three languages—French, English, and Spanish. Most artists and intellectuals supported the Left, but some did not. Since the Spanish war, the same cleavage in opinion has appeared again and again.

One thing that strikes you as you read through the historical literature on the Spanish Civil War is its utter failure to give a plausible description of the motives of the Nationalists. It's not that the writers don't try. Hugh Thomas is an able scholar, and he has read the documents. His major work, *The Spanish Civil War* (1961), was subjected to a great many criticisms on points of detail by reviewers and scholars, and when these were valid, Thomas corrected his text in later editions. But as historian, his disabling flaw is that he is utterly unable to think himself into the shoes of those on the Nationalist side. The enemy remains opaque. The motives he assigns to the Nationalists are, in effect, liberal and secular ones: they were wealthy and protecting their interests; they were military and asserting the interest of the army; they were priests and protecting the ecclesiastical interest; they were middle class and protecting the property interest. No doubt such motives existed, but if those were the only incentives, there would have been no war. What you discern in such liberal-left historians, then, is an incapacity for writing the history of the war at all. They cannot explain why the other side fought. A great gap opens, and they cannot cross to its other side. This incapacity is evident in detail after detail.

Hugh Thomas, for example, has also produced an illustrated volume on Spanish history and culture in the *Life* magazine series on world history. It is a handsome, even an opulent book and well worth owning: it is full of splendid photographs of Spain and of

Spanish life, and for the most part, its facts are accurate. But on page 81 there is a picture of some Spanish farmers carrying an image of the Virgin through their fields, evidently singing as they go. It is a fine photograph, and in color. The caption reads: "Frenzied worshippers shout and sing while carrying a statue." *Frenzied.* Not passionate or joyful or devoted. If history is an effort to illuminate what happened, you can't write history this way. Given his built-in denigrative reflex, Thomas cannot understand the "interests" such laborers were protecting when they fought for the Nationalists, much less understand why they won.

To be sure, a number of other writers of great power and authority have written on Spain—Malraux, Hemingway, Koestler, and Orwell come instantly to mind. Their works dealing with the Spanish war have many virtues; how, indeed, could it be otherwise? Yet the opacity remains. Orwell, for example, had been established as virtually the official interpreter of the war to the Anglo-American mind, and *Homage to Catalonia* is now a minor classic. Orwell is everyone's "honest man"—the very texture of his prose advances the claim—and when he finds that the Stalinists are evil and that they are running the show in Barcelona, he does not hesitate to tell us so. Yet he was also capable of saying that "the broad truth about the war is simple enough. The Spanish bourgeoisie saw their chance of crushing the labor movement and took it, aided by the Nazis and the forces of reaction all over the world. It is doubtful whether more than that will ever be established."

No, Gironella has been involved with Spain and with Spanish history in a deeper way than any of the historians or novelists generally accessible to us. He has long meditated upon his material, and in *The Cypresses Believe in God,* he has produced a major work of art, a major embodiment of consciousness, in which every detail is informed by the imaginative integrity of the whole and which is implacable because it is true.

Wartime, I
The Nazi Hour

Before it gets forgotten through the passage of time and through mortality, I would like to attest to the distinctive quality of the Nazi idea as it emerged in the 1930s. It possessed a powerful appeal to many at the time, both here and in Europe. No one then knew about the apocalyptic horrors of the death camps, though some certainly intuited that death camps were inferrable from the whole Nazi idea. The word "Nazi" has now been emptied of all content, becoming a term used as rhetorical bullying. Lyndon Johnson was not a Nazi, and neither was Richard Nixon. If those who throw the word "Nazi" around for rhetorical advantage against wholly democratic opponents met a real Nazi, they would probably experience cardiac arrest. The original Nazi idea was novel, menacing, radical.

I have done a lot of research on this subject in connection with my recent book, *From This Moment On: America in 1940* (1988). The first concrete thing I remember about the Nazis was a remark of my father's: "The Hitler Youth," he said, "isn't the Boy Scouts. They would tell you what to do and when to do it. You would have no choice at all." This was probably 1938, and that idea of Hitler Youth did not appeal to me at all. I preferred sandlot baseball and tennis on the local public courts.

Oddly enough, I met my first Nazi idealist in 1939 or 1940 at a YMCA in Flushing, Long Island. I was about ten at the time and a passionate camera nut. The YMCA had a camera club, complete with a darkroom, enlarger, and so on, and the director was a sandy-haired man in his thirties—let's call him Dieter Schultz. He was a photographic ace, a state-of-the-art man of great precision, and he prided himself on his "scientific" coldness. The light for the "correct" photograph had to be "just so." The developing bath had to be "exactly this." But to this ten-year old, his vocabulary possessed oddities. What he considered bad or sloppy was "bourgeois." Who knew what that meant? When I mentioned this "bourgeois" business to my parents, they said that Mr. Schultz must be a Communist, a reasonable inference.

When I returned to the YMCA camera club, I asked Mr. Schultz if he was a Communist. "Get out of the room," he snapped harshly. We were back on an even keel later that day as we leaned over a developing bath, but what Mr. Schultz was at the time was an idealistic and a believing Nazi. His world view was as opposed to anything "bourgeois" as Trotsky's was. His vision of the desirable future consisted of precision, science, technology, modernization, and cold efficiency, and he had a sense of unshakable superiority. He coldly and passionately believed that the future belonged to people designed on his described mode. He was a genuine Nazi radical.

Kodak cameras? Bourgeois. *Zeiss!* Kodak film? Bourgeois. *Agfa!* This man was very helpful to me in a photographic way, but you could not really say that he was either nice or not nice. He was neither. He was almost a piece of machinery, which was in a way his ideal. He was anything but a barrel of laughs. Years later, Lionel Trilling would remark to me that to understand the Nazis, you had to realize that they were *idealists.*

In the summer of 1940, France fell to the *Wehrmacht* in eight weeks. Mr. Dieter Schultz was coldly enthusiastic. "England is next," he said, as if announcing a correct shutter aperture. England? England? All those pictures of King George on the stamps in my album? Those pictures of the *Queen Mary* in the rotogravure sections? England? "Bourgeois"?

This man Dieter Schultz was entirely unlike the German war veterans I later met vacationing in Spain and Switzerland and Latin America. The once-young men who had flown the *Luftwaffe*'s planes or fought with the Afrika Corp were not much different from the Englishmen I met who had flown Spitfires in the Battle of Britain or routed Rommel with Montgomery's Eighth Army. One former *Wehrmacht* colonel, now in the lingerie business in West Germany, had been the military governor of a small French city during the war. He is still a hero in that city and returns every year at Christmas for a *gemütlich* celebration. Apparently his administration was the best the locals can remember. A former *Luftwaffe* pilot, now in insurance, was shot down over Soviet territory in a photographic reconnaissance plane, a burning phosphorous bullet in his stomach. He was hidden and sheltered by Russian peasants and then picked up when the German offensive rolled by. Later he flew for Rommel. These men, old now, were not Nazis. They were young Germans; the country was at war, and they went. They did not have much choice in the matter.

The Nazi idea, puritanical and often ascetic in its "scientific" way, did draw some of its energy from something real and specifically German, though in the Nazi ideologization it became fanaticized. I learned the following from a recent book about German scientists by Tom Bower called *The Paperclip Conspiracy* (1987). As soon as the war ended, the United States, the United Kingdom, the U.S.S.R., and France engaged in a desperate competition to recruit or kidnap German scientists. We came out ahead.

The barrel of the American 50-caliber machine gun eroded after eight hundred rounds, while German barrels lasted for five thousand. American bazookas and anti-tank guns were ineffective compared with the German hollow-charge heavy rockets and high-performance anti-tank weapons.

Bourgeois! The Germans developed the first jet fighter and the V-1 and V-2 rockets (and it was very good luck that we got to their big rocket base at Peenemunde before the Russians did). The Germans were first with infrared aircraft detectors for night fighting and made a breakthrough with the astonishing nerve gas Tabun. The British got to radar first and also sonar—or asdic, as they called it—but of course the Germans were not very interested in antisubmarine warfare.

Virginia Woolf, shortly before she killed herself, took notice of the special Nazi vitality. As the panzer motorized columns rushed across northern France, Woolf noticed the perfection of detail. The German parachutists wore sky-blue uniforms, and the undersides of their parachutes were sky blue. They were using *glider* troops, for heaven's sake! The Stuka dive bombers, with their gull wings, were equipped with *sirens,* harmless but terrifying, which screamed as they dove. The Dutch flooded the country by rupturing the dikes, but the Germans were on hand with rubber boats and pontoon bridges.

Rubber boats, though, were no surprise to this ten-year old. The first collapsible boat I had seen appeared one summer in, of all places, Great Neck, Long Island. The *foldbot,* as it was called, was being boastfully shown off at the beach by a group of young Nazis from the German consulate. The *foldbot* packed up into a canvas bag about the size of a tennis racquet case. But out it came, very fine fabric and aluminum struts, and, by George, it became a canoe. The three tanned and lean young Nazis paddled off into Long Island Sound, laughing in their superiority. The *foldbot* was not just an aquatic craft, it was a statement.

During the Depression era, another symbol of Nazi modernism and efficiency was the great airship *Hindenburg*. In his quasi-autobiographic novel *World's Fair* (1985), E. L. Doctorow wrote a memorable passage—probably fantacized—about the *Hindenburg* flying low over the largely Jewish Bronx:

Over the roofs of the private houses that bordered the right side of Mt. Eden Avenue, across the street from the park, the nose of the great silver *Hindenburg* appeared. My mouth dropped open. She sailed incredibly over the housetops, and came right toward me, just a few hundred feet in the air, and kept coming and still no sight of the tail of her. She was tilted over me as if she were an enormous animal leaping from the sky in monumental slow motion. Some sort of line lagged under her, like a halyard, under the cupola. Then, as I blinked, she was visible in her entirety, tacking off some degrees to the east, and I saw her in all her silver-skinned length; the ribbed planes of her cylindrical balloon, thick in the middle, narrowed at each end, reflected the sunlight. . . . I heard her now, the propellers alongside her cupola whirring like fans in the sky. She did not make the harsh raspy snarl of an airplane, but seemed to whisper. . . . I could see little people in the cabin; they were looking out the window and I waved at them.

In those days, the *Hindenburg* was a regular sight over Manhattan, always arriving exactly on time—precision! science!—and circling the Empire State Building in tribute or challenge before heading south to Lakehurst, New Jersey, where it docked. Everyone saw those huge red tailfins with the black swastika in the white circle. The *Hindenburg* was a powerful symbol of the Nazi idea. It appears established that it was blown up in Lakehurst in 1937 by a time bomb placed there by a Communist crewman.

It is worth recalling that one of the notable exhibits at the New York World's Fair of 1939–1940 was a live, beating chicken heart, kept functioning by a pump designed by Charles Lindbergh in partnership with the French biological scientist Alexis Carrel. Carrel was a Nazi sympathizer. The chicken heart adumbrated the whole field of organ transplants. Lindbergh himself, after the kidnapping trauma, moved to England and became an anglophile—they respected his privacy—but he was also much impressed, perhaps too much so, by the *Luftwaffe*.

One of the best pavilions at the 1939–1940 World's Fair, by wide consensus, was the Italian. In its design, it staked a brilliant architectural claim to the future, a design evoking at once the ancient Roman past and the futurist ideas of F. T. Marinetti. At the top of its huge central tower was a statue of the goddess Roma. From a point two hundred-feet high on this tower, a cascade of water flowed down an arrangement of steps, tumbling into a pool at the base of a monument to the inventor Marconi. From Roma to electricity and the telegraph: the future! The Italians also exhibited a train that went one hundred miles per hour, very modern, with red leather upholstery. We should be grateful that we had the wonderful Trylon and Perisphere to answer the fascist claims.

G. Gordon Liddy, perhaps only half-consciously, has delivered to us an Americanized version of the Nazi idea in his autobiography entitled, significantly enough, *Will* (Leni Riefenstahl's great Nazi movie was, of course, entitled *The Triumph of the Will*). When Liddy was sent to the District of Columbia jail, he gained psychological ascendancy over the jail's black thug population by singing in the shower—the *"Horst Wessel* Song," in German: *"Die fanner hof, Die fanner hof."* The other prisoners decided to let Liddy alone. Liddy married his "Nordic" wife for "eugenic" reasons. He willed away his childhood fear of rats by eating one. He willed away his fear of lightning by sitting out a thunderstorm in a tree. At the prison in Danbury, he dealt with the homosexual rape initiation with great directness: Liddy is a karate expert, and when a large black prisoner started to manhandle him, he broke both the man's arms. Liddy is an ace with a pistol, and he held his palm to that candle flame. After Watergate, he offered himself to the Nixon White House for execution, promising to turn up at a given street corner to be rubbed out. He regularly flies—or at least used to—the air force's forget-the-sound-barrier jet fighters. "If you make a mistake," he says, "you're in northern Canada." With Gordon Liddy you feel that you are in a time warp, back in the 1930s, with *foldbots,* blue parachutes, and the strength-through-joy German movement.

In my research regarding the year 1940, I discovered that one of Adolf Hitler's favorite and often-used expressions was "icy cold and lightning fast." In 1934 Hitler decided to get rid of Ernst Roehm and his Nazi leftist brownshirt S.A. The extermination was "icy cold and lightning fast," though his S.S. executioners under Heinrich Himmler became over-enthusiastic in the midst of the slaughter and Hitler had to execute some of *them* for form's sake. Poland, Norway, France: "icy cold and lightning fast." A chilly detail: before the invasion of Poland, Hitler ordered the termination of the moribund in German hospitals through lethal injection. He needed the beds for the expected wounded soldiers.

ii

On June 21, 1941, Joe DiMaggio hit safely for the thirty-fourth time before a Saturday crowd in Yankee Stadium. The same day, off a New Jersey beach, I bobbed around all day on an air mattress, sometimes rolling off it for a swim. The next day, boiled to a sunburned, painful crisp and wrapped in wet towels in our hotel room, I read in the daily paper about the greatest invasion in the history of the world. At 3:30 P.M. on the day DiMaggio hit number thirty-five, it was sunrise in the Baltic. Rudolph Hess had flown to England to try to get the British realigned and on board for Hitler's greatest project, the destruction of communism. Hess failed, but England really did not matter much at that point to Hitler. Territory was what mattered. At dawn on June 22, Hitler threw 146 infantry, panzer, and motorized divisions against Stalin. In addition, the Finns, still seething over Stalin's 1939 war against them, invaded Russia across the Karelian isthmus. Fourteen Rumanian divisions joined the attack, which rushed forward in three huge thrusts along a thousand-mile front as entire Soviet armies were encircled and slaughtered. Nine million men were fighting. Even Hitler was impressed. In the midst of the chaos, Stalin arrested and executed his commander, General Pavlov. Hitler was so confident of a quick victory that he did not equip the *Wehrmacht* with winter uniforms. The Russians were a rotten barrel; just give it a kick.

Of course, there was the usual Nazi touch. As the invasion rolled forward at twenty-five miles a day, the Nazis butchered entire villages, lining up and shooting thousands of people beside long burial ditches in the local forests. Hitler planned to Germanize the captured territories by resettling the former Slav areas, *Lebensraum,* the Greater Reich. "Icy cold and lightning fast." But something had slipped. The Nazi intelligence services had underestimated Stalin's available reserves by six million. Six million! So much for Nazi precision.

As for me, then and even more so now that so much we did not know then has come out, I much, very much, prefer Winston

Churchill—whom the vegetarian Hitler considered a decadent drunk—and Franklin Roosevelt, both democratic leaders much more loosely put together than Mr. Icy Cold and Lightning Fast. Indeed, in the end, the British and the Americans were actually *tougher* than the Nazis. I call here upon Ernie Pyle's in *Ernie's War* (1986) description of the British Eighth Army, which routed Erwin Rommel's Afrika Corp and chased it across North Africa until it was trapped and surrendered.

Since Montgomery has chased Rommel all the way from Egypt in one of the great military achievements of history, it is only right that the British should have the kill.

The 8th army is a magnificent organization. We correspondents have been thrilled by its perfection. So have our troops. It must surely be one of the outstanding armies of all time. We trailed it several days up the Tunisian coast, and we came to look upon it almost with awe.

Its organization for continuous movement is so perfect that it seems more like a big business firm than a destructive army. The men of the 8th are brown-skinned and white-eyebrowed from the desert sun. Most of them are in shorts, and they are a healthy-looking lot. Their spirit is tonic. The spirit of our own troops is good, but these boys from the burning sands are throbbing with the vitality of conquerors.

They are friendly, cocky, and confident. They've been three years in the desert. We envy them, and are proud of them.

The Nazi idea ended in horror and disaster. The Japanese, who also had an ideology of racial superiority, ran into the Australians in the fighting for the Owen-Stanley Mountains in New Guinea and were profoundly shocked. The rapists and bayonetters of Nanking and the organizers of the Bataan death march found themselves fighting against Australians who went into battle wearing Japanese skulls dangling from their belts, and then they met United States Marines who liked to collect Japanese gold teeth. None other than General MacArthur said that the fighting on Okinawa was "awful, just awful," and it was.

The Nazis had no monopoly on toughness. Yet, in their cult of nerveless rationality, their worship of hard efficiency, their sense that cruelty and superiority were inseparable, they did posses at least a corner of the spirit of the age, a corner that of course became infinitely corruptible. Where that sensibility is concerned, I think of two poetic texts, both eloquent in their way, both of them appealing and also true, if dealt with judiciously. In Canto XXX, Ezra Pound is saying that the humanitarian emotion of *pity* can be corrupting, as indeed it can:

> Compleynt, compleynt I hearde upon a day,
> Artemis singing, Artemis, Artemis
> Against Pity lifted her wail:
> Pity causeth the forests to fail,
> Pity slayeth my nymphs,
> Pity spareth so many an evil thing,
> Pity befouleth April.

And, in what amounts to a manifesto of a "cold" aestheticism, Yeats in "The Fisherman" (1919) celebrates "The freckled man who goes / To a grey place on a hill / In grey Connemara clothes / At dawn to cast his flies." This fisherman is certainly not bourgeois or humanitarian, and the poet concludes, "A man who does not exist, / A man who is but a dream." But he vows: "Before I am old / I shall have written him one / poem maybe as cold / And passionate as the dawn."

The entire Nazi-Fascist enterprise ended in horror and disgrace, and we must hope it will never be repeated. But it did represent in its time a highly distinctive movement with a particular and memorable sensibility.

iii

A review of the case of the late Paul de Man, literary critic and Yale professor, thrusts upon us a long repressed memory of that brief Nazi hour. In his later phase at Yale, Paul de Man was a beloved, some even said saintly, professor and scholar. His influence in academic criticism has been very wide. But, after his death, it suddenly emerged that between 1939 and 1943 he had been, as a brilliant young literary intellectual, *on the other side.* He was then a regular contributor to the major Belgian, and pro-Nazi, newspaper *Le Soir.* Nor had he confined himself to literature. He wrote antisemitic and culturally Nazi articles. These pieces make strange reading today, but with the Nazis apparently on the verge of victory in Europe, such may well have seemed the thing for an ambitious young man to do. Other aspects of Paul de Man's career indicate, at least until its Yale phase, a fundamentally amoral character. On the other hand, the Nazi propaganda directed at the intellectual elite was far from crude. Its principal theme was that the Nazification of a country such as Belgium was the furthest thing from their thoughts. Nazi propaganda, at its elite levels, celebrated the cultural particularity of Belgium, France, and the other conquered nations in the West—though not in the East.

In academic circles today, Paul de Man's pro-Nazi journalism is on ongoing scandal, and it certainly is a moral scandal. But de Man was far from unique during that period. Historians have documented the appeal of the Nazi idea among intellectuals—and, of course, among collaborationist politicians—but this information is far from having been culturally absorbed. If it had been so absorbed, the academic world at Yale and elsewhere would not have been "shocked."

Writing in *The New Republic,* the historian Zeev Sternhell, who teaches at the Hebrew University in Jerusalem, sets us straight about the Nazi hour. He by no means suspends judgment, but his essay represents tragic historical awareness. I will quote from this fine essay as briefly as possible.

The case of Paul de Man is important, in the end, because it is an example. De Man is an instructive illustration of a major phenomenon of European history during the interwar period: the rejection of the democratic order by a large part of the intellectual elite. This respected and admired individual, a major thinker and a charismatic scholar of great authority, participated during his youth in a great movement of revolt against the whole of the liberal, individualistic and humanist political culture. . . .

The ideas of this young journalist reflected something important: a confrontation between two rival political traditions that fought each other in the French intellectual sphere of influence throughout the period between the two world wars. At the end of the nineteenth century, a second tradition developed in France, which rebelled against the classical universalistic heritage, against rationalism, humanism, and liberalism.

Professor Sternhell has no trouble listing the advocates of this particularist tradition, who after the war went on to high governmental posts and vast cultural esteem. Paul de Man covered up his past and went on to Yale.

A principal vehicle for this rival tradition was the movement led by Charles Maurras, *Action Francais,* which was quasi-fascist in a highbrow way. An admirer of Maurras was T. S. Eliot, and also, none other than Charles de Gaulle. When de Gaulle opposed the integration of Europe and dropped out of NATO, he did it in the Maurassian name of "the Europe of the fatherlands."

iv

An enormous amount of distinguished research has been devoted to the phenomenon of "modernism" in the arts, including the political connections and implications of artistic modernism. On any given evening during the later nineteenth and early twentieth centuries people were reading—perhaps aloud, in a family circle—such staple authors as Galsworthy, Wells, Conrad, or Tennyson. Soon, however, they witnessed the outrageous appearance of Cubism and went on to riot over Stravinski's *Le Sacre du Printemps,* to denounce *Ulysses,* and to fume over the aggressive obscurities of *The Waste Land.* The connection, if any, between all of this and the Nazi hour will seem tenuous and probably obnoxious. Certainly no one wishes to blame Joyce, Picasso, or even Nietzsche for the historical phenomena of Hitler and Nazism. But a cultural connection is persuasively made in a profound book by a Canadian scholar, Modris Eksteins, *The Rites of Spring: The Great War and the Birth of the Modern Age* (1989). Professor Eksteins explores artistic modernism in terms of its relationship to its intended audience. That relationship was one of fully declared warfare, and it erupted long before 1914. Picasso painted his Cubist *Demoiselles of Avignon* in 1908. It depicted a group of prostitutes in *African* mode. During the first decade of the twentieth century, as Professor Eksteins abundantly documents, an aesthetic and moral fury against middle-class and establishment materialism and complacency became widespread in the modernist avant-garde. The French term *bourgeois* entered the English language as an epithet of contempt. A principal aim of artistic modernism was to shock and outrage its prosperous "bourgeois" audience.

And this it certainly did. When Stravinsky's *Le Sacre de Printems* was performed in Paris in 1913, its opera audience *rioted.* They were outraged by Stravinsky's musical discords, but perhaps more so by Nijinsky's flat-footed and knock-kneed, deliberately ugly dancing. The socially powerful patrons of the opera had been deliberately insulted, and they knew it. Merchants, stockbrokers, and even princesses threw punches and broke seats. The spirit of artistic modernism was one of revolt against Victorian middle-class certitudes and the styles they generated.

The Germans in World War I, Eksteins points out, fought the war believing that Germany was the first modernist country, preeminent in philosophy, music, engineering, and especially theoretical and applied science. They considered materialism, hypocrisy, and banality to be "English" traits. On that famous Christmas Day in 1914, when the British and German troops met in no man's land to exchange cigarettes and Christmas greetings, Eksteins notices a difference in manners. The British soldiers came forward first, moved by such traditional and conservative values as sportsmanship and Christmas spirit. The British were honoring such values and defending the status quo, the political and moral European order. The Germans were fighting to upset just that status quo. Eksteins even views the Tommies' sixty-pound pack as a possible metaphor for the encumbrance of an older tradition.

V

In the brief Nazi hour, the Germans, many of them at any rate, seemed to themselves and to many others to be a modernizing force. The artistic modernists wanted to "make it new," and they did so triumphantly. Their works represent, arguably, the greatest and most concentrated artistic achievements since the Renaissance. They were built on a foundation of hatred for the Victorian bourgeoisie.

One of Hitler's most energizing slogans was *"Deutchland Erwache!"*—Germany awake! He meant, "awaken from bourgeois torpor." And for the Nazi hour, the Germans certainly did, with, Autobahns, Volkswagens, Blitzkriegs, Stukas, rocket bombs, and death camps.

The old bourgeois values look a lot better since the Nazi political "modernists." The Nazi hour ended in catastrophe. Historians now instruct us that Nazi efficiency was an illusion, and that Berlin was an administrative chaos. Nazism's twin hater of the bourgeoisie, Marxist-Leninism, is now, fifty years after the Nazi hour, a historical shambles. Both were colossal, twentieth-century murderous mistakes.

Bourgeois values such as humaneness, privacy, moral responsibility, comfort, economic well-being, and domesticity do not look today as contemptible as they did to the artistic and political modernists. But do not blame it on James Joyce, or even on Paul de Man. What the artistic modernists really had to say was that bourgeois virtues are not exciting or heroic enough, that there is something more. In that, they were surely right, and it is to be sought in the whole central tradition of Western thought and creativity.

Wartime, II
The Deadly Hiatus, 1945

The soldiers and the sailors came home. They came home from the Normandy landing, the Ardennes, home from North Africa and the butchering Italian campaign, home from those deadly coral atolls in the Pacific, home from Okinawa. Home. The fighting on Okinawa had been so ghastly that it turned the stomach of no less than General Douglas MacArthur. "It was just awful," he said. "Just awful." Though the Japanese had lost Okinawa, they thought that the battle had really been a victory, in that the American casualties had been so heavy. The Americans would be demoralized by the Japanese will to kill and die. This estimate was naive.

MacArthur had been a humane commander. In military history, his New Guinea campaign is a classic, as is his Inchon flanking move in the Korean war. MacArthur did not hit the Japanese frontally in New Guinea. He leap-frogged them, taking this port and that city, skipping their forces, saving their lives and the lives of his own men. But war is war. The Japanese had planned to invade Australia. The Australians were not hospitable to that idea, and in the fighting in the Owen Stanley Mountains in New Guinea the Australian soldiers went into battle with Japanese skulls tied to their belts, and took no prisoners. The rapists and bayonetters of Nanking were shocked. This was going too far.

We all knew in 1942 about the Bataan Death March. The Japanese were bayonetting the wounded and burying American soldiers alive. We responded. I later met former U.S. Marines who had collections of Japanese gold teeth.

But in that summer of 1946, the war was over. Everyone was coming home. I remember playing tennis with a young man who had been the youngest Marine colonel in the Pacific, and who earlier had been captain of the tennis team at the University of North Carolina. He did not get to be a regimental commander in the Pacific by filling out a job application. His senior officers had all died in battle against the Japanese.

In retrospect, I do not think the Japanese knew how hard the Americans and the Australians would fight. They probably were genuinely shocked by their fate. They had enjoyed kicking the Chinese around in Manchuria. But the American war machine was a vast industrial operation, relentless, grinding on, unstoppable. The Henry Kaiser shipyards were launching "a ship a day." President Roosevelt was putting a thousand planes a month into the air. The U.S. Navy "crossed the T" in the Battle of Suriago Strait, and sank much of what was left of the Japanese Navy. The home islands were isolated without their navy.

When the American navy "crossed the T" that day, it was a classic moment in Naval history. Horatio Nelson had perfected the maneuver in the war against Napoleon, but it had always been a difficult thing. The point is to bring the maximum fire-power of your ships up against the minimum fire-power of the enemy. That means, your fleet should try to be at the top of the *T,* all guns firing. It also means that the enemy ships have been maneuvered into the line leading up to the top of the T. This ideal situation is very difficult to achieve. The American and Japanese admirals were commanding vast fleets, with the battleships at their center. To maneuver such a fleet is an enormous undertaking. With Horatio Nelson smiling overhead, the Americans outsailed the Japanese. The T was crossed. All of the available American fire-power was brought to bear on individual Japanese warships, as they sailed in confusion up the T. We need not celebrate here the predictable results.

It was the last such battle in naval history. Today we fight naval wars with electronics and with missiles. The T is gone.

We had not gone to war joyfully. I remember from 1939 the anguished emotions. Americans who were not even yet middle-aged had fought in World War I. There were thousands of destroyed soldiers in the veterans' hospitals, men who had been gassed, men with their arms and legs shot off. No one wanted war.

I remember with crystal clarity the day the war started. It was in September 1939. Hitler had defied a British ultimatum and moved his troops across the Polish border. Hitler had defied *the British Empire.*

I was home from school, in bed with a cold, my ear close to my tiny radio. The newsman was speaking from France. Static. The

French soldiers were assembling, static, coming from their homes on their bicycles. The French regiments were falling into line, static, and within days the French would have four million men at the front. The British fleet had sailed to sea from its great base at Scapa Flow, movements secret. Was the British fleet going to invade the North Sea and explode the German coast? Unfortunately, they had no such thing in mind. They were afraid of U-Boats and air-raids.

And then France fell, Hitler lost the air war over England, and the Japanese attacked Pearl Harbor.

But then it was over. In that summer of 1946, when all of the soldiers and sailors came home, the war was really over. Finished. I recall that for those young men it was considered bad form to tell "war stories." The damned thing was *over.*

In 1917, we had gone to war with *brio.* Americans had forgotten the slaughters at Cold Harbor and Antietam. Our 1898 war with Spain had been a turkey shoot, a military farce. *And we won't come back until it's over over there.* As the U.S. soldiers marched through Manhattan to the transport ships waiting at the docks, Enrico Caruso stood on a balcony at the old *Herald Tribune* building and sang in the languages of all the allies Irving Berlin's war hymn, "Over There."

In 1941, after Pearl Harbor, the mood was very different. It veered between "migod, not again," and "those little yellow bastards." But the national mood settled into "let's get the job done, and fast." The American war culture then was anything but joyful. There were Bill Mauldin's cartoons in *Stars and Stripes,* the soldiers Willie and Joe looking like bag women. The songs said things like "coming in on a wing and a prayer" and "You'll be so nice to come home to, home by the fire."

I remember crashing, as a teen-ager, a party at the Hotel Lexington in Manhattan. The men were all submarine personnel, in their naval uniforms, none of them over thirty. Everyone knew that most or even all of them would die in the Pacific. It was like a New Year's Eve party. "Auld Lang Sine." "Anchors Away." And big-band sounds of the 1940s. A lot of champagne was drunk. Undoubtedly there was romance. The next day, the navy men were on their way to Hawaii and their submarines. There was a job to be done, out there in a different time zone, out in Hawaii, Wake Island, Midway, the Solomons, the Marianas, the Philippines, Okinawa, Japan itself. Toward the end of the war there were so many American submarines in

Tokyo Bay that you could have gone on a morning stroll from deck to deck.

And then it was over. The awful war was over, and the job had been done. On the deck of the battleship *Missouri,* lying at anchor in Tokyo Bay, Douglas MacArthur with matchless magnanimity— and he knew about the Bataan Death March—announced that "our differences have been settled on the field of battle." MacArthur then went on to become a sort of Emperor of Japan, re-inventing the nation from his office in the Dai-Ichi Building, perhaps the kindest proconsul in the history of the world. He saved Hirohito's life. Dean Acheson, J. K. Galbraith and many others in Washington wanted to try Hirohito and hang him.

But as the young soldiers and sailors came home under those blue summer skies of 1946, hitting tennis balls and throwing baseballs and humming Rodgers and Hammerstein tunes, something had gone terribly wrong at the top of the American political pyramid. Franklin Roosevelt had won a fourth term in November 1944, but had been a desperately sick man. His personal physician knew that the president had a serious and degenerative disease of the arteries, but this was concealed not only from the American public but from Roosevelt's own colleagues. In these crucial months, as the war was ending, the American president was not functional. "I can personally handle Stalin," this dying president said. At the mature peak of his powers, Franklin Roosevelt would have entertained no such sentimental notion. With his mature wits about him, Roosevelt would have known that he could "personally" handle Stalin in about the way he would have had to handle Al Capone.

We now know from multiple sources that Franklin Roosevelt was not of sound mind in 1944–45. He drifted. The personal drama here is of Shakespearean quality. Eighteen days before Adolf Hitler committed suicide in his bunker, Franklin Roosevelt died in Warm Springs, Georgia. He had been rapidly weakening. He was having his portrait painted. The great love of his life was with him, not Eleanor.

Remember the term "the deadly hiatus." This refers to the period at the end of the war when *no one was in charge.* General George Marshall was making day-by-day decisions. In an eerie resemblance to Woodrow Wilson in 1919, when Wilson was incapacitated by a stroke and his wife signed his name to state papers, Franklin Roosevelt, because of arterial deterioration, was fading mentally. Momentous decisions were taken about the conduct of the war, which, in retrospect seem almost insane: the Italian campaign, the misbegotten invasion of the south of France, the incredible decision not to seize Berlin before the Russians did, the handling of the Polish problem.

Vice President Harry Truman had been in office only since November 1944. He had nothing to say on policy and little access to Roosevelt. He was not even told of the development of the atomic bomb. When Roosevelt died, Truman, who was a vigorous and decent man, took charge of policy. But much had gone over the dam.

Winston Churchill's private secretary John Colville has recalled the deadly hiatus. "I did not go to Yalta, but went to meet the returning British delegation and drove to London with Anthony Eden. I asked how things had gone. He replied that as Roosevelt was the sole head of state present, Churchill and Stalin being only heads of government, Roosevelt had been the chairman at every plenary session. That, said Eden, had been most hampering, for the president's powers were obviously failing and Eden had the impression that half the time he was unable to concentrate. So the deadly hiatus was already beginning to have its effect."

In his authoritative book *Roosevelt and Stalin* (1988), Robert Nisbet has thoroughly analyzed the vacuum that developed at the pinnacle of the American executive function in 1945.

This in my judgment was a global tragedy eerily resembling that of 1918. In 1917, the Americans went to war singing, and fought ferociously. In 1920, they voted overwhelmingly for Warren Harding and the "return to normalcy." But the war itself meant that there was no "normalcy" in Europe. Even as we voted for "normalcy," the returned German veterans were seething with resentment, and they found their orator. "Normalcy" was an illusion—in 1920 and in 1945.

The deadly hiatus of leadership in 1945 led to the loss of Eastern Europe, once known as Middle Europe, and to the calculations of the other side that led to Korea and Vietnam, to Cuba and Nicaragua.

International politics is like physics. The only brake on force is counterforce. If an initiative is doomed to failure, the initiative will not be made. On any power move, the odds must be calculated. If the enormous French army had smashed Hitler's move into the Rhineland, Hitler today would be an obscure name, removed from power by the German army as a dangerous gambler. I would not have listened on my radio to the news of the French soldiers assembling with their bicycles that long-ago September. The Polish cavalry would not have charged against the German tanks.

In the summer of 1946, the American soldiers and sailors had come home. They had "done the job," and they didn't want to talk about it. You could feel their sense of relief that now they were going to live. They had their lives before them.

I can still see the blue skies of the summer of 1946. I can still hear the pok-pok of the tennis balls, hit by ex-Marines and ex-fighter pilots. There was no hatred that I can recall for their former Japanese and German enemies. I think they felt that those poor bastards had been in it with the rest of us. Many of them brought back Japanese and German wives.

No one wanted to fight the Russians, but no one realized the truth about the deadly hiatus at the top of American decision making.

For that deadly hiatus, the bill has been very large, paid by the people of Eastern (Middle) Europe, by the dead of Korea and Vietnam, and the mounting dead today of Central America. There was no president at the top of the U.S. government.

But the young men and women who came home in that summer of 1946 had done their job, and they had a lot to remember. Colin Kelly. Pappy Boyington. Joe Foss. The British Eighth Army, considered by many military historians the finest fighting force in history. Lean, sun-burned, cocky, eye-brows desert-bleached, highly organized for continuous battle, the British of the Eighth Army had chased Erwin Rommel and his Afrika Corps all the way across North Africa and then destroyed what was left of that army. Rommel got out in a plane. And there was Admiral Spruance's brilliant naval victory over the Japanese at Midway. There were those young men who ran up those beaches firing assault weapons, and the men who sailed the ships.

When the young men came home in 1945–46, they had fought quite a war. They were comrades of Caesar and Lee and Grant and Pershing.

Johnson, Boswell, and Modernity

"Maybe there never was anyone so young as Boswell was in the spring of 1763," Christopher Morley remarks in his preface to the *London Journal,* and certainly it is that quality of youthfulness that makes this record of Boswell's early adventures in London so appealing and so poignant. Yet note how Morley uses the word "never," advisedly, I think—there "never was anyone so young as Boswell." And here we touch upon an aspect of the *London Journal* that endows it with an importance that goes beyond charm and poignancy. "When we came upon Highgate Hill," writes Boswell of his first approach to London, "I was all life and joy." A few months later, some songs in a play evoke the same emotions: "The songs revived in my mind many gay ideas, and recalled in the most lively colors to my imagination the time when I was first in London, when all was new to me, when I felt the warm glow of youthful feeling and was full of curiosity and wonder." It is easy enough to discover in his *Journal* the sources of that joy and wonder; one sees that they were the result of a sudden and liberating awareness of possibility, an awareness that in London one could, if one had sufficient powers of imagination, be anything one liked.

In Scotland, which lay behind him, Boswell's identity was relatively fixed: he would eventually practice the law, preside over Auchinleck, and marry the proper sort of wife. But in the great city, he could experiment with different selves, each of which was the creation of his imagination. "I patrolled up and down Fleet Street, thinking on London, the seat of Parliament and the seat of pleasure, and seeming to myself as one of the wits in King Charles the Second's time." In such moods as this, he plays the rake: "I should have mentioned last night that I met with a monstrous big whore in the strand." At another time, he imagines himself a blackguard: "It was the King's birthnight, and I resolved to be a blackguard and to see all that was to be seen." He can be a lover in the high style—the liaison with Louisa, one feels, was invented by Wycherley—or he can be a literary man, or a respectable and pious citizen, or a crony of Wilkes, or the friend of aristocrats, or even—it glitters on his horizon—a commissioned officer in the guards. The modes in which he conceives himself seemingly have no limits. Martin Price has noticed that in some passages of the *Journal* he speaks in the voice of Tristram Shandy, that in others he catches the note of Fielding or of Addison; and Frederick Pottle observes that the figure of John Gay's Macheath lurks behind much of the book.

Boswell, then, made the romantic discovery of the "god-like" power of the imagination: we are not *really* the creations of parents or social class or other circumstance; we invent ourselves. "By our own spirits," as Wordsworth wrote, "are we deified" or made creators, made our own authors. For Boswell this discovery was inseparable from London, from the circumstances of the modern city, and the spiritual descendants of Boswell, during the next century and a half, were to explore as he did the transformations of the self that the conditions of the modern city do so much to encourage: Pip, in *Great Expectations,* becomes a gentleman; Julien Sorel plays a succession of roles and scales the heights of society; James Gatz becomes Jay Gatsby, Oxford man and military hero. Lionel Trilling has called this sort of figure the Young Man from the Provinces: "a provincial birth and rearing suggest the simplicity and high hopes he begins with—he starts with a great demand upon life and a great wonder about its complexity and promise," and he moves from his obscure position to one of eminence in Paris and London. He touches "the life of the rulers of the earth."

It is this story that is told in Boswell's *Journal* and in the *Confessions* of Rousseau, as in some of the most powerful novels of the nineteenth century—*The Red and the Black, Pere Goriot, Great Expectations, Sentimental Education,* and *The Princess Casamassima.* The experience with which all these books are concerned is certainly connected with the emergence of the modern city—that is, experiencing the modern city becomes a possibility sometime during the middle years of the eighteenth century. Before that time, one may see, social status and social role were too clearly defined for Boswell's histrionics to have much validity: in London, as elsewhere, one was too quickly categorized. London was a kind of extension of the provinces. But by the middle of the century, the city had grown sufficiently—there was the necessary mobility and just enough anonymity—for an exceptional young man to entertain the diverse possibilities of selfhood that we meet in the pages of Boswell's *Journal.** As Ian Watt has written in *The Rise of the Novel* (1957):

Instead of the countryman's unchanging landscape, dominated by the regular alternation of the seasons, and the established hierarchy of social and moral order symbolized by the manor house, the parish church and the village green, the citizen of eighteenth century London had a horizon that was in many ways like that of modern urban man.

Max Weber has noticed that, with the breakdown of a social hierarchy, a certain theatrical element entered into social identity: to a greater degree than before, one was taken for what one appeared to be. For the determination of status, style of life became more of a determining element. As Weber puts it, social identity came to involve a kind of stylistic "usurpation." An adept individual such as Boswell or the agile protagonist of a novel by Defoe could imaginatively usurp one or more social identities. Georg Simmel has argued that this aspect of modernity explains why so many modern artists have an aesthetic preference for an older form of society: under the traditional arrangement of a society, appearance and reality are drawn more closely together—a person is more likely to appear to be what he actually is. In the modern form of society, a person is what he appears to be. As Simmel points out, the separation of thing and sign, reality and appearance, is counter to the essence of the artistic.

The discovery that one could invent oneself is the discovery that Boswell makes when he comes to London; it is this that produces

---

*As might be expected, the question of the size of London at different periods has been a matter of considerable controversy and debate. After the Great Fire of 1666, many observers were struck by the expansion of London beyond the limits of Westminster and London. Max Beloff (*Public Order and Public Disturbances, 1660–1714*) concludes that this growth was perhaps the most important feature of the social history of the late Stuart period (see Watt, *The Rise of the Novel*, p. 178). It is beyond dispute, however, that the most dramatic growth occurred much later. Between 170 and 1800 the population of Great Britain apparently doubled, from about 8 million to about 15 million, and this was "accentuated in the years after 1750" (David Ogg, *Europe of the Ancien Regime, 1715–1783*, pp. 14–15). Furthermore, since the number of deaths in the cities, as measured by the bills of mortality, often exceeded the number of births, it is clear that the population was to an unusual degree made up of immigrants from the countryside. This factor must have contributed to the unstable and inorganic character of social life in the cities, preeminent among which was London.

in him that wonder and joy upon first seeing the city from Highgate
Hill. He felt about London much as, a century and a half later, Nick
Carraway was to feel about New York:

The city seen from the Queensboro Bridge is always the city seen for the
first time, in its first wild promise of all the mystery and beauty in the world.
. . . "Anything can happen now that we've slid over this bridge," I thought,
"anything at all."

The extraordinary appeal of the *London Journal* may in part be
accounted for by the fact that it does express this sense of the city,
that it evokes for us the modern city in its idea and in its ideal, that
it recalls the city as it seemed before it passed from promise to
threat—for now we are more aware of the dehumanizing forces of
the city than of its promise, more aware of impossibility than of
opportunity. No writer of the present time celebrates the city as a
reservoir of infinite potentiality. Our city is the one in the later
novels of Dickens, and the same polluted river flows through it as
flows through the London of *The Waste Land.*

We know too a darker truth, which Boswell eventually discovered: that if one can be anything one wishes, one might never
achieve any true identity at all. "Know thyself," says Boswell at the
beginning of his *London Journal,* "for surely this knowledge is of
all the most important." His *Journals,* monstrous in length, constitute the record of his long search for himself, a search never to be
crowned with success, for he *had* no self. The aging Boswell remains
a Young Man from the Provinces, open to all the possibilities of
imagination, of intellect, of social role, and in the end he is defeated
by them. We remember him savoring Hume's skepticism, carousing
with Wilkes, courting noblewomen, fornicating with whores, responding to Ossian, behaving like a high churchman or else like a
disciple of Rousseau. He had been converted to Roman Catholicism
in his youth and had renounced it, but then, in 1773, amid the ruins
of a chapel on St. Kenneth's Island, he felt that earlier self return: "I
walked out in the dark to the cross, knelt before it, and holding it
with both my hands, I prayed with strong devotion. . . . I said '*Sancte
Columbe, ora pro me.*' "

Because Boswell in his long search never succeeds in knowing
himself, he frequently finds himself plunged into despair. "This was
one of the blackest days that I ever passed. . . . I had lost all relish of
London." Again and again this note recurs. As for Gatsby, the dream

of infinite possibility has an alarming capacity to turn to ashes, and Wordsworth's memorable line, "By our own spirits are we deified," is susceptible to an ironic reading.

During the second half of the eighteenth century, there occurred in other cultural areas a comparable dissolving of traditional definitions and settled distinctions. The older theory of literary genres, for example, rested, as Paul Fussell has shown, on certain widely held assumptions: that human nature is uniform and that the various capacities of the "common" human mind are served by the characteristic literary genres. The part of the mind that responds to melancholy is served by the elegy; the part that is gratified by enthusiasm and praise responds to the ode; the sense of justice is served by satire and tragedy; and comedy supplies occasion for laughter. Naturally, this account oversimplifies, and the assumptions did not become pedantic, but it was assumed that the genres collectively constituted an analogue or model of the fixed potentialities of the mind. And since human nature is constant, the genres of the ancients are still valid in the present. But during the second half of the eighteenth century, the genres broke down. We see a rich variety of experiments with poetic prose and rhapsody, pastiches of Oriental and Persian matter, a general mingling and transcendence of traditional forms. In the painter's assertion of color and mass against line we see a related phenomenon, as well as in the growing estrangement from traditional doctrines of natural law and in religion with its emphasis upon intensity of personal experience at the expense of precise doctrinal definition.

ii

Unlike Boswell, whose *Journals* record a long and unrewarded search for a self, Johnson possessed a formidable one. His life in London—he arrived twenty-five years earlier than Boswell—turned out to be a long defense of the values of Augustan humanism against the pressure of other possibilities. In contrast to Boswell, Johnson possesses an identity not because he has gone in search of one, but because of his allegiance to a set of assumptions that he regards as objectively true. Johnson's intellectual and moral outline was this sharp, moreover, because he was so continuously under siege, so often forced into definition by a confrontation.

The values and assumptions he devoted himself to defending define a traditional and wholly coherent vision of existence. He considered human nature to be uniform and the literature and the history of the past therefore relevant to the present. Because human nature is fallen, the ethical responsibilities of literature are of primary concern, and as a moralist, therefore, the man of letters has a recognized place in society. His attitude on this point is identical to the one implicit in the description of the poet in Ben Jonson's *To Penshurst,* whose recognized function assures him of a "station" in that model of the social order. Johnson's value judgments imply a set of traditional hierarchies: some literary genres, some human activities, and some periods of history are higher than others. Such judgments, he considered, do not derive from personal whims but are based on the nature of things. He approved of subordination and considered respect for rank important for the stability of society. He was contemptuous of novel theories of government; he thought that although society might in time become more commodious, there had been no overall moral improvement in human nature, and he believed that most human problems are ultimately intractable. Finally, he believed fervently in the moral and metaphysical truth of Christianity.* The coherence and seriousness of this vision lies behind the special authority of his prose, as in the somber music of the opening sentence of *Rasselas,* surely one of the great openings in literature:

Ye who listen with credulity to the whispers of fancy, and pursue with eagerness the phantoms of hope, who expect that age will perform the promises of youth, and that the deficiencies of the present day will be supplied by the morrow, attend to the history of Rasselas, Prince of Abyssinia.

The *opening* sentence, but its effect—a matter of rhythm, of periodicity, but also, one feels, of the weight of experienced truth—is rather as if a gate had closed.

The defense of these assumptions—against an increasing religious skepticism, against optimism, against sentimental views of human nature, against egalitarian feeling—enlisted all the combativeness of Johnson's nature. Everyone has noticed this combativeness, and when Carlyle argued that Johnson was a moral hero, he had something almost military in mind—Johnson's irreducibility, the strength

---

*Paul Fussell, in *The Rhetorical World of Augustan Humanism* (Oxford, 1965), demonstrates the continuity of most of these assumptions in Swift, Pope, Gibbon, Johnson, Burke, and Reynolds.

of will that enabled him to conquer his "vile melancholy," to hold at bay his fears and his guilt, to fend off all attacks upon his besieged but superbly designed intellectual citadel. As Boswell observed, accurately and beautifully, in *The Life of Johnson*:

[Johnson's] mind resembled the vast amphitheatre, the Coliseum at Rome. In the center stood his judgment, which like a mighty gladiator, combatted those apprehensions that, like the wild beasts of the Arena, were all around him in cells, ready to be let out upon him. After a conflict, he drives them back into their dens; but not killing them, they were still assailing him.

Boswell's characterization of Johnson as a gladiator is perfect, for combat was indeed central to his intellectual and moral life. As he once remarked to Boswell about the art of conversation, no dialogue can occur

but one or the other will come off superior. I do not mean that the victor must have the better of the argument, for he may take the weak side; but his superiority of parts and knowledge will necessarily appear: and he to whom he thus shows himself superior is lessened in the eyes of the young men.

Nor was Johnson combative only in conversation. His defiance of Macpherson is well known: "I hope I shall not be deterred from detecting what I think a cheat by the menaces of a ruffian." Here he was defending the idea of the man of letters against the practice of a fraud, much as he had, in the famous letter of Chesterfield, defended it against the condescension of a patron.

Johnson was humble before the Lord Jesus Christ, as Medford Evans has aptly remarked, but not before any other lord, not even Lord Chesterfield, and perhaps the two attitudes are not unrelated. Nor was his intellectual and moral courage, refined and delicate though it could be when circumstances required, so very different from his extraordinary physical courage, many examples of which Boswell's *Life* provides. Johnson "feared death," says Boswell, "but he feared nothing else, not even what might occasion death."

Still, there is something further that has not been sufficiently recognized, perhaps because of the weight of Johnson's affirmations; something that makes Johnson's defensive battle more complex and still more impressive. Johnson responds not only deeply but sympathetically to what is powerful and attractive in the adversary, and it is this response that makes his final affirmation all the more weighty.

iii

Unlike Boswell, who views society as a kind of stage upon which to act out his various roles and who otherwise has no very clear idea of or interest in society, Johnson, like Gibbon and Burke among his own contemporaries and like Swift and Pope in an earlier generation, had the ability to view society disinterestedly and as a whole, to stand outside it and view it as a social *order.* "I consider myself as acting a part in the great system of society," said Johnson. "I would behave to a nobleman as I should expect he would behave to me, were I a nobleman and he Sam. Johnson." As F. R. Leavis has observed, "Johnson is not, like the Romantic poet, the enemy of society, but consciously its representative and its voice, and it is his strength—something inseparable from his greatness—to be so."

Johnson's ability to view society as a whole, as a social order, is implicit throughout his work, and it enables him to endow the individual act with a wider, a general significance, but it is especially manifest in the one book in which he deliberately set out to reflect analytically upon an entire society, his *Journey to the Western Islands.* In this book, moreover, Johnson's method provides an instructive contrast with Boswell's approach to the same subject in a book of his own. Boswell's account of the famous tour through Scotland is anecdotal, and one can open his book almost anywhere and find memorable incidents dramatizing what was Boswell's chief interest—personality. Who will ever forget in Boswell that encounter with the ancient highland widow who fearfully expected to be raped by Johnson? Equally memorable in Boswell's book is the conversation between Johnson and the Reverend Hector MacLean—"about seventy-seven years of age, a decent ecclesiastick, dressed in a full suit of black clothes, and a black wig"—a conversation in which the participants, because both were hard of hearing, spoke simultaneously, "each continuing to maintain his own argument, without hearing exactly what the other said."

Boswell's account is rich in this kind of thing and immensely enjoyable, but Johnson's *Journey* has an entirely different perspective. It tries to depict whtat is going on in an entire society, and it uses its analysis to reflect upon the situation in England. Scotland is Boswell's country, but in a sense Johnson is more interested in it. There has been some ill-natured controversy about the meaning of Johnson's *Journey,* but it is difficult to see why there should have been, for Johnson himself tells us the theme of his book. That passage from the *Life* is important enough to quote in full:

We dined together with Mr. Scott (now Sir William Scott, His Majesty's Advocate-General), at his chambers in the Temple, nobody else there. The company being small, Johnson was not in such spirits as he had been the preceding day, and for a considerable time little was said. At last he burst forth: "Subordination is sadly broken down in this age. No man now, has the same authority which his father had,—except a jailer. No master has it over his servants: it is diminished in our colleges, nay, in our grammar schools." BOSWELL: "What is the cause of this, Sir?" JOHNSON: "Why, the coming in of the Scotch" (laughing sarcastically). BOSWELL: "That is to say, things have been turned topsy-turvey. But your serious cause." JOHNSON: "Why, Sir, there are many causes, the chief of which is, I think, the great increase of money. No man now depends upon the Lord of a Manor, when he can send to another country and fetch provisions. The shoe-black at the entry of my court does not depend on me. I can deprive him but of a penny a day, which he hopes somebody else will bring him; and that penny I must carry to another shoe-black, so the trade suffers nothing. I have explained in my *Journey to the Hebrides,* how gold and silver destroy feudal subordination. But, besides, there is a general relaxation of reverence. No son depends upon his father, as in former times. Paternity used to be considered as of itself a great thing, which had a right to many claims. That is, in general, reduced to very small bounds. My hope is, that as anarchy produces tyranny, this extreme relaxation will produce *freni stricto.*"

iv

Johnson's ability to view society as a whole, as a social order, resulted, as is well known, in his affirmation of subordination in society. Subordination he connected with "reverence," with "authority," with stability. Men, he elsewhere remarked to Boswell, "are happier in a state of inequality and subordination. Were they to be in this pretty state of equality, they would soon degenerate into brutes." In a similar vein, he once remarked to Mrs. Thrale: "You are to consider, Madam, that it is our duty to maintain the subordination of civilized society; and when there is a gross and shameful deviation from rank, it should be punished so as to deter others from the same perversion." Disinterestedly, he considered such subordination necessary to society: "I am for supporting the principle, and am disinterested in doing it, as I have no such right." As a psychological and moral realist, he recognized the value of family tradition, though again, there could have been no personal motive for him to do so:

But, surely, it is much easier to respect a man who has always had respect than to respect a man who we know was last year no better than ourselves, and will be no better next year. . . . Riches do not gain hearty respect; they only procure external attention. A very rich man, from low beginnings, may buy his election in a borough; but, *ceteris paribus,* a man of family will be preferred.

But for all his praise of subordination, and despite the weight that must be given to his elegaic treatment of older social modes in his *Journey to the Western Islands of Scotland,* there are indications of internal conflict. He is engaged, as it were, in an inner debate, one which is resolved in the end in favor of continuities with the past but which is always felt by the reader to be *present.* Coming down out of the highlands into the bustling city of Glasgow—in the narrative at this point one feels that one is entering another world altogether—Johnson sees that in Glasgow one encounters thriving commerce and obvious prosperity, and he remarks upon "the greatest of many private houses." More interesting still, and this is not generally recognized, he responds deeply to the new kind of world that is emerging in the metropolis, and no one has ever expressed in so eloquent a phrase as Johnson's the spirit of the new and insurgent capitalism.

When Thrale died after making his fortune as a brewer, Johnson assisted at the sale of the brewery:

[Johnson] appeared bustling about, with an inkhorn and pen in his button-hole, like an exciseman; and on being asked what he really considered to be the value of the property which was to be disposed of, answered, "We are not here to sell a parcel of boilers and vats, but the potentiality of growing rich beyond the dreams of avarice."

He saw long before Goethe that capitalism was not really utilitarian but Faustian, and, perhaps in spite of himself, he responded to that vision. Thus, though he was passionately devoted to the traditional idea of order, to the values of subordination, reverence, and family loyalty, he also responded to the possibilities that worked counter to them. He knew the beauty and value of order but also the excitement of aspiration: one should, he said, "fly at the eagle." It is for this reason that his acts of judgment, when they finally are made, are so impressive.

V

Johnson's judgments concerning literature exhibit a similar tension. His allegiance was to the main tradition of neoclassicism or, as

Paul Fussell calls it, the rhetorical tradition of Augustan humanism. That this literary allegiance has wider implications is clear enough. It is in Johnson's verse, writes F. R. Leavis,

> that we can see most clearly the extremely positive civilization to which Johnson belonged expressing itself as literary convention. ... For most eighteenth-century verse, and all verse of the Augustan tradition, has a social movement—a movement that suggests company deportment, social gesture, and a code of manners.

Fussell argues convincingly indeed that Johnson's modifications of the Augustan tradition often in fact only confirm his central allegiance to it. The intense seriousness with which he goes about justifying the mixture of comedy and tragedy, as against the assumption that they should be kept separate, demonstrates the seriousness with which he takes the entire *rationale* of genres.

The Augustan tradition begins for Johnson with Denham and Waller, continues through Dryden, and culminates in Pope.

> By perusing the works of Dryden, [Pope] discovered the most perfect fabric of English verse, and habituated himself to that only which he found the best. ... New sentiments and new images others may produce; but to attempt any further improvement of versification will be dangerous.

It is clear that this is not merely a *literary* judgment but is involved with a whole series of social assumptions. Johnson condemns deviations from the mode epitomized by Pope. The metaphysicals "endeavoured to be singular in their thoughts and were careless of their diction." Milton had, both in prose and verse, "formed his style by a perverse and pedantic principle." The language of Gray is "too luxuriant" and "a little ... beyond common apprehension." Collins seemed to think "with some later candidates for fame, that not to write prose is certainly to write poetry."

In the famous tenth chapter of *Rasselas,* Johnson gave the most eloquent expression we have of the neoclassical spirit in poetry.

> [The poet] is to examine not the individual, but the species. He does not number the streaks of the tulip, or describe the different shades in the verdure of the forest: he is to exhibit in his portraits of nature such prominent and striking features, as recall the original to every mind. ... He must disregard present laws and opinions, and rise to general and transcendental truths, which will always be the same.

We cannot suppose, as some have, that this opinion is Imlac's rather than Johnson's, for Johnson applies the same standard in his critical essays. "Great thoughts," he observes in his commentary on the metaphysicals, "are always general, and consist in positions not limited by exceptions, and in descriptions not descending to minuteness."

Yet even so, when it came to biography, he knew, as Boswell said, the value of a "minute selection of characteristical circumstances" that serves to distinguish particular experience from general. Here, as in his *Journey to the Western Islands,* he shows the influence of that increasing concern with the *historical* that marked the second half of the century, a concern with the flux of time and the uniqueness of the moment that was ultimately so subversive of the neoclassical attempt to focus upon the permanent in experience, upon the general as distinguished from the particular truth. Again, when he used the word *nature* to define the difference betweeen Richardson and Fielding, he was adding a psychological, subjective dimension to the neoclassical sense of that word. "Sir," he said,

there is all the difference in the world between characters of nature and characters of manners; and *there* is the difference between those of Fielding and those of Richardson. Characters of manners are very entertaining; but they are to be understood by a more superficial observer than characters of nature, where a man must dive into the recesses of the human heart.

Here, as in his social views, we see him, despite his allegiances, attracted to insurgent and even potentially revolutionary forces. And, oddly enough, it is the insurgent, often, that evokes his most eloquent, his most memorable phrases: "the potentiality of growing rich beyond the dreams of avarice," and "a man must dive into the recesses of the human heart."

vi

Nowhere more clearly than in their religious beliefs and their results do the differences between Johnson and Boswell shine forth. Johnson was not concerned with what was dramatic, with what stimulated his "sentiments," with what made for an effective "personality." What mattered to him was what was true, and that truth was objective, outside himself. It has long been said that some of the most striking aspects of Johnson's behavior might be traced to neurosis, but it is now accepted that certain of these traits have more to do with his relationship—a changing one—to theological doctrine. In this connection, Maurice Quinlan's study of Johnson's religious development is indispensable.

Johnson's famous melancholy, for example, and his fear of death, for both of which a variety of fanciful explanations have been put forward, were in fact deeply involved with his interpretation of the doctrine of the Atonement. Some writers, such as William Law, who was perhaps the most important influence on Johnson's religious thought, held that Christ's sacrifice was exemplary: we achieve salvation by attempting to imitate Christ's perfect sanctity. Until late in life, Johnson subscribed to this view, and its rigors are obvious. If Christ is an ideal to be imitated, one must inevitably fall far short. Furthermore, one is in the position of atoning for one's own sins, for that immense distance by which one *has* fallen short—and how can a scrupulous man ever be sure that his propitiatory acts have been in proportion to his sins? We remember Johnson performing such extraordinary acts of penance as standing bareheaded in the rain at Uttoxeter to expiate a boyish misdemeanor committed sixty years before.

But Christian tradition contains another and, as it happens, more orthodox view—that Christ's sacrifice was *expiatory*: He took upon Himself the sins of the world. Eighteenth-century Anglicanism witnessed a tropical growth of theologies and personalities, and Johnson found convincing arguments for this interpretation in the most unlikely of places. The saintly William Law, otherwise orthodox, had been eccentric on the Atonement, but the writings of Samuel Clarke, a heterodox rationalist ("Nobody doubted the existence of God," a wit said of him, "until Dr. Clarke strove to prove it"), convinced Johnson of the orthodox view. Under the influence of Clarke's work and of a religious experience at Easter 1776, he changed his mind and began to scandalize his friends by recommending Clarke to them, saying that Clarke had "made him a Christian." His anxieties eased to a degree, and his terror of death was softened: what must have seemed hopeless was now at least possible.

All his life Johnson struggled with the problems presented to him by the fragmented Christian tradition, and he took these problems with intense, with final, seriousness. His attitude toward the Dissenters is well known. Refusing to attend the church of Dr. Robertson in Edinburgh, he remarked pungently, "I will hear him . . . if he will get into a tree and preach; but I will not give a sanction, by my presence, to a Presbyterian assembly." Still, in one important respect, he agreed with the Nonconformists and stood against the high Anglicans and the Catholics. On commonsense grounds, he did not believe in the Real Presence in the Eucharist and thought that Christ was present only symbolically. To be sure, he might have been charged with inconsistency here for, though he deemed the Trinity inexplicable, he nevertheless believed in it, justifying his belief by distinguishing between "doctrines contrary to reason and doctrines above reason."

On quite a few issues, however, especially as he grew older, his attitudes had a Roman Catholic coloration. Though he remained firmly within the Church of England, the changes in his religious opinions always involved a heightening, if one may put it that way, of his religious position. Johnson found, at least where deathbed repentance was concerned, that he had to modify the position of the Reformers that actual amendment of life was necessary for one's sins to be forgiven. He shifted away from the characteristic Protestant position on the mode of administering the Eucharist. He apparently believed in Purgatory and looked with favor on the invocation of saints, and though he thought the "perfection of religious life" required active goodness, he also had a genuine sympathy for the contemplative life. He told Boswell that he never read of a monastery without in imagination falling on his knees, and there is even evidence that during the last year of his life he considered returning to Paris to end his days at the Benedictine monastery he had visited years earlier.

In his religious views, as in other areas of his thought, Johnson leaves us with the impression that he was, perhaps excepting Burke, a larger entity than the men around him. Wider in his sympathies than the eighteenth-century establishment, more intense and learned than other laymen, he seems a survival from an earlier and more Christian period, a man on the scale, imaginatively, of Milton or Herbert.

vii

Boswell's relationship to Johnson has what might be called a classic quality. They were very different and even opposite kinds of men, but the point is that their differences have a representative quality. Both came from the provinces to London, but when Johnson came to London in 1737 he brought with him, from his reading and his reflections, the assumptions of the Augustan tradition. He committed himself to and defined himself by the defense of those values. Boswell, in contrast, adumbrated the future and assumed, without attempting to reconcile them, disparate sets of values. His commitment was not to truth but to the dramatization of self, and whatever might for the moment serve that end was true. Johnson was, unlike Boswell, a violent man, a defender of order because he knew what the absence of order meant. When he was twenty, so Boswell tells us, he had a severe nervous collapse:

While he was at Litchfield, in the college vacation year of 1729, he felt himself overwhelmed with a horrible hypochondria, with perpetual irritation, fretfulness, and impatience; and with a dejection, gloom, and despair, which made existence misery. From this dismal malady he never afterward was perfectly relieved.

Johnson found himself threatened, in fact, by a recurrence. "About this time [1764] he was afflicted with a severe return of the hypochondriac disorder."

Despite this ever-present chaos, the great sane propositions prevailed: perhaps the chaos made all the more passionate his commitment to them. Like the other great writers in the Augustan tradition—Dryden, Swift, Pope, Gibbon, and Burke—Johnson retained the ability to view society as a whole, to stand outside it and view it as a social order, of which he imagined himself a part. This entailed no diminution of his energies, a fact one can never forget, as is revealed in the episode of Langston's will:

Johnson could not stop his merriment, but continued it all the way till he got without the Temple-gate. He then burst into such a fit of laughter that he appeared to be almost in a convulsion; and, in order to support himself, laid hold of one of the posts at the side of the foot pavement, and sent forth peals so loud, that in the silence of the night his voice seemed to resound from Temple Bar to Fleet Ditch.

Johnson's sense of the social order entailed no diminution of his own being, no lessening of his own energies, and it allowed him to endow the individual act with a wider, a general significance, to evaluate it in terms of larger relations. As Johnson said, "I consider myself as acting a part in the great system of society."

But Boswell—like Sterne, for example—had almost no sense of society as a social order, could not achieve the imaginative perspective of the great Augustans, could not rise to meanings that transcended the self. The social order for Boswell was not a system of moral relations; rather, it existed as a limitless, dramatic reservoir of possible identities. Johnson knows the social function of the aristocrat, but he never supposes that he is one. Boswell, in contrast, and with politically sinister implications, is capable of impersonating an aristocrat. Johnson's entire intellectual career was involved with the defense of social and intellectual values that required a man to have a particular character, to behave according to established principles. But what Boswell found in London, what evoked feelings of joy and wonder in him, was precisely the liberation from those requirements.

The struggle, both inner and outer, that gave weight to Johnson's rhetoric, that made it the unmistakably personal expression of a self attempting to order its experience, disappears in Boswell, and we find instead a perfect—indeed, a selfless—lucidity. The possibilities of experience do not conflict for Boswell as they do for Johnson, nor do they have implications beyond themselves, any reference to a wider order of meanings. They do not conflict; they merely succeed one another cinematically; Tory, libertine, *litterateur,* Scottish laird, sentimentalist, skeptic, Roman Catholic. And it is the selfless lucidity of Boswell's prose that enables us to see so clearly the unforgettable, the intrasigent being of Johnson.

Herbert's "The Collar" Re-read

The Collar

I struck the board, and cry'd, No more.
    I will abroad.
    What? shall I ever sigh and pine?
My lines and life are free; free as the rode,
    Loose as the winde, as large as store.
      Shall I be still in suit?
    Have I no harvest but a thorn
    To let me bloud, and not restore
What have I lost with cordiall fruit?
      Sure there was wine
Before my signs did drie it: there was corn
    Before my tears did drown it.
Is the yeare onely lost to me?
      Have I no bayes to crown it?
No flowers, no garlands gay? all blasted?
      All wasted?
    Not so, my heart: but there is fruit,
    And thou hast hands.
Recover all thy sigh-blown age
On double pleasures: leave thy cold dispute
Of what is fit, and not. Forsake thy cage,
    The rope of sands,
Which pettie thoughts have made, and made to thee
    Good cable, to enforce and draw,
      And be thy law
While thou didst wink and wouldst not see,
      Away; take heed:
    I will abroad.
Call in thy deaths head there: tie up thy fears.
      He that forbears
    To suit and serve his need,

This article first appeared in *Studies in Romanticism* and is reprinted with permission.

> Deserves his load.
> But as I rav'd and grew more fierce and wilde
> At every word,
> Me thoughts I heard one calling, *Child!*
> And I reply'd, *My Lord.*

According to the interpretations usually offered, "The Collar" describes the struggle between discipline and pleasure, between the duties of a clergyman and the satisfactions to be derived from the natural life or, as Joseph Summers puts it, the struggle between God's will and the speaker's rebellious heart. But to leave the matter here is to miss, I think, the full import of the poem. Properly read—read, that is, in the context of Herbert's other poems and with reference to the tradition that fills his imagery with meaning—the poem gains in complexity and power. It can be seen to represent in psychological terms the events of the Christian moral drama—the Fall, the Atonement, and the Redemption.

It is certainly true that the speaker, under the influence of the heart, rebels against discipline. But in reaching for the "fruit," as did Adam, he simultaneously reaches for the supernatural fruit, the fruit of the Cross. Paradoxically, the "natural" imagery of the poem, the fruit and wine and corn, in pursuit of which the speaker rebels, is also the imagery traditionally associated with the Eucharist. Therefore we may describe the moral events of the poem in this way: just as the moral disorder entailed by the rebellion of Adam and Eve was overcome by Christ's sacrifice, so the moral disorder of the speaker's rebellion is to be finally overcome by the sacrament of the Eucharist. Part of the brilliance of the poem lies in the fact that it expresses rebellion and atonement in the same vocabulary and, by so doing, epitomizes its central idea: that rebellion necessarily entails, because of God's justice and mercy, atonement.

In *George Herbert: His Religion and Art* (1954), Joseph Summers has described very well the structure of the poem. It is divided into four sections of argument. First the speaker, under the influence of the heart, complains, then the will answers that there is "fruit" if the heart will seek it. Next the heart repeats its complaint and its rebellious intention, and finally there is resolution. But if we look closely at the imagery, the precise nature of the resolution becomes clear. We see, furthermore, that both heart and will are the unconscious instruments of God's will and that His intention, latent from the start, gradually becomes manifest. Lines 6–12 contain the unmistakable references:

> Shall I be still in suit?
> Have I no harvest but a thorn
> To let me bloud, and not restore
> What I have lost with cordiall fruit?
> Sure there was wine
> Before my sighs did drie it: there was corn
> Before my tears did drown it.

"Suit" in line 6 suggests a petitioner. The speaker, as if in a court of law, seeks something that as yet is not forthcoming. The word also carries the sense of enforced attendance, the attitude of a courtier who has little to hope for. But as one analyzes the poem and becomes aware of its full implication, one realizes that the important word in this line is not "suit" but "still." The speaker is not a litigant in an earthly court, and he is not in suit before a secular prince: his suit is before a supernatural king and is to be decided according to transcendent laws. He should, in other words, be *still,* although he does not know it, and at the end of the poem we are indeed aware of a kind of stillness: the speaker no longer needs all those words.

In the next six lines we encounter a series of references that would have presented no difficulties to Herbert's contemporaries. The speaker's suit yields him a harvest only of thorn. I do not wish to insist upon a minor point, since the poem is clearly theological in its bearing, but I cannot suppose that the mixing of metaphors here, the legal and courtly suit entailing the unfortunate agricultural harvest, is entirely without social meaning. However this may be, we are told that the speaker's harvest yields only "a thorn" that makes him bleed. At the moment of his rebellion, the speaker understands his words in some such sense as this: my discipline is painful; in blocking the satisfaction of my desires, it makes me bleed and sigh, and to make matters worse, it brings no reward.

However, the word he uses have an alternative signification. The thorn suggests the imperfections introduced into the world by the Fall, the damaging of the *rose sine spina* of paradise. Such an association for "thorn" was commonplace. Bishop Bayly, for example, referred to "thornes, the first fruits of the curse," in his *Practice of Pietie* (1613), and Milton points out in *Paradise Lost* that Eden before the Fall boasted "Flow'rs of all hue, and without Thorn the Rose." Thus the thorn, which in its primary meaning in the poem signifies the discomforts the speaker experiences when his desires conflict with his discipline, also suggests the results of the Fall. Just as Adam, rebelling against the original "discipline" of Eden, introduced thorns into Eden, so the speaker, rebelling against *his* discipline, finds a thorn rather than fruit.

But—and here is the third signification of "thorn"—the thorn is not only the result of the sin of rebellion but is also associated with the means of its redemption. The speaker's harvest, the thorns that make him bleed, though at present bringing only pain, foreshadow the mode of his redemption: they are also the thorns of Christ's crown.

To summarize: the speaker is linked in his rebellion with Adam, and like Adam, he longs for "fruit"; his longing and rebellion lead to "thorns," but, as with Adam, the means of recovery is implicit in the act. The thorns are the thorns of Eden after the Fall; they are the thorns of the speaker's pain; and they are also the thorns of Christ's crown, the symbol of *His* pain and therefore of the means of man's redemption.

The speaker is not aware of all this, however, at the moment the thoughts described in these lines occur. The full meaning of his rebellion, as defined by the *double entendres,* does not become clear to him until the end of the poem. In lines 8 and 9 he says merely that there is no relief for him, that his harvest is only of thorn. He is not aware, although we are, of the irony present in "only"—*only* Christ's crown. As far as the speaker knows at this moment, he has no harvest that will "restore / What I have lost with cordiall fruit."

To Herbert's contemporaries, the pun involved in "cordiall" would have been a routine matter: *cor, cordis.* "Cordiall" therefore alludes to that which comes from the heart, or blood. But what of "fruit"? "Cordiall fruit," the restorative fruit for which the speaker longs, is thus "bloody fruit." This would not have been a difficult allusion for a seventeenth-century reader to unravel. The Fall occurred when fruit was plucked from the forbidden tree. Because this theft introduced death into the world, the fruit Adam stole might plausibly be described as bloody. But Christ was the fruit that grew on a later tree. As Thomas Middleton put it, "The tree of Good and Evil brought forth an apple to cast us all away, and the Tree of

Shame bare a fruit to save us all forever." An old carol can count on a common understanding of this conceit and thus begins, "An earthly tree a heavenly fruit it bare." Christ's body and blood thus constitute one meaning of the bloody fruit, or "cordiall fruit," of the poem. It is "cordiall fruit" in this sense that atones for man's rebellion, either the original rebellion of Adam or the rebellions that occur in every self, much as they occur in the speaker of *The Collar.*

The next three lines are fraught with implication and, further-more, elaborate upon the theme of the Eucharistic sacrifice.

> Sure there was wine
> Before my sighs did drie it: there was corn
> Before my tears did drown it.

Let us consider the possibilities present here. Wine and corn can represent natural food and drink, the pleasures of eating that the speaker has denied himself because of his ascetic discipline. Consid-ered in this way, they are the natural pleasures he longs for, objects of desire comparable to "fruit." But wine and corn (wheat) are also, of course, the elements of the Eucharist, wine and bread.

At first the speaker seems to be saying that he desires the natural pleasures, the pleasures from which he has been cut off by discipline. But he simultaneously says that his tears and sighs are the manifesta-tion of his need for the restorative, reordering powers of the sacra-ment. To put it another way: he *thinks* he desires natural pleasure, but the real object of his desire is supernatural, the cordial fruit of the Eucharist. Here, as in Dante, the true object of desire is not the earthly and the mutable but the eternal.

There is also an implication here that the speaker's tears and sighs have damaged the wine and corn. This could mean that the rigors of the speaker's discipline have denied him sensuous pleasure, and it can mean that the speaker's emotional turmoil has cut him off from an awareness of the restorative powers of the sacrament.

Now that we have identified the controlling imagery of the poem as Eucharistic, we can give certain details a fuller explication than they have yet received. According to Hutchinson, the "collar was in common use to express discipline, and 'to slip the collar' was often used figuratively. Preachers would use the word *collar* of the re-straint imposed by conscience." The speaker, it is clear, thinks of himself as a kind of prisoner, and like a prisoner, he wishes to free himself from the restraints that have been imposed upon him. The

"collar" of his discipline punishes him much as a criminal is punished
by having to wear a real collar. The comparison implicit in the title,
between the speaker who is suffering amid tears and sighs and a
criminal anxious to "slip the collar" of his punishment, was not
unusual, for man, the descendant of Adam, was in fact guilty of a
robbery and was a "prisoner" because of it. As Herbert put it in "The
Sacrifice," where Christ Himself is the speaker, "Man stole the fruit,
but I must climb the tree." The rebellion of the speaker in "The
Collar" is a version of Adam's rebellion, or theft, and must be re-
dressed in the same way.

It may be that the "board" in line 1 is Christ's table, the Communion table. The speaker, under the influence of the rebellious heart,
turns from the Communion table and entertains the possibility of
gaining a kind of freedom through rebellion. He asserts argumenta-
tively that he *is* free, that in effect he has not fallen: "I will abroad.
. . . My lines and life are free; free as the rode, / Loose as the winde,
as large as store." Entertaining the notion of his own guiltlessness,
supposing that his life, "as large as store," need not be "restored,"
he proceeds to reenact psychologically the events of the Fall. He
has only to stretch forth his hand to pluck the fruit, he tells himself:
"there is fruit, / and thou hast hands." The irony implicit here is that,
in reaching for one fruit, as Adam did, he will simultaneously reach
for the other fruit, the cordial fruit that grew on the Cross. Rebellion
sets in motion, unknown to the rebel, the process that leads to
atonement, and at the very moment of his psychological rebellion,
the speaker sets forth the elements that define the mode of his
redemption.

The series of questions beginning in line 13 admit of the answer
"no" in two different senses:

> Is the yeare onely lost to me?
> Have I no bayes to crown it?
> No flowers, no garlands gay? all blasted?
> All wasted?

The rebellious heart intends these to be rhetorical questions, ex-
pects the obvious answer that, no, the speaker has hands and can
reach for the fruit. But the fruit here, as we have seen, is not only
the fruit that is the object of rebellion but is also the fruit of the
Cross, the "cordiall fruit" of the Eucharist. Another answer therefore
suggests itself: no, the speaker has hands and can reach for the

chalice. Thus lines 17–18 can be read in two different ways. They can represent *agreement* with the heart, the assent of the will, now corrupted, to be heart's rebellious argument; or they can suggest the truth at which the speaker eventually will arrive. The phrase "thou has hands," therefore, signifies not only the hands that can rebelliously reach out for the fruit or the hands that *might* reach for the chalice, but the hands that *were* nailed to the Cross.

Similarly, in view of the pun on "cordiall," the word "heart" in line 17 can also be identified with Christ. Christ is, in a sense, the speaker's "real" heart. These double meanings, themselves a kind of transubstantiation, the interpretation of two realms, anticipate the conclusion of the poem in which the speaker and Christ are united analogically, both being "children" of God.

In addition, a third category of reference can be discerned here. The poem is also about the writing of poetry. The imagery of the questions just dealt with—bays, flowers, garlands—has traditionally been associated with poetry, as they were, for example, in "Lycidas" and in Carew's "An Elegy upon the Death of the Dean of Paul's, Dr. John Donne." Herbert's use of such imagery suggests a connection between loss of poetic power and the speaker's separation from the restorative powers of the Eucharist. The Eucharist, indeed, linking as it did two disparate realms, might be seen as the perfect symbol for the metaphysical conceit. Furthermore, if we consider the flower imagery to be associated with poetry, we can see that the rebellious heart is longing for the *wrong* kind of poetry. In "Jordan," we recall, Herbert rejected the pastoral mode, among others, as "false" and asserted that, in plainly saying "My God, My King," he was expressing truth directly. In a similar way, the pastoral imagery employed by the rebellious heart in "The Collar" is to be replaced by the "plain" truth of the last line.

"The Collar" also implies that the *form* of poetry is a kind of analogue of the order epitomized by the Eucharist. When the poet's "lines are free"—that is, when his rhetoric escapes poetic form—he has no bays and garlands, or poems, to crown the year. The rebellious heart, ironically enough, does not see that even "false" poetry, pastoral poetry, requires the order of poetic form, does not see that rebellion against order is ultimately destructive even of inferior poetry. Helen White has pointed out that after these lines about garlands and bays, the imagery becomes more vulgar, as the emotion expressed grows "more fierce and wilde." At the end of the poem, when the speaker's impulse toward rebellion has been overcome and he has recovered his sense of his relation to God, his lines begin to lose their "freedom" and poetic order returns along with moral and theological order.

In lines 19–34, the heart goes on with its counsel of rebellion, oblivious to the implications we have found in line 17–18. The heart urges the poet-priest to seek "double pleasure," to regard the law (which, ironically, is operating silently in the very vocabulary of the poem) as a "rope of sands." "Leave thy cold dispute / Of what is fit, and not," the heart urges. These lines are illuminated by Herbert's remark in "A Priest to the Temple" that "Contentiousness in a feast of Charity is more scandal than any posture." The "dispute" that, according to the heart, the poet-priest has been engaged in is alien to the spirit of the sacrament. Perhaps these lines suggest that it has been "cold dispute" that has, at least in part, caused the poet-priest to lose his sense of the power of the Eucharist, a sense recovered by the "childlike" consciousness of the poem's conclusion (compare "Unless you become like children . . .," Matthew 18:3–4).

At any rate, in lines 19–34 the heart urges rebellion in preemptory terms. A chief result of the Fall, mortality, should not be feared: "Call in thy death's head there." But double meanings here, as previously, provide an undercurrent of ironic commentary on the heart's speech. "He that forbears / To suit and serve his need, / Deserves his load" seems at first merely to justify rebellion. But looked at again, "suit" takes on the color of "Shall I be still in suit" (line 6), and the lines might suggest that "he that does not seek redemption deserves the burden of his sin."

Yet, even as the speaker, under the influence of the rebellious heart, raves and grows more wild, the ironies of the earlier line are asserting themselves for his benefit. The line endings, we notice, reflect a gathering order. Starting with line 27, earlier random endings are succeeded by a steady pattern of assonances (heed/abroad, fears/forebears, need/load, wilde/word, Christ/Lord). This reassertion of pattern is heralded by the unsubtle *a b b a* rhyme of thee/draw/law/see, which brings to an abrupt end the chaotic rhyming of the first half of the poem. As Joseph Summers has summarized the function of form in this poem:

Until the final four lines, the poem dramatizes expertly and convincingly the revolt of the heart, and its imitation of colloquial speech almost convinces us of the justice of the cause. But the disorder of the poem provides a constant implicit criticism, and with the final lines we recognize that *The Collar* is a narrative in the past tense: the message of the present concerns the necessity of order.

We may now see that law obtains at the supernatural court in which the speaker, unaware, was "in suit." The reestablishment of order follows upon, is entailed by, rebellion. The speaker began by asserting the validity of rebellion. He then identified himself with Adam, imagined himself reaching for the fruit that brought about man's Fall. But the law remained in operation: the hands that reach for the fruit of rebellion reach also, unknown to the speaker when he is under the influence of the heart, for Christ. They reach for the chalice ("cordiall fruit," "corn," "wine") that—such is God's power—restores the speaker to his proper relationship to God. Line 34, indeed, admits of two interpretations. The speaker grows more fierce and wild "at every word," but also "at every word" in the poem he now hears the voice of God: "Me thoughts I heard one calling, *Child* / And I reply'd, *My Lord*." The speaker's heart, previously united with Christ by means of *double entrendre,* is now united with Him in a relationship that is part of the speaker's awareness: both Christ and His surrogate, the priest who administers the Eucharist, are children of God. The moral hierarchy, epitomized in the hierarchy of father and son and of Father and Son, has been restored.

Ideas in Culture

We all live in the midst of ideas. We espouse some and attack others. Ideas manifest themselves as opinions, as slogans, as parts of seemingly coherent structures, and they exist at the core of many of our attitudes. Yet ideas are stranger things than they may at first appear. "Certain sentiments," writes Lionel Trilling,

consort only with certain ideas and not with others. What is more, sentiments become ideas by a natural and imperceptible process. "Our continued influxes of feeling," said Wordsworth, "are modified and directed by our thoughts, which are indeed representatives of all our past feelings." And Charles Peguy said, *"Tout commence en mystique et finit en politique"*— everything begins in sentiment and assumption and finds its issue in political action and institutions. The converse is also true: just as sentiments become ideas, ideas eventually establish themselves as sentiments.

In the following remarks, I want to begin a process of reflection upon ideas, especially upon political ideas but upon other kinds as well. I say I want to begin a process of reflection because in truth I myself have only begun this process myself, and what I can say here is necessarily limited by my own thought and experience. Many of the things I have to say will point down roads that I myself have not yet traveled. However, the questions I want to raise here are about what ideas actually are, how they actually function, and why in the life of our culture some ideas seem to prevail and some do not. In the title of a famous book, the late Richard Weaver asserted that *Ideas Have Consequences.* That is true, of course, but it might be still more accurate to say that some ideas have consequences. Why is that so?

I will argue here that ideas often stand in an illuminating relationship to some objective reality, but often, perhaps most of the time, that is not their primary function. Instead, they become vehicles of social communion, symbols of social status, claims to moral superi-

This article first appeared in *Imprimis.*

ority, instruments of the will to power, and thrilling consumer items. In this functional chaos, the whole question of the truth of an idea can easily become a kind of embarrassment.

It may be that the truth of an idea is not the most interesting and valuable thing about it. I myself do not finally believe that, but of course the moral claim of truth has been an issue since the beginning of conscious reflection upon ideas. It certainly was the issue between Socrates and the Athenians, and we know how that disagreement ended. Socrates' ideas had merit, but they were difficult to live with.

By way of a preliminary, I would like to relate three stories, or little items, arising out of what a social scientist would call my own "raw experience." Each item contributed to my own education concerning ideas as they function in actual human existence.

Number one: During the year 1968, I worked as a political speech-writer in the presidential campaign of Richard Nixon. Until then, I had been largely literary and academic, and my view of the political process was essentially the same as that of the standard civics class or the League of Women Voters. That is to say, if I had bothered to formulate the matter to myself at all, I would have said that the candidates identify leading "issues" and then take "positions" on those issues, that the voters then assess the "positions" taken and decide which of the candidates is preferable. I might not have agreed with the League of Women Voters on the positions to be preferred, but I certainly agreed with them on the importance of political "issues," "positions," "principles," "ideas."

Then I ate the apple. In actually writing political speeches, it gradually dawned on me that the ideas in a political speech are not there to illuminate reality for the benefit of an audience but rather to establish a sense of communion between the speaker and the audience. It helps if the ideas have merit, if they are in some sense true, but that is not the finally important thing about them. Interestingly enough, Nelson Rockefeller never grasped this point, though he probably paid more cash per word for his political speeches than any politician in history. They sounded as if they had been processed through an academic department and polished by a think tank. They bristled with thoughts and statistics, but they tended to be hopeless. The real function of ideas in a political speech, as I just remarked, is to establish a sense of communion between speaker and audience.

Ideas are the magnets attracting the iron filings of emotion. They
make the audience feel that the speaker understands them, sympa-
thizes with their condition, loves and hates what they love and hate,
shares their view of the world.

Ideas, I thus began to understand, are not at all pure; they are not
hard intellectual pellets. Their status in actual existence is not purely
rational.

Number two: Here, I am at an academic cocktail party, a very
congenial occasion, and I am surrounded by colleagues and the
usual chit-chat. The touchy subject of South Africa comes up. I
myself am hardly enamored of the present regime there, but the
situation does strike me as complicated, and on this occasion the
devil is in me, and I begin making assertions: that, in fact, the original
Dutch and English settlers were there first and then defeated the
Zulus to make good their claim to the territory; that the blacks there
today are undoubtedly better off than blacks, say, in Mozambique;
that the current white regime, though obviously repressive, is probably the only thing that keeps the various tribes from slaughtering
one another; and that, when and if the present regime is overthrown,
the place will certainly not get majority rule but some sort of black
dictatorship, most likely horrendous. In sober truth, these assertions,
though they may have some merit, might be largely irrelevant.
Debater's points, after all, may be entertaining at the Oxford Union,
but the historical process tends to ignore them. My assertions,
however, were not addressed on grounds of merit at the cocktail
party, nor were they criticized as irrelevant on grounds of *realpoli-
tik*. Instead, a full professor drew himself up to his full tweedy
height, harrumphed like some Colonel Blimp, and announced, "Sir,
no gentleman could have a good word to say about the white racist
regime in South Africa."

This was a moment of illumination. Political ideas in this circumstance were not true or false or some mixture of the two. They were
badges of status, symbols of respectability. And, by George, it was
absolutely true. Nice people, people wearing tweedy jackets and
regimental-striped ties, did not in fact have a nice word to say about
the South African regime, or for that matter about the one in Chile,
just as nice people did not make a big noise about abortion, say, or
busing or pornography. Ideas on such subjects were not so much
true or false as either respectable or socially disreputable.

Finally, I turn to item *number three*. We have all noticed that various groups of people tend to sound alike. Sinclair Lewis, for example, had a very good ear, and he had a lot of fun at the expense of Coolidge-era businessmen and their clichés when he wrote *Babbitt*. But all cultural subgroups tend to sound alike when they give verbal expression to their ideas and sentiments.

Not surprisingly, therefore, I have noticed that liberals in the academy and elsewhere tend to sound alike. The signals are quite uniform. Certainly there is a wonderful irony present here in particular, since the liberal's myth of himself depicts him as a fiercely independent thinker, one who even puts a high valuation on heretical opinion. Nevertheless, when these fiercely independent thinkers turn up to nail their heretical theses to the door of the cathedral, we find that they have all arrived at the same theses. We may therefore be permitted to think that these theses have less to do with some lonely vision of the truth than with group self-interest, group identity, and group cohesion. Their ideas, as Samuel Johnson put it, "are not propagated by reason but caught by contagion." They are part of what sociologists like Peter Berger and Thomas Luckman call "the social construction of reality"—that is, they constitute an accepted and more or less official body of doctrine that might advance the interests of the group but certainly make the members feel comfortable.

ii

It is important to grasp the degree to which ideas are in fact social constructions serving social needs. One of the fundamental propositions of the sociology of knowledge holds that the plausibility of a view of reality depends upon the social support it receives. We obtain our notions about the world largely from other people, and these notions continue to be plausible to us because other people continue to affirm them. A person whose "plausibility structures" were entirely internal would be some kind of madman.

Suppose you were suddenly set down in a society in which everyone assumed the truth of astrology, while you assumed its falsity. In this society, everyone except you explains all occurrences with reference to the movement of the planets and stars. There is no doubt that in due course you would begin to question the bases of your own skepticism. You might not really admit the fundamental importance of Pisces and Scorpio, but you would at least soon begin to show some deference toward the official truth. Even if you wished

to express skepticism, you would be obliged, merely to avoid ostra-
cism, to provide elaborate signals of that deference. You would say
things like, "This may sound foolish to you . . ." or "I know that this
is just my own opinion . . ."

One might think that the propositions derived from the physical
sciences, at least, would be exempt from social conditioning; but
not so. The late C. S. Lewis argued brilliantly in his posthumously
published Cambridge University lectures on cosmology, which have
been gathered in the book *The Discarded Image,* that they are not
exempt. There turn out to be cultural styles in cosmology and
biology. We all know that sometime during the seventeenth century
the old Ptolemaic model of the universe, with the earth at the center,
was dropped in favor of the heliocentric Copernican theory. We
also know that during the nineteenth century the natural selection
theory of biological evolution came to be generally accepted. We
connect both events with the supposed discovery of new facts.
Lewis takes a different view.

The old astronomy was not, in any exact sense, "refuted" by the telescope.
The scarred surface of the moon and the satellites of Jupiter can, if one
wants, be fitted into a geocentric scheme. Even the enormous, and enormously different, distances of the stars can be accommodated if you are
prepared to make their "sphere," the *stellatum* of a vast thickness. . . . But
the change of Models did not involve astronomy alone. It involved also, in
biology, the change—arguably more important—from a devolutionary to
an evolutionary scheme. . . . This revolution was certainly not brought about
by the discovery of new facts. When I was a boy I believed that "Darwin
discovered evolution" [but] in Keats, in Wagner's tetralogy, in Goethe, in
Herder, the change to a new point of view had already taken place. Its
growth can be traced far further back in Leibniz, Akenside, Kant, Maupertius,
Diderot. Already in 1786, Robinet believed in an "active principle" which
overcomes brute matter, and *la progression n'est pas finie.* For him, as for
Bergson or de Chardin, the "gates of the future are wide open." The
demand for a developing world—a demand obviously in harmony with
the revolutionary and the romantic temper—grows up first; when it is
full grown the scientists go to work and discover the evidence on which
our belief in that sort of universe would now be held to rest. There is
no question here of the old Model's being shattered by the inrush of
new phenomena. The truth would seem to be the reverse; that when
changes in the human mind produce a sufficient disrelish of the old
Model and a sufficient hankering for some new one, phenomena to
support that new one will obediently turn up. I do not mean at all that
these new phenomena are illusory. Nature has all sorts of phenomena in
stock and can suit many different ideas.

iii

As should now come as no surprise, the same kind of sociocultural analysis can be applied to theological opinion. Theology, the former Queen of the Sciences, like the sciences themselves, has always been deeply embedded in the cultural matrix.

Both theistic and atheistic philosophies have of course been available since time immemorial. There is nothing new about either position. But one or the other position acquires authority under concrete historical circumstances. We are all familiar with the famous Victorian crisis of faith, as a result of which thousands of individuals passed from some form of theism to some form of agnosticism or atheism. It would be naive to assume, however, that the crisis of faith occurred because Hume on miracles or the Biblical scholarship of Tubingen suddenly swept the mass market and that everyone, upon reading this material, closed the volumes with an eureka-like forehead-slapping agreement. No, it was not the aristocratic skepticism of the philosophies that prevailed, nor even the academic skepticism of the Biblical critics, but rather the bourgeois atheism of the marketplace.

Sir Francis Bacon, Thomas Hobbes, John Locke, Jeremy Bentham, John Stuart Mill, and the other formulators of the new ethos did not refute Anselm or Aquinas; they merely ignored them. George Santayana has quite truly said that "intellectual progress," as it is called, takes place not because of what we learn but because of what we forget. The great project of the seventeenth- and eighteenth-century bourgeoisie was not to understand existence but to make a living in it. The cultural focus shifted sharply toward the physical world. Anselm's ontological argument does not do much for the trade in spices or tobacco, but navigation certainly does. Metaphysical ultimates, at least in the short run, proved to be irrelevant to the economic enterprise. The empirical and utilitarian philosophies, which reflected the dominance of this culture, were designed not so much to understand the world as to control and possess it, and, at least in the short run, they were triumphantly successful.

I do not mean to condescend to these phenomena. Ideas in any actual human circumstance are always largely instrumental in character. Always and everywhere people tend to think that ideas are current because they are true. Actually, they are current because they are convenient.

Parenthetically, if you would like to experience a rare intellectual pleasure as well as a genuine epiphany, I would recommend John Murray Cuddihy's book *The Ordeal of Civility* (Basic Books, 1974). This work is a stunning application of the sociology of ideas to the work of Sigmund Freud. It was among the National Book Award nominees in 1975, but because of its subversive potency, it has become a kind of underground classic.

iv

I now turn to the ideas and attitudes of a particular contemporary subculture and attempt a rudimentary sociocultural analysis of the ideas familiar in the liberalism of the ordinary academic community. This is important, I think, even though those ideas themselves are relatively uninteresting, because such liberalism radiates outward from the academic hub to the various spokes of the cultural wheel—to the media, of course, but also to the professions and to what is called "educated" and "enlightened" opinion generally.

You will notice that the effect of this process will be to de-mythologize and de-absolutize the liberal ideas, which are normally asserted as gleaming, self-evident axioms of universal validity. Under closer inspection, however, they turn out to be epiphenomena of circumstance and self-interest. To undertake this procedure is to reperceive liberalism as, in its own way, provincial. While we are at it, moreover, we will attempt to discern beneath these slogans and platitudes the almost-never-avowed assumptions that inform them. In this pleasant exercise, I examine three aspects of the liberal idea pattern as it manifests itself in culture. Those aspects are: (1) psychological, (2) economic, and (3) consumerist.

First, the *psychological:* The mood in the academy naturally fluctuates with changing circumstances. Across the nation, that mood is now very different from what it was a half-dozen years ago. Nevertheless, all experience testifies to, and all objective surveys confirm, the fact that academic opinion tends to be startlingly more liberal than opinion in the surrounding society. This liberalism shows up not only in the political candidates preferred by professors but in a whole range of issues and attitudes.

But why? The academic liberal has a ready explanation: academics tend to be liberal because they are better informed, more rational and far-sighted, and less selfish than other people. No one who has ever sat through a faculty meeting can accept that explanation however. Most college professors, though perfectly competent in their academic field, are by no means remarkably intelligent or even especially well informed outside their field. A good mathematician is likely to be what I would call sub-*Atlantic Monthly* in range of information and general culture. The resident campus poet is only too likely to be an intellectual monstrosity.

What, then, is the explanation for the liberal character of academic culture? You will note that a college faculty is by no means a random sample of the general population. It is, rather, a self-selected and rather special sample. In my opinion, the original act of career choice is probably fundamental here. The choice of an academic career is, at the same time, a negative decision—as much a choice *not* to be a lawyer, a general, or a businessman as to be a Shakespearean, an scholar or an expert in structural linguistics. I do not think the academy makes people liberals, but that individuals who are already on uneasy terms with ordinary society tend to choose the academy.

Naturally, the choice is dressed up as something much more flattering to the ego. The academic individual is a "critic of society" and an "independent thinker." Within their own environment, however, we do not seem to encounter much criticism or independence—merely a lot of people who tend, as noted before, to "sound the same."

Second, the *economic motive:* Nothing in the above psychological observation necessarily predicts the content of liberal opinion. After all, it would be possible for these individuals to "sound the same" and also separate themselves doctrinally from the rest of us if they were all devotees of Nietzsche or Buddha. One answer to the liberal content of academic opinion, applicable over the last century or more, takes a "history of ideas" form. It argues that the traditional attitudes and ideas of Western culture form, so to speak, the thesis, while liberalism constitutes the antithesis, the negative image. Thus, from the liberal perspective, most traditional virtues become negative qualities. If the traditional thesis is Christian, the liberal antithesis must be secularist. If ordinary human nature admires victory, the liberal cherishes victims, real and contrived. If the ordinary fellow roots for the Marines and the cowboys, the liberal roots for the Vietcong or the Indians. The sense of alienation from customary attitude is total. You can sense this alienation in the language itself, and language always carries cultural values in it. The English word "abortion" possesses powerful negative overtones—you simply cannot say, " I had a marvelous abortion the other day." In his negative culture, the liberal converts abortion into a positive cause. Figures who are pariahs in the ordinary culture—the pornographer, the Communist, or whatever—become in the negative liberal culture the objects of special solicitude.

This thesis-antithesis relationship has long been there, I think, but in recent years it has been reinforced by powerful economic motives. As Kevin Phillips and others have explained, familiar liberal ideas now provide the rationale for a virtual new class of exploiters. This new class has established itself at exactly the same time as we have seen an enormous growth in academia. This new class, or postindustrial elite, is in the business of selling a social environment.

This particular enterprise has long been with us, of course, but the really huge boom started around 1960, and it gave rise to a new and expanding class of persons consisting of professionals in education, urban planning, welfare, social research, rehabilitation, compensatory programs of all sorts, poverty law, informational systems, innovative textbook design and publication, computer software application, various kinds of communications and media ventures, and so on. After Lyndon Johnson's 1964 landslide, the lopsidedly Democratic Congress enacted a cascade of social programs. Education, housing, and urban outlays soared. Enactment of the War Against Poverty alone brought expenditures of two billion dollars a year and rising. As a spin-off effect, it called into being about a hundred new firms in the Washington area, and many others elsewhere, functioning as consultants on the subject of poverty.

As the federal billions began to flow into the "social concern" sector, private enterprise was quick to sniff out the opportunities. Corporations began to find educational innovation, urban studies, and assorted rehabilitation schemes immensely profitable. Any social concern became a gold rush; the victim of society was a virtual Klondike. We saw the mushrooming of new economic entities— what might be called Social Concern Conglomerates. There is a genuine parallel here to the big Bull Market of the late 1920s, the so-called Coolidge Prosperity. In the big Bull Social Concern Market of the years after 1960, Wall Street investment houses gobbled up securities with names redolent of scientific technology related to social problems. This entire enterprise, of course, has an immediate and voracious interest in large and increasing federal expenditures. The budget of HHS long ago passed that of the Pentagon. In the struggle among competing elites, the military-industrial complex—and I am no apologist for that elite—is losing the budgetary battle to the social concern elite.

Naturally, this new class of social concern entrepreneurs is ideologically liberal for as I have said, it is in the social change business. Without social change, social problems, programs, solutions, and goals, this new class certainly would be in bankruptcy proceedings. Social change is to the new class of social problem solvers as inventory turnover was to the old mercantile class or a good cotton crop to a still earlier plantation elite.

The uncomfortable truth here is that most people do not want their social environment processed according to theory, let alone theory originating in the academy.

In the antiquated Marxist model, capitalist society is supposed to resemble a pyramid, with a tiny capitalist elite at the top exploiting the masses toiling below. This Marxist model hardly describes our present reality. Of course, as C. S. Lewis has explained, a model can be stretched. More and more people and institutions can be crowded into that exploitative peak of the pyramid. Nevertheless, American society today does not so much resemble a pyramid as it does an egg. It is broadest in the social middle. At the top, struggling for power with increasing success, is the new class of social concern exploiters, busy reordering our priorities.

The liberal ideas, no doubt generated elsewhere back in time, ideas conceived under other circumstances, now legitimate and protect this new postindustrial social concern industry.

V

The *consumerist* aspects: I turn now to my third and last analytical point, which has to do with the way in which ideas circulate given the concrete circumstances of our culture.

At the time of the French Revolution, ideas were circulated largely by intellectual popularizers such as journalists, pamphleteers, and the philosophers in the Parisian salons. This Republic of Letters, as it was sometimes called, was also called the Fourth Estate. It functioned, that is, as a fourth, extra-constitutional power in the political equation, the other three estates being the nobility, clergy, and commoners. The Fourth Estate was, of course, a prime generator of revolutionary energy. In our own time, the media have emerged as a vastly more potent Fourth Estate—both the printed and the electronic media—and they are continuously involved in the marketing of ideas and attitudes. I would argue that there is something in the very nature of a liberal idea that renders it especially suitable for such marketing by the media.

You will have noticed that conservative ideas do not—usually, at any rate—come into "vogue." They do not characteristically become the subject of fashionable chit-chat, and their progenitors do not star on talk shows. In contrast, it is possible to identify a succession of liberal "vogues." Consider a few of the liberal and/or radical ideas that have had notable currency in recent years. The early Kennedy years glittered with the promise of a technological utopia. The think-tankers at Rand and Hudson had banished the irrational. Cost-accounting, computers, and options dominated the scene. McNamara was rationalizing the military, Lindsay was rationalizing New York, and Neustadt was rationalizing presidential power. The theologians jumped into this think tank—not only did Harvey Cox invite us to live in the gleaming Secular City, but the Vatican, heavily influenced by social scientists, junked the old liturgy and provided its constituency with a rationalized new one.

To be sure, the results in actuality were quite dim. McNamara failed in Vietnam, Lindsay failed in New York, Congress frustrated Neustadt's designs. An epoch in modern theology lasts about five years, and Harvey Cox, when last spotted, was some sort of mystical guru. The technological promise of utopia, Professor Cox's "secular city," gave way to utopia through charismatic, revolutionary gurus: Che Guevara, Mao, Castro, Ho, Malcolm X, Frantz Fanon. Their baleful faces gazed out from poster and paperback. Then, poof, that gave way to another cast of characters. More mystical gurus came on the scene, some from the East, some from the chemical laboratory. Utopia was mystical; it was chemical; or it demanded closeness to nature. In his 1960s best-seller, *The Greening of America,* Charles Reich—in real life a professor of law at Yale—told us that we were going to be saved by virtuous and unrepressed college students, an amazing idea.

In a certain sense, all of these and other such currents were novel and therefore "interesting." Herbert Marcuse's doctrine that the West is "repressive" precisely because it is tolerant—its very tolerance preventing revolution—is certainly interesting. The contrasting idea, that the freedoms of the West, given the limits of human nature, represent a considerable civilizational achievement, actually seems banal by comparison. It is much more interesting to be told by James Coleman in his earlier phase that black children can be improved by busing than to be told by Edward Banfield and James Coleman in a later phase that they cannot. John Locke's *tabula rasa,* an early metaphor for the position that we can achieve felicity by innovation in the social environment, is inherently interesting. A contrasting stress on things like heredity or an anthropological stress on the density and intractibility of culture seems dull and depressing by comparison. It is much more interesting to be told by George Leonard in *Education and Ecstasy* (1969) that education will save the child than to be told by Christopher Jencks that it will not. Conservatives tend to stress things like the immutability of human nature and its flawed nature, the lessons of experience, the complexity of a given situation. Not very exciting.

We thus arrive at the following paradox. The liberal and/or radical idea is striking and interesting because it describes an unreality. The conservative idea or attitude often tends to seem banal and boring because it has greater affinity for reality. But the very novelty of the liberal-radical idea gives it tremendous impetus in a media-oriented culture that thrives on the marketing of novelty. If you are running a television talk show, a weekly news magazine, or even a boutique, Malcolm X and the earlier Tim Leary are much more valuable entertainment properties than Edward Fanfield or Michael Oakeshott.

vi

The liberal idea within our culture, then, possesses certain psychological, economic, and structural advantages. It also possesses a large vulnerability, and it is here that it can be most effectively attacked.

You will notice that other cultural ideals, past and present, have not been reluctant to define and even celebrate themselves. We know what Socratic Man was and Chivalric Man. The latter was celebrated in song and story. The Christian churches have always been quite explicit about the individual they are trying to fashion. We know what a gentleman is, and we even know what Maoist Man is. Why is it that there is no similarly clear outline regarding Liberal Man?

I think we are on to something important here. We can, with a little effort, deduce Liberal Man from the assorted ideas, attitudes, and positions with which we are familiar, but that we are obliged to do this is most revealing. When we make explicit the liberal perception of man, it turns out to be base, shameful, and ignominious. Almost as soon as he is formulated, he tries to slink away into the shadows, embarrassed. No wonder his advocates resist such an effort at formulation.

My colleague at *National Review,* Joseph Sobran, however, has assayed the task, and in conclusion, I would like to draw upon the words in one of his recent essays. The liberal, he writes, possesses an "integral world view" that

sees man as an animal; an animal whose destiny is a life of pleasure and comfort. Those who view things in this light tend to believe that this destiny can be achieved by means of enlightened governmental direction in removing (and discrediting) old taboos, and in establishing a new economic order wherein wealth will be distributed more evenly. It is interesting to note that they describe such a redistribution as being "more equitable," because that suggests [note: the environmental thesis again] that they ascribe inequalities of wealth to differences in circumstances rather than ambition, intelligence, fortitude, or any of the myriad other moral virtues that may lead to fortune. . . .

It is interesting to note, too . . . that they never deride or censure human behavior as "bestial" or "animal," because they see man himself as an animal in essence, and cannot be indignant about behavior proper to an animal. They *are* indignant about suffering, which is to say animal suffering—pain, hunger, physical discomfort—and the frustration of animal appetites in general. . . .

This is a morally passive view of man. . . . The middle-class virtues are assumed to blossom spontaneously under the right material conditions; progress comes inevitably, so long as there are not reactionaries "impeding" it. . . . Although [this view] asserts the obligation of those who are well off to share their abundance with the "less fortunate," they can never make demands of the less fortunate themselves. . . . It is characteristic of them to invoke the poor early in any public discussion. . . . As James Burnham has penetratingly put it, the liberal feels himself morally disarmed before anyone he regards as less well off than himself. . . . If pleasure is man's destiny, it is his right. Nobody should have to endure hardship, even if he brings it on himself. Parenthood, when it comes unlooked for, is cruel and unusual punishment, and people who fornicate no more deserve to be assigned its duties than a man who kills somebody deserves to be hanged.

Well, there we have the larger strategic vulnerability that, in due course, will overwhelm the tactical strengths of liberal ideas. Of all the conceptions of human nature and of man's destiny down through the ages, this one must be, morally and aesthetically, the most ignominious and derisory.

Christ and Apollo
The Modern Debate

If one tries to name the theologians who speak most persuasively to the contemporary audience, the names Kierkegaard, Tillich, Niebuhr, Barth, and Bultmann come at once to mind. It is they who are felt to be especially relevant. They are the ones most often discussed in the quarterlies, and even in the popular press, and it is they who prevail, one gathers, in the Protestant seminaries as well as with those students and general readers who are attracted to religious thought.

To the specialist in literature, however, there is something odd about all this, for the religious temperament of the modern writers, and especially the poets, who have made a point of religion in the system of their thought has been markedly different from the theologians' listed above. One considers, for example, Eliot, Tate, Robert Lowell, C. S. Lewis, Auden, Wimsatt, Waugh, and one notices that the religious values of these men—they are not professional theologians of course, but they are intensely concerned with religion—tend to be rather less *protestant* than the views of those theologians. All of these writers, in fact, are either Anglo-Catholics or Roman Catholics. These religious writers seem to differ from the theologians for a particular reason, one that can be found in the relationship between Christianity, a distinctive religion, and the nature of literature, in the relationship that obtains between the distinctive doctrine of Christianity, the doctrine of the Incarnation, and the distinctively literary act.

Perhaps the best way to approach this matter, though it may at first appear an excessively technical method in comparison with so large a subject, is to consider the nature of metaphor. In the popular view, a metaphor merely decorates with suitable imagery a truth

"Christ and Apollo: The Modern Debate" by Jeffrey Hart first appeared in *Renascence*, Winter 1964, and is reprinted with permission.

quite communicable in some other form. "The prevailing view since
Aristotle's *Rhetoric,*" according to Morris R. Cohen, "regards metaphor as an analogy from which the words of comparison, *like* or *as,*
etc., are omitted. This presupposes that the recognition of literal
truth precedes the metaphor, which is always a conscious transfer-
ence of the properties of one thing to another." It is certainly true,
moreover, that writers do sometimes use metaphors in a manner to
which such a description is more or less adequate:

> On life's vast ocean diversely we sail,
> Reason the card, but Passion is the gale.
> (Alexander Pope, *An Essay on Man*)

Such metaphor, comparing life to a ship, does not primarily enlarge
our knowledge; it merely embellishes it, and no doubt makes it
more attractive and more memorable. Thus conceived, a metaphor
is primarily an ingenious device for recommending a truth already
known to the mind by other means. This conception of metaphor,
which is, implicitly at least, a theory of our way of knowing, assumes
that what we know can be delivered by means of a statement, a
statement that, if one so desires, can be made palatable or vivid by
means of concrete imagery. This conception of metaphor, as it
appears in Aristotle or in neoclassical aesthetics, follows from the
notion, so pervasive in classical culture, that it is *ideas* that are real
and valuable in contrast to mutable concrete phenomena.

But this conception of phenomena, though it does describe a way
in which it is often employed, does not describe that use of metaphor
that poets and critics consider most important: the use of metaphor
as a vehicle of discovery. Both anthropology and psychology suggest
that the association of concrete images occurs prior to the formulation of discursive statement—that we learn, in fact, concretely.
Metaphor, accordingly, may be thought of as a way, and perhaps as
the way, of pushing forward into an awareness of meanings and
relationships that could not be apprehended in any other way. A
metaphor thus conceived does not represent what has "oft been
said but ne'er so well expressed," but rather, what could not have
been said, could not have been expressed at all, before. Metaphor
becomes an instrument of insight, a mode of knowing, and not
merely a way of decorating what one already knows. It is the revelation of a small mystery, and such a use of metaphor is at the heart
of language itself. Matthew Arnold made a spiritual meaning con-

crete by talking of sweetness and light. We are able to think about electricity, evidently a rather mysterious thing, by comparing it to a stream. We speak of an electric "current," and thinking of it in this way, we can apprehend something of its nature. There is no doubt, indeed, that science and poetry are equally metaphorical. The main difference would seem to be that science has employed a series of metaphors, each provisional and many of them abandoned for others, while poetry can be described as a number of metaphors, each valued as an end in itself and none deducible from another or to be rejected for another.

This second view of metaphor is central to the modern discussion of poetry. It derives from the practice of the seventeenth-century metaphysical poets and the nineteenth-century symbolist poets, and, philosophically, from Kant and Coleridge. But metaphor so viewed may be seen to be, in an unexpected way, analogous to what lies at the center of the Gospel story, the Incarnation. Like a metaphor in a poem or in science, the story of the Incarnation reveals, brings into being as far as human intelligence is concerned, a previously unknown conception of God's relationship to history and to the material creation. The Old Testament prophets, to be sure, were inspired or spoke with God; God appeared in a burning bush or in a whirlwind. But none of these things is the same as the Incarnation. It is for this reason that Augustine thought of the Old Testament as striving toward the New and of the New as revealing something only adumbrated in the Old, a new relationship between matter and spirit, the fact that they could be *one*. The word, or *logos,* became flesh and, as such, is fully known, just as within its own scale of intention the meaning of a metaphor, its *idea,* is known only through its concrete embodiment. It is not too much to say, accordingly, that the study of poetry, of the way language actually functions in literature, can lead by means of analogy to an understanding of other modes of knowing, whether scientific or religious, and that the study of poetry, carried on with sufficient intensity, can render this central Christian doctrine both intelligible and relevant.

ii

The entire subject of the relationship between religious doctrine and imaginative activity has received very little attention. To my knowledge, only Erich Auerbach, F. D. Wilhelmsen, and William Lynch have recently explored in any extended way the imaginative implications of theological propositions. Yet, this matter is of central importance. We might well speculate, for example, about whether the vitality of Western science is connected with the hospitality of Western Christendom to the concretizing of ideas. Greek and Roman culture, in contrast, preferring to let ideas remain transcendent, produced a science that, from our own perspective, seems static and limited.

Newman in *The Development of Christian Doctrine* called the doctrine of the Incarnation "the central aspect of Christianity." It is indeed a doctrine fraught with cultural implications, for does not, in Christopher Dawson's words, "the visible manifestation of the Divine Logos in the flesh involve a sanctification of material things, and the visible representation of spiritual realities?" Attacks upon this central doctrine have characteristically taken the form of an attack upon the dignity of the creation, refusing to countenance the notion that spirit could take on material embodiment. They have moved in the direction of the denigration of matter; they have spiritualized; they have sought to split asunder the fusion implied by the Incarnation.

It will be recognized that a theology hospitable to the idea that spirit can be embodied—a theology, that is, that stresses the doctrine of the Incarnation—will put a higher value on culture and find another dimension to art, to literature, to sculpture, as well as to more ordinary acts such as birth, marriage, and death, than one that does not. Such a theology tends to sanctify the material realm, to draw religion and culture, religion and life, closer together.

An eloquent expression of this religious temperament may be found in Eliot's *Notes Toward the Definition of Culture.* We might ask, writes Eliot, "whether what we call the culture, and what we call the religion of the people are not different aspects of the same thing: the culture being essentially the incarnation (so to speak) of the religion of a people." Notice Eliot's use of the word "incarnation." He thinks of culture as standing in a metaphorical relationship to spirit, of culture as a way of apprehending spirit; it does not seem repugnant to him that spirit can thus be materialized. His "theology" proceeds from his relationship to language, from his involvement with English poetry, from, that is, his perception that the mental habit of Christendom is, at the center, metaphorical, that it conceives of meaning as being *embodied.* The language of a culture embodies its characteristic perceptions, and the poet who fully possesses that language inherits these perceptions.

Eliot's conception of "incarnation," the fusion of spirit and matter, is as central to his aesthetic thought, where it appears as the doctrine that form and content ought to be one, as it is to his religious and cultural thought. Thus his attack on Milton's verse, carried out in aesthetic terms, is also a cultural and religious attack. He finds in Milton a "dissociation of sensibility," which means that the sense of the words is not fused with the rhetoric, with the sound and rhythm of the lines. Milton must be read, Eliot said, once for the meaning and once for the music. And he is right. Milton's rhetoric, he might well have said, does not incarnate his meaning. The body of his verse is one thing, its mind quite another.

When we turn from Milton's verse to his theology, to the statement of his beliefs as opposed to their poetic acting out, we find, as might have been expected, that he maintained a heterodox Christology and was inclined to separate Christ from, by subordinating Him to, God the Father. His other opinions were consistent in spirit with his poetry and his theology. There was to be no *visible* church, he thought. The community of believers, to be pure, could only be spiritual. Even to pay ministers, he argued, was to corrupt the spirit with evident materiality: ministers must support themselves by other means—the realm of spirit and meaning is entirely independent of the ordinary affairs of life. Marriage, in Milton's view, was the experience of intense harmony between husband and wife, a harmony mainly of mind, or else it was nothing. Vows, ceremonies, the observances of church and state—all these had nothing to do with marriage, purely conceived. There was no marriage when that harmony of minds broke down. It may be seen that this desire to free marriage, as he would religion, from all relationship to externals, from all laws, institutions, vows, and contracts, and to make it an experience only, a sentiment in the mind, proceeds from his desire to purify it of things, to separate it from material representations and connections of any kind. Externals are to be thought of as corrupting rather than as expressing intention.

Those seventeenth-century writers whose "unified" and concretizing sensibilities Eliot finds so congenial (they felt their thought, he says in a famous phrase, as immediately as the odor of a rose) are notable for their use of the conceit, the rhetorical device by which "heterogeneous ideas are yoked by violence together," characteristically to bring together and identify disparate realms of experience. Now this is a task metaphor has always performed, and it is the insistent use these seventeenth-century writers make of the device that must be explained. In fact, we can interpret the conceit as the weapon such writers employed against the forces in their culture that were prying apart experience, making disparate realms out of it, the forces to which Milton responded sympathetically. The conceit was stressed in the seventeenth century because the very view of experience implied by it was under attack. In Eliot's own formulation, "the poets of the seventeenth century, the successors of the dramatists of the sixteenth, possessed a mechanism of sensibility which could devour any kind of experience," but "something happened to the mind of England between the time of Donne or Lord Herbert of Cherbury and the time of Tennyson or Browning. . . . In the seventeenth century a dissociation of sensibility set in from which we have never recovered."

iii

Allen Tate agrees in the main with Eliot's diagnosis. He considers that the "symbolic imagination"—by which he means the disposition to embody meanings in concrete images—depended upon a recognition of the limits of human rationality, a recognition that prevailed in the West, he says, until the seventeenth century. Honoring these limits, men recognized that the intellect could not have "direct knowledge of essences," rather, an image must mediate. But during the seventeenth century, in Tate's account, a kind of mind prevailed that attempted to transcend the mediation of images, "to disintegrate or to circumvent the image of the illusory pursuit of essence." This kind of mind "has intellect and will without feeling"; it "loses its human paradigm, and is dissolved in the worship of intellectual power, the surrogate of divinity that worships itself." This analysis, though employing a rather different vocabulary, is clearly the same as Eliot's, and Tate, extending the specificities of Eliot's critique, quite correctly recognizes in Descartes a dematerializing impulse analogous to that which, as we will see, is found in Puritanism.

It is not too much to say, I think, that the temperament of the Reformation itself (and Milton was one of its great and heroic exemplars) constantly strove to separate matter and spirit in the interest of purifying spirit. That is the definition, if any so various a phenomenon can be said to have a definition, of Puritanism. And it explains why the Puritans tended to find the Old Testament so much more congenial than the New. Edmund Wilson might go too far when he remarks that "one feels that it would have been easier for Calvin if the Gospels did not exist—he is obliged to explain so much of them away," but one sees what Wilson means when one samples Calvinist culture at key points. A good example can be found in the familiar "Battle Hymn of the Republic," written with a particular spontaneity, as if through inspiration, by Julia Ward Howe:

> In the beauty of the lilies Christ was born across the sea,
> With a glory in his bosom that transfigures you and me:
> As he died to make men holy, let us die to make men free,
> While God is marching on.

Wilson's comment on this stanza is worth quoting. It is, he says,

particularly interesting on account of its treatment of Jesus, so characteristic of Calvinism. As is so often the case with Calvinists, Mrs. Howe, though she feels she must bring Him in, gives Him a place which is merely peripheral. He is really irrelevant to her picture, for Christ died to make men holy; but this not what God is having us do. .... Note that Christ is situated "across the sea"; He is not present on the battlefield with His Father.

The Puritanical New Englanders went so far in their rejection of the New Testament, Wilson points out, that they began to assimilate it into the Old. Calvin Stowe, the colorful husband of the author of *Uncle Tom's Cabin* and an eccentric Calvinist,

allowed his beard and his hair to grow and wore habitually a rabbinical skull-cap, and ... liked to pose with a New Testament—in some curious unbooklike form, perhaps masquerading as a Torah scroll—held up before him like Moses' Tablets. His wife was in the habit of referring to him as "my old rabbi" or simply "Old Rab."

Given this resistance to the central aspect of the New Testament, the idea that the spirit can become concrete, we need not be surprised that the great artistic achievements of Puritanism were in music, the least carnal of the arts. The Reformation, so to speak, gave us the hymnal and Bach, while Catholicism responded to the dematerializing temper of the Reformation with the massive arrangements of Baroque painting, architecture, and sculpture, which constituted the aesthetic gesture of its insistence upon the carnal. This division is carried down even into modern ecclesiastical manners. The crucifix that depicts the *body* of Christ is recognizably (with

the special exception of Lutheranism) un-Protestant. We have come
far from Breughel and Durer, but then the central tendency of an
idea does not appear in all clarity until that idea has been refined
by history.

As I have said, I think it is precisely because they are poets and
writers that Eliot and the other Anglo and Roman Catholics I have
mentioned hold the views they do on the relationship between
religion and culture. Seeing deeply into the relationships in a good
poem, they are hospitable to analogous views regarding metaphysical relationships. In the most influential modern Protestant thought,
however—Kierkegaard, Barth, Bultmann, Niebuhr, and Tillich—it
is the *otherness* of God that is stressed. Culture and spirit are viewed
not as continuous but rather as radically divided and even as irrecon-
cilably opposed. This essential dichotomy is reflected in their most
characteristic titles: *Either-Or, The Word of God and the Word of
Man, Christ and Adam.* As a matter of fact, one often senses in
such writers a kind of resentment over the fact that culture *is* so
particular, so historical and material. They seem to lack love for the
material particulars of a culture, of a way of life, an attitude deriving
no doubt from the fact that the particulars of a culture, by their very
nature, fail of transcendence. And this attitude toward culture must
go far toward accounting for the political "neutralism" of men like
Barth and Niemoeller. If what really matters is entirely transcendent,
entirely *other,* we need scarcely be concerned with victories and
defeats that are merely historical. It is this attitude, no doubt, that
makes theologians of this kind so attractive to the paperback intelligentsia, whose hostility toward culture and whose impulse to reject
it, however, spring from sources having little enough to do with the
transcendence of God.

Even Reinhold Niebuhr, a cogent critic of Barth in political matters, shows a certain hostility, a certain Puritanism, toward culture
itself. Particular institutions and customs he regards from a purely
utilitarian point of view. It obviously is necessary, he seems to say,
to live in this world and be engaged in its struggles, but after all, the
necessity is a grim one and at no point to be celebrated. As one
might expect, Niebuhr does not, as Barth and Bultmann and Tillich
do not, stress the doctrine of the Incarnation. (Barth's attitude
toward Christ should by no means be oversimplified. Henri Bouil-
lard's *Karl Barth,* 3 vols. [Paris, 1957], a sympathetic study of Barth,

proposes that Barth has moved from the position that "He sacrifices to the incomparably Greater and to the invisibly Other every claim to genius and every human heroic or aesthetic possibility, because there is no conceivable human possibility of which He did not rid Himself" to an interpretation more receptive to the notion of the humanity of Christ.)

Niebuhr, like the earlier Calvinists alluded to, seems more at home in the world of the Old Testament and its prophets than in the world of the New Testament. He is more inclined to talk of a "biblical" rather than of a specifically Christian way of life. At least once, moreover, when giving up in principle (and not merely as an aspect of democratic manners) any missionary activity directed at the Jews, he seems to undercut the New Testament entirely:

Christian missionary activities among the Jews ... are wrong not only because they are futile and have little fruit to boast for their exertions. They are wrong because the two faiths despite differences are sufficiently alike for the Jew to find God more easily in terms of his own religious heritage than by subjecting himself to the hazards of guilt feeling involved in a conversion to a faith which, whatever its excellencies, must appear to him as a symbol of an oppressive majority culture.

Now the important thing to notice about this position is not its historical untruth. The doctrinally interesting thing is what Niebuhr's position does to the conception of the Incarnation. The Puritan tendency has worked itself out: the Incarnation here becomes a "historic symbol" that may be discarded to alleviate "guilt." One may well wonder about Niebuhr's phrase, employed with respect to Christianity, "whatever its excellencies."

At any rate, although it seems clear enough to me that, considered as the expression of a comprehensive attitude toward experience, a theology that goes so far as to eliminate the doctrine of the Incarnation is inadequate and unattractive (is not even, for example, adequate to the felt experience of the Protestant culture of a New England town, whatever the explicit doctrine that culture sprang from), it nevertheless remains true that one can understand the genesis of such a theology and sympathize with and preserve what is true in it. These theologians are theologians of crisis and cultural extremity. They reflect and, in doing so, paradoxically criticize a time from which God indeed seems to have fled to some impenetrable fastness. Furthermore, they may be sympathetically understood as rejecting the complacent identification of religion with ethics characteristic of liberal Protestantism, and in this rejection they perform a valuable critical and corrective function. We know, of course, that culture and religion, though they overlap, though they are continuous and interpenetrating, are nevertheless not the same. They most surely are related; they sometimes seem the same, as to Eliot, but they are also different. Culture concerns itself with ethics, as does religion. But the religious man is something more than the ethical man, and the ethical man need not be religious. It was such a distinction that Christopher Dawson intended when he said that the difference between the religious and the irreligious man is not a difference in levels of culture but in levels of consciousness: the religious person has commitments of another kind.

Culture transmits and may adorn religion. Religion makes use of culture and may inform it with purpose. Yet, at the extreme margin, a margin in which the contemporary theology I have been discussing seems to operate, religion does differ from culture, and those who stress so forcefully the otherness of God clearly tell us not to lose sight of that difference. Even Eliot, though, concerned as he is with the incarnation of values, is far from ignorant of the separateness of religion and culture. When the identification of culture and religion is complete, he writes, "it means in actual societies both an inferior culture and an inferior religion."

Reflections
on Pornography

The subject of pornography has come in for a good deal of attention lately, and for a variety of reasons. There is more of this kind of product visible in the marketplace than heretofore, and in fact, it is a major industry. Many people object to it from different perspectives, and indeed, they mean different things by the term. Pornography for some has become a political issue, for others it is a moral and even a religious one. On pornography, the Moral Majority and Gloria Steinem agree—for once. The whole issue goes far beyond the rather narrow definitions established in current case law, in which the courts have defined the pornographic as: (1) appealing entirely to "prurient" interest; (2) focusing on the representation of human genitalia; and (3) having no redeeming social or scientific value. Those definitions, when we come to actual works of representation, are difficult to apply. In any event, the concerns of Jerry Falwell or Gloria Steinem are entirely different.

My own effort here will be one of clarification, both intellectual and semantic. My interest in this subject was awakened several years ago when I moderated a debate on it between D. Keith Mano, the novelist, and Ernest van den Haag, the social philosopher. I have since read a great deal of the literature on the subject. I offer these reflections tentatively, but also out of a sense that all of the discussion I have read has been in various ways inadequate. I would also wish to make it clear that I consider hard-core pornography of the *Hustler* sort profoundly repellent, and of course, there is much worse than even *Hustler.*

It seems to me that the extension of First Amendment protection to this material has been a very serious mistake. We were not "less free" before the Supreme Court decision in the case of *Roth,* which

"Reflections on Pornography" first appeared in *Partisan Review,* Vol LII, No. 4, 1985. Reprinted with permission.

opened the floodgates. Under the present legal circumstances, perhaps community boycotts of stores stocking repellent material is the best we can do. On the other hand, in a series of court cases during the 1950s, it became legally permissible to publish *Lolita* and other works of erotic content. It is ironic that this legal breakthrough came in the 1950s—that allegedly repressive era. However, there is little doubt in my mind that we ought to be able to read *Lolita,* and no doubt either that *Lolita* is different from a "snuff" movie. That distinctions can be difficult to make sometimes does not mean that we should not make them.

In a recently collected essay, for example, Gloria Steinem characterizes as pornographic any work in which a woman is exhibited as an unwilling victim. One understands her political impulse here. But after all, people—men, women, children—are sometimes victims. The disposition of power in a given relationship is not always equal. Such a situation ought to be available to representation. Steinem would be the most restrictive critic of *Othello* since Thomas Rhymer.

In her recent book, *Pornography and Silence,* Susan Griffin writes from what could fairly be called a feminist perspective, and she— a writer of genuine poetic power—has marvelous things to say about this subject. Her central thesis or insight is a useful one, though not in the way she handles it. Griffin argues that the spread of pornography is not the result of the so-called "sexual revolution" and is by no means a celebration of eros. It is, in fact, the opposite— the negation of the erotic. In its exploitativeness, its reductionism, its imitativeness within the genre, its essential redundancy, it is the opposite of genuinely erotic expression. Susan Griffin is onto something here, and I will come back to it in a minute.

Perhaps the most useful book I have read in this area is Steven Marcus' *The Other Victorians: A Study of Sexuality and Pornography in Mid-Nineteenth-Century England* (1964). Marcus has surveyed a great deal of subliterary material, and he has turned up some colorful underground Victorian characters. He has also deployed a fine critical and historical intelligence. He notes, for example, that in the pornography we find much that was *left out,* self-censored, by the great Victorian novelists—for example, the often affectionate sexual relations undertaken with working-class women by men of the middle and upper classes, and, for a further example, the way people actually talked and actually behaved in a working-class pub in 1850. The eighteenth-century artist Thomas Rowlandson could depict this; Dickens could not. I was led by Marcus to reflect upon *Oliver Twist*. Surely in that milieu presided over by Fagin, and with Bill Sykes in a prominent role, those boys would not have been primarily sneak thieves. Fagin and Sykes would have been selling them.

Marcus concludes, however, that for the most part pornography has a number of recognizable but severely limiting characteristics—and I point out here that he is dealing only with prose narrative and not with the visual arts at all. Marcus finds that pornography, sentence by sentence, strings together cliches. The consumer of pornography apparently prefers dead to fresh language. When you survey a great deal of it, as Marcus did, you find that the same situations keep reappearing. Within this genre, there is a great deal of self-imitation, even plagiarism. Its interest in characterization is feeble, as is its interest in external nature. Fantasy plays a large role, as in the amazing sexual performance of the males, and in some ways this pornography is like the Keystone Cops and other comedies: things that, in reality, would put you in the intensive care unit are routinely shrugged off. As in Voltaire's *Candide,* no one ever gets seriously injured.

So far, so good, and it is here that I wish to take my point of departure. What Susan Griffin and Steven Marcus seem to me to be describing is not some special and isolated category called "pornography" but bad art in general. Bad art exhibits precisely the characteristics that Griffin and Marcus have identified.

Take the genre of the detective story. At its highest reaches, as in *Crime and Punishment,* it exhibits enormous power and complexity. Raskolnikov is a St. Petersburg Hamlet, and—come to think of it—*Hamlet* is also a detective story. We can move down from *Crime and Punishment* through good but much lesser writers such as Graham Grelene, Conan Doyle, Wilkie Collins, Dashiell Hammett, and so forth. But there is an immense literature much lower still, and it resembles Marcus' and Griffin's sense of the pornographic: full of cliches, imitative, with feeble characterization, fantasy, and unlikely feats.

Wuthering Heights and *Jane Eyre* are great Gothic romances, investing the "dark male" and the "passionate but unawakened woman" with virtual mythic power. And, speaking of the things that could not be said in the Victorian novel, Emily Brontë went much further in print than the sexually hyperactive Charles Dickens. The north-country novelist actually has Cathy and Heathcliffe spiritually free on "Pennistone Crag." Here, in the Brontës, we are at the top of the Gothic genre, and we can descend to Mary Shelley, Horace Walpole, Bram Stoker, and others in whom there are good things, and we can descend still further to the junky Gothic romance you can purchase at the airport—full of cliches, imitativeness, and improbabilities.

War and Peace and *The Red Badge of Courage* are great works of literature and deal with the subject of warfare. But of course much war fiction and many war movies are also garbage—full of cliches, and so on.

It is not at all surprising that Susan Griffin believes pornography to be hostile to eros. Bad art *does* make you feel bad. It is the central point of Alexander Pope's *Dunciad* that bad art is hostile to life itself, and in his great poem *MacFlecknoe,* John Dryden equated the bad poetry of Thomas Shadwell with excrement, constructing a typographical pun by printing Shadwell's name as Shitwell. I am not claiming for myself anything approaching the sensitivity of Mozart, who became physically ill if someone played a note out of tune, but I think most people have had the experience of being offended and angered by, say, a really stupid and banal movie. Pornography is merely bad erotic art.

Though the whole matter is charged with peculiarly intense emotion, it seems to me that it would be an aid to intellectual clarity for us to put aside for a moment the word "pornography" and hold it, so to speak, in reserve.

I would argue that all areas of human experience should be—and have been, as a matter of fact—available for artistic representation. There are, indeed, extreme forms of human experience such as the battlefield, religious ecstasy, and the surgical operating room that might prove shocking or disturbing, but that is no reason to exclude them from the realm of art. I can even imagine making a college faculty meeting the subject of a work of art, though the treatment would inevitably be satirical. And there is no reason why art cannot deal with erotic experience. We can make the customary analyses and judgments within the field of erotic art. How well is it executed? Is it tragic or comic? What is its meaning? Does it possess originality? Of what kind? What is its relationship to the artist's other work?

I have before me as I write seven items of erotic art. I do not doubt that many people would consider one or more of them "pornographic," and it is even possible that some would fall within the legal definition of pornography as currently applied by the courts, though I am not certain about that. All seven items, however, seem to me interesting and valid works of the imagination, and I will describe them briefly:

1. A book called *Eros in Antiquity,* published in 1978, consists of splendid photographs, in color, by Antonia Mulas. They depict Greek and Roman works of sculpture characterized by erotic motifs. There are vases and urns, medallions, bas relief representations, and three-dimensional statues. The sexual acts being represented are very explicit and sometimes complicated. There is no doubt that many of these items are works of art of a very high order—indeed, priceless. Looking at some of these urns, one wonders afresh just exactly what was going on in the frieze on Keats' Grecian urn: "Bold lover, never, never canst thou kiss, / Though winning near the goal. . . ."

2. An etching done by Picasso in 1968 exhibits a sexual act, with a voyeur peeking through a curtain into the boudoir. The style of the etching is elegant and witty and continuous with Picasso's style in other etchings of the same period about other kinds of behavior. It would certainly be impossible to argue that this erotic drawing is not a work of art.

3. A 1969 pencil drawing by the American artist Betty Dodson, a powerful piece of realism, depicts a couple engaged in oral sex. Dodson's execution is magnificent and, incidentally, destroys the contention that erotic art is exclusively produced by males.

4. A collection of photographs by the great photographer E. J. Bellocq, a sort of photographic Toulouse-Lautrec, taken around 1912, portrays prostitutes in bordellos. Bellocq, who was deformed, spent his days in Storyville, a district in New Orleans where prostitution at that time was legal. The photographs are enormously evocative, individualized, full of the pathos of times past and of mortality, and they even evoke the Virgilian emotion of celebrating the deeds of times long gone. The cover photograph depicts one of the most notable and desired of Storyville's prostitutes (who was, incidentally, the subject of the movie *Pretty Baby* starring Brooke Shields).

5. A collection of photographs entitled *100 Years of Erotica,* edited by Paul Aratow and published in 1981, covers the years

1845–1945. As might be expected, they vary widely in quality, but there is a sequence of photographs taken in 1910 in Paris depicting a young couple in eight different sexual postures. The young woman wears a headband to keep her hair from flying around, which it undoubtedly would have done otherwise. The photographs are interesting and moving, and again we have an additional aesthetic element introduced by the passage of time. If that young man and woman are still alive, they would be in their nineties, but, given the apparent age of the young man in 1910, it is much more likely that he was mixed up with the mud of Verdun or some such place. One is glad that they evidently enjoyed themselves while they could.

6. More modest in artistic ambition, but by no means contemptible, are the drawings by Charles Raymond and Christopher Foss in the contemporary, best-selling sex manual by Alex Comfort, *More Joy of Sex*. Though these drawings, both pastels and black and whites, are intended to be instructional within the intention of the book, they also have considerable delicacy and flair.

7. Finally, I have before me the March 1979 issue of *Playboy,* with a characteristic centerfold depicting one Denise McConnell. She is without doubt a beautiful human being, and the photography is technically accomplished, though the message of the props is obvious mass-audience: Miss McConnell, mostly nude, has her right hand on the latch of a door, presumably to the bedroom. I am certainly not sorry that this photograph exists, and, indeed, the world would be a poorer place if Miss McConnell were not in it.

We could, of course, descend to *Penthouse, Hustler, Playmate, Screw,* and to still lower levels, and we could easily specify the nature of their artistic inferiority to the works we have been discussing above. But the point is that we would be dealing with *bad art,* comparable to that described by Steven Marcus.

There is, though, the fact that a special anxiety appears to surround this issue. After all, we are not so exercised morally and politically over "bad art" in the detective story or in science fiction, so I am led to a moment of reflection about my initial view that "all" of human experience is available to artistic representation. Is it possible that sexuality is so unique, so utterly different from other forms of extreme experience that it must be "out of bounds"?

In an important essay entitled "The Pornographic Imagination,"

Susan Sontag drives a kind of wedge between erotic art and other art by defining sexuality as, in some way, "other." In a key passage:

Human sexuality is, quite apart from Christian repressions, a highly questionable phenomenon, and belongs, at least potentially, among the extreme rather than the ordinary experiences of humanity. . . . Even on the level of simple physical sensation and mood, making love surely resembles having an epileptic fit at least as much, if not more, than it does eating a meal or conversing with someone.

While our judgment is suspended, we read on: "Everyone has felt (at least in fantasy) the erotic glamor of physical cruelty and an erotic lure in things that are vile and repulsive."

I do not think "everyone" has felt that, nor has "everyone" felt that making love is akin to "an epileptic fit." St. Paul might have agreed with Miss Sontag; still, there are few eras in human history that do agree, with the singular modern exception of the nineteenth century. It is interesting to ask whether we are still, somehow, living in the long aftermath of unique, nineteenth-century assumptions about both art and sex. The nineteenth century emphatically did not believe that all of human experience is available to representation—at least not officially. They put pantaloons on the legs of pianos and referred to human legs politely as "limbs." It strikes me that the restrictions here are unique in human history—or at least in Western history, thinking of the disturbing figure of the Ayatollah.

It seems clear that "pornography" is useless as a descriptive term as regards erotic art. When we use it, we really mean that we want to "do something" about the erotic art, usually about the bad erotic art, though the Victorians "did something" about the entire range of erotic art—in the process, hobbling some of their greatest artists. Indeed, as recently as the late 1940s, books by Henry Miller and D. H. Lawrence had to be bootlegged through the United States customs inspectors, and the legitimacy of *Ulysses* had been established not long before—an entirely absurd situation. What we want to "do about," for example, *Hustler* is entirely a policy matter. My own answer would be that for any number of excellent reasons, the federal government should probably do nothing.

I see no reason, however, why a local community of whatever size—from, say, Newport Beach, California, to New York City—should not establish, if it wishes, that *Hustler* be sold under the counter and not exhibited. A political community can, of course, zone its acreage to suit its idea of itself, and it does not have to accept a tannery on its Main Street. It can exclude alcohol, as does Ocean Grove, New Jersey, a fact that gives a unique serenity to that seacoast town. The press freedoms of the First Amendment do not give me the right to pin the photograph of Denise McConnell to the front of the Supreme Court bench.

My central point, however, is that all of human experience from birth through death, including the joys, the pains, the ambiguities of the erotic, ought to be available to artistic representation in the various media: narrative, painting, sculpture, photography, and so forth. When we use the term "pornography," we are not really talking about the specific object before us but about our often unanalyzed intentions toward it.

The Ivory Foxhole

I suppose I have always been a conservative of some sort. Sitting in the press gallery at Kemper Auditorium in Kansas City and watching tanned, articulate Alf Landon address the Republican convention, I suddenly had almost total recall of the first presidential campaign I was actually aware of—Landon's, in 1936, when he carried Maine and Vermont against Franklin D. Roosevelt. During that campaign, in a bitter Depression year, I wore a brown Landon button. It had a beautiful orange border made of felt, so as to suggest a Kansas sunflower. The Democrats among my classmates in the kindergarten called me an Economic Royalist, a mysterious phrase being bruited about by FDR that year.

Earlier than 1936, I was essentially nonpolitical. Nevertheless, I dimly recall confronting and failing to solve, as an infant, a political problem. My infant mind grasped the fact, no doubt from dinner-table conversation, that something called "Hoover" was running the country. The perplexing problem arose from the fact that the family vacuum cleaner was also called "The Hoover," just as one might call a camera "The Kodak." The Hoover resided menacingly in a closet, and periodically it howled down the long and gloomy corridors of our Brooklyn apartment. I now think that I understood, even then, that the vacuum cleaner did not run the country, but further than that my bemused brain failed to penetrate.

The years since my Hoover problem, which must have occurred around 1932, sharpened at least to some degree my political perceptions.

My friend the editor has asked me to comment on my own experience as a conservative in the academic world—certainly an interesting topic—and so I had better begin by specifying just what kind of conservative I am. The conservative breed comes in many gorgeous varieties—more, I am sure, that I can detect among the

This article first appeared in the *Dartmouth Alumni Magazine* and is reprinted with permission.

liberals, a grayer and more predictable group altogether. About my own conservatism I would like to make three brief points. The first one will be spiritual-aesthetic, the second, substantively political, and the third, briefest of all, touching upon foreign policy. In each of these three areas I find myself sharply at odds with many of my academic colleagues.

First, the spiritual-aesthetic. In my own experience, liberalism is relentlessly moralistic, even puritanical. I groan inwardly at a general meeting of the Dartmouth faculty, listening to them moralize away about virtually everything. Liberals are perpetually engaged in a kind of moral Easter-egg hunt, seeking out supposed victims. These victims, hereafter known as Victims, must be rescued from supposed oppressors, whom we will now call Oppressors. In this melodrama the result is always predictable and therefore boring.

The human emotion of pity is valid, of course, but it cannot be allowed to preempt all other emotions and values. The liberal converts pity into a kind of nervous tic, the habitual response to everything. The liberal seems constantly to be rejecting the spectrum of powerful and valid human emotions that have nothing to do with pity. There really do exist values in the world other than concern for Victims, real or phony. Such potent worldly values include vitality, form, style, beauty in all its modes, heroism, pleasure, freedom, wealth, creativity, and joy. The liberal seems constantly to be repressing or ignoring all of those in favor of routinized and quickly boring pity. I recall, a couple of years ago, a moralistic attack from the liberals upon the notion of choosing a Carnival Queen. They charged that the girl was being singled out on the basis of "mere beauty." That language—"mere beauty"—just about tells it all. Mere beauty happens to be intensely important to me.

In the search for a new symbol to replace the bushwacked Dartmouth Indian, it has occurred to me that we might consider The Liberal. Various astonishing skits could be devised for this figure, all of them self-abasing and moralistic. We might even commission a Cigar-Store Liberal, life-sized, carved out of wood. This Cigar-Store Liberal—unisex, of course—might be posed rejecting a bunch of grapes, or forcing a kid onto a bus, or surrendering, or kissing the foot of some Third World windbag.

So much for my first, or spiritual-aesthetic point. I now turn to substance and theory.

As applied to the United States, my own conservatism consists of a doctrine about how decisions ought to be made. It appears to be procedural, but it has plenty of substance. A theory about how decisions ought to be made may sound pretty tame, but believe me, it is not. This is a fighting issue, and it could even conceivably become a bloody one.

It certainly was in 1776, and at the present time it is useful to attempt to put ourselves in the shoes of those Founding Fathers. They looked back, from their late eighteenth-century perspective, upon a broad landscape of history stretching back to Rome, of course—Rome of the Republic. Still earlier political examples existed, and those men of Virginia and Massachusetts knew their Livy but, also, their Thucydides. Those planters and merchants and militiamen, absorbing history, their own experience, and the best thought of their time, came up with something entirely novel. They were intellectually pregnant with an enormous project. They would consciously create the largest self-governing republic since ancient Rome. It is extremely important to understand the theory to which they subscribed. This theory, today, remains the central issue of our politics.

The United States Constitution devised at Philadelphia during that hot summer of 1787 is a Deliberate Sense document. It assumes that people, in living their lives, accumulate experience and knowledge. It means to prevent them from converting temporary judgments into public policy. Waves of popular feeling will not prevail. This novel instrument of government puts all sorts of buffers in the path of popular feeling. There is no need to remind you of them: a bicameral legislature, presidential veto, a Supreme Court, a federal system of states, and so on. These procedural buffers were intended to insure that the "sense" of the people would indeed be "deliberate." Nothing really serious could happen without reflection. Nevertheless, in the end, the "sense" of the people would actually prevail. I do not suppose I need to say that I revere that theory of government and also the men who devised it.

Nevertheless, there has grown up in our midst, like a viper in the bosom, an entirely different and contradictory theory. This viper theory appeals not to the deliberate sense of the people but to theoretical absolutes. It is certainly plausible to discern in this viper theory of theoretical absolutes exactly the kind of thing the men of Massachusetts and Virginia and the other states defeated on the battlefield and rejected at Philadelphia in 1787 in the name of self-government. The viper theory proposes a government based not upon the deliberate sense of the people, as refined through the careful buffers of the constitutional mechanism, but upon theoretical absolutes and bureaucratic fiat.

These theoretical absolutes are not found in the plain language of the Constitution, and indeed, they contradict the "deliberate sense" political theory upon which the Constitution is based. An absolute is an imperative, not the product of deliberation. The theoretical absolutes are first discernable in the "created equal" clause of the Declaration—though such a reading of that clause is utterly unhistorical—and in the First and Fourteenth Amendments—needless to say, by tortured interpretation.

My assertions in this regard are neither eccentric nor original. They are completely supported by such specialists as the late Alexander Bickel of Yale, Professor George Carey of Georgetown, and Professor Raoul Berger of Harvard. Berger's monumental book on the Fourteenth Amendment, by the way, scandalized liberaldom.

The conflict between "deliberate sense" and "theoretical absolutes" is a profound matter. The people, in their deliberate sense, on the basis of their lived experience, will, in my opinion and the opinion of the founders, affirm what is true and valuable. That deliberate sense, however, will not effectuate a whole spectrum of liberal projects, both egalitarian and libertine. The deliberate sense tradition, therefore, is being derailed by a heretical "rights" theory that has no constitutional legitimacy and that is imposing upon the people things that go against the grain of their common sense. An interpretation of the First Amendment, for example, that legitimizes every excess—which, as Irving Kristol has remarked, says that it is legal for an adult woman to have sexual intercourse on a public stage as long as she is paid the minimum wage—is not government according to the principles of the founders. Americans, I hope, will not continue to put up with it, any more than they long endured a capricious rule from England during the eighteenth century.

Most things have an economic aspect, and the liberal exploitation of pity, not surprisingly, turns out upon closer examination to be a kind of Gold Rush, as I have earlier pointed out. The rhetoric of liberal idealism justifies and protects those who are currently mining the Pity Klondike. This enterprise gave rise to a virtual "new class" of persons, a postindustrial elite consisting of professionals in education, urban planning, welfare, social research, compensatory programs of all sorts, rehabilitation, poverty law, communications, and similar enterprises.

After Lyndon Johnson's 1964 landslide, the lopsidedly Democratic Congress enacted a cascade of social programs. Education, housing, welfare, and urban outlays soared. Enactment of the War Against Poverty alone brought early expenditures of two billion dollars a year, rapidly rising. As a spin-off effect, it also called into being a hundred firms in the greater Washington area—and of course swarms of others elsewhere—functioning as consultants in the poverty area. As the federal billions began to flow into the "social concern" sector, private enterprise was quick to sniff out the opportunities. Corporations began to find educational innovation (so-called), urban studies, and assorted rehabilitation schemes immensely profitable. We saw the mushrooming of new social-economic entities—what might be called Social Concern Conglomerates. A few years ago, Robert Kruger estimated the social services market as a seven billion dollar per year concern, and growing exponentially. In the big Bull Social Concern Market of 1965–1968, Wall Street investment houses gobbled up securities with names redolent of scientific technology, environmental purification, research, planning, advanced educational techniques, computer software, informational systems, and so on.

Linked on the one hand to a surging social welfare bureaucracy in Washington (and to innumerable related agencies) and on the other to myriad allies in the academy and in the printed and electronic media, this new class has consolidated its political and social power. Naturally, it has an immediate and voracious interest in large and increasing federal expenditures.

Naturally this new class is ideologically liberal. It is, in fact, in the social change business. Without social problems and social solutions, goals, and programs, it would be out of business. Social change is as important to the new class as inventory turnover was to the old mercantile elite or a good cotton crop to the still earlier planter elite.

Most social change items on our recent and present agenda had their theoretical foundations laid in the academy. They were publicized and sold by the media. The myriad programs and projects occasionally do some good, but generally they do not—and, indeed, recent empirical studies have begun to confirm common sense in this regard. Often, by any reasonable measure, the programs and projects are outright disasters. They include, of course, busing, but also expensive programs of criminal rehabilitation that show no results—elaborate, compensatory schemes for the "poor" that do no good, urban renewal and model city schemes that are counter-productive, affirmative action hiring and "experimental" textbooks that outrage the normal person, and so on. Each program sustains thousands of administrators and other professionals. Because so much of this action is either useless or actually disastrous, it all has to be sold to us as "moral," "compassionate," or "liberal," rather than on the grounds of results achieved.

Notice that this new class is in the business of manufacturing a social environment. By monkeying with the social environment, the new class will, it implicitly claims, increase human felicity. Of course, such social engineering turns out to be devilishly expensive, but no matter—it is "moral." Notice, too, that if some heretic steps forward to question the absolute claims of "environment," the new class defends itself against him savagely. If perfectly respectable academicians, such as Jencks and Herrenstein at Harvard and Jensen at Berkeley, murmur dark things about "heredity," thus directly threatening new class social-environmental claims, the response is vicious. For the new class, to call such heretics "racists" is the precise analogue of the epithet "Bolshevik" as employed by the old capitalist elite. Real economic and class interests are thus defended by moral slander.

A further point, touching upon foreign policy, can be put much more briefly. It seems to me that the American Left (liberals and on over to radicals) has been, since World War II at least, in some disarray on the freedom issue. No doubt the Soviet Union has very few apologists anywhere these days—the stench from the Gulag as well as visible economic failure has ended such apologies. Mao's China, however, had in its day plenty of admirers; many also actively desired and worked for a Communist triumph in Vietnam; and many admire the various Third World "liberation" movements, most of which are Marxist and totalitarian in character. It may be a small point, but I sat through the entire Democratic Convention at Madison Square Garden and did not hear the word "freedom" mentioned once—though of course "compassion" was a key word in all speeches. Yes, yes, I know—I will address myself to Franco and Pinochet in a moment.

As I was meditating upon a subject for my regular newspaper

column, my gaze fell upon a headline in, as it happened, the *New York Times* sports section: "Miss Navratilova Cries Some a Year After Defection." Miss Navratilova is the Czech tennis star who defected and now resides mostly in the United States. Like everyone else, I had read the words "defect" and "defector" thousands of times before, but this time they struck me with the force of revelation, and I grasped their true meaning for the first time.

If I were to travel abroad for an extended period—if I took a job in Paris, say, and moved my belongings there—I would not be called a "defector." I would be "an American living abroad"—as thousands in fact do. T. S. Eliot who, though born in St. Louis, became a British subject is not known as "Eliot, the famous defector." The use of the term to describe Navratilova and others like her really implies the Communist state claim to total control over the individual. She is not working for the CIA; she merely wants to play tennis where she pleases. You can unpack the term "defector" and find within it the walls and barbed wire, armed towers and checkpoints, the entire repressive apparatus of the state that is designed to enforce that total control. The word "defector" is also pejorative. When we use it, we accept the Communist valuation of the act. It is almost military in character (you can defect only to an *enemy*), and it therefore implies the unremitting hostility of the Communist state to everything outside it.

The Communist claim to total control seems almost historically unique, the single possible qualification to such uniqueness being the case of Nazi Germany. Under Franco, in contrast, tens of thousands of Spaniards worked abroad, traveling back and forth across the border without interference. There is no wall around Chile, as there is none around the other non-Communist authoritarian states. This distinction seems to me absolutely momentous. It means that these authoritarian states stand in an entirely different relationship to their citizens. Yet the American liberal and radical has been almost invariably more hostile to Franco's Spain or Pinochet's Chile than he is to any Communist state.

I would like to add, however, that I myself am not obsessed with the Communist problem—as some of the older generation of American rightists, such as Whitaker Chambers and Frank Meyer, seem to have been. After they broke with the Party, they hated communism while also somehow respecting it. For my generation of conservatives, communism was never the "central experience" it was for Chambers, Meyer, and others. I myself, for example, was born in 1930 and grew up in a normal, middle-class environment. Communism was just not a real option. It seemed a repellant and self-evidently alien phenomenon. The few Communists I met during the 1930s and 1940s, usually in the public school system or some Work Projects Administration enterprise, confirmed this impression of alienness. They looked as if they had just gotten off the boat and would do very well to get right back on it. Their books and pamphlets sounded as if they had been translated from Hungarian, and perhaps they were. I have always regarded the Soviet Union as a bleak and disgraceful tyranny, run by gray men with steel jaws, wide trousers, and shoulder holsters. As a seven-year old, I rooted for the Finns.

Well, there you have it. But given this spectrum of opinions and attitudes, how do I get along in the predominantly liberal atmosphere of the contemporary campus? The answer is, very nicely, thank you. First of all, liberalism at Dartmouth is relatively benign and, like liberalism generally, on the defensive intellectually. Hanover in no way resembles, for example, the People's Republic of Berkeley. The presence here of a cohort of New Leftists and Marxists remains an annoyance, but they usually are too busy screaming and yelling about El Salvador or racism to do any serious academic work.

Let me hasten to add that I would not mind it a bit if a competent scholar taught history of literature from a Marxist perspective. Eugene Genovese, for example, describes himself as a Marxist, and as a historian he would be an asset to any institution. Marx himself maintained, however, that the task of intellect is not to understand the world but to change it. Of course, understanding would then be subordinate to political action, and no academic institution can accept that set of priorities. The task of the academician is precisely to "understand" the world. Inquiry must be free, even if it damages someone's "cause." I would have to say that, unlike Eugene Genovese, the Marxist and New Left academicians I have known did in fact suppress other points of view and treated their classrooms like political soapboxes. A campus where that sort of thing remained a powerful presence would be intolerable. Bringing politics into the classroom in a style of advocacy seems to me to constitute academic malpractice and also to be seriously infra dig, the sign of intellectual bad breeding. During the decade of intense United States involvement in Vietnam, for example, I cannot recall mentioning the word "Vietnam" once in the classroom.

My academic subject helps here, of course, as does my methodology. I tend to stay close to the literary text itself. How would you, even if you so desired, bring Vietnam into the analysis of a poem by Alexander Pope? It also helps, I suppose, that I do not lack opportunities for political self-expression elsewhere. I am a senior editor of *National Review;* my syndicated political column appears in many newspapers; a president, two governors, a senator, and several cabinet officers have delivered speeches I have written. I have even published a couple of essays in *The New Republic.* So I do not feel that I have to get into fights at cocktail parties.

Finally, some people manage to get along, and some just do not. Civility and good humor rank high with me. My personality does not resemble that of Thorstein Veblen. I am sure that I am detested by some, mostly silently, and that many regard my opinions as deplorable, but in the latter group, many also like to ski, play tennis, or hang around football practice with me. Existence, thank God, includes much more than opinions.

Burke and
Radical Freedom

In the period following World War II, as everyone knows, an enormous revival of interest in Edmund Burke took place. Scholars, to be sure, have always been interested in him, and he was widely admired for his style and, by some, for his "practical wisdom" during the nineteenth century. But in our time he has come to be read not merely as one among a large number of other important figures in the history of political thought but as a thinker of intense, of special, contemporary relevance. Burke is our contemporary—he is an *issue* in a way that Locke is not and Leibniz is not and even Mill is not. Burke has not receded into what Lovejoy called the pathos of time, by which he meant that benign and even tender feeling we have for thought that is now completely, forever, a part of the past and so neither defines us nor menaces us.

In part, of course, Burke is a beneficiary of the revival of critical and scholarly esteem for eighteenth-century writing generally, and especially for eighteenth-century writing on the conservative side. Like Dryden and Pope and Swift and Johnson, he speaks, we see, for civilization, for a high, elegant, and traditional civilization, and this is a welcome voice to us in our age of cultural democratization and the corruption of manners. In part, too, Burke is a beneficiary—as is conservative thought generally—of the fact that in the world arena today America is irreversibly a conservative nation, with everything to gain from the maintenance of order and nothing from its dissolution. Yet neither of these reasons quite accounts for the atmosphere of passion and polemic that surrounds the subject of Burke. Attitudes toward him among otherwise sober-seeming scholars tend to suggest total commitment—for him or against him.

This article first appeared in *The Review of Politics,* Vol. 29, No. 2 (1967), and is reprinted with permission. © *The Review of Politics.*

Individuals whom one would never suspect of much capacity for feeling transform themselves when the question of Burke is brought up. This passion, I maintain, occurs because Burke was the first to recognize the deep moral division of the West, which was just then opening up and which today, across the board, is decisive in our moral, political, and metaphysical opinions, and because Burke, having recognized the division and defined its doctrinal grounds, took sides.

ii

Burke's break with Charles James Fox in 1791 may be taken as a kind of symbol of the division then forming in the West itself, and I think that Burke himself so understood it. Burke had always been known as an advocate of reform. He had urged a moderate and conciliatory policy toward the American colonies. A recently uncovered note among his papers at Sheffield in England demonstrates that Burke actually had a good deal of sympathy with the American Revolution. "The Americans," he noted,

as I have and do repute them the first of men, to whom I owe eternal thanks for making me think better of my nature—tho they have been obliged to fall down at present before the professional armies of Germany, have yet afforded a dawning hope by the stand they have made, that in some corner of the globe, at some time, or in some circumstance or other, the Citizen may not be the slave of the Soldier.

In his parliamentary career, Burke had fought for the independence of Parliament against what he thought was the unconstitutional influence of the Crown. In economic matters, Burke was reformist as opposed to the older mercantilist economic theory; he inclined to the theories of Adam Smith who said, indeed, that Burke was the only man in England who really understood him. Burke's reformist politics even involved him in some friendly friction with his associates in Dr. Johnson's circle, who were very largely Tories. (Dr. Johnson, you will recall, remarked only half-playfully that the first Whig was the Devil and that Patriotism—by which he meant the so-called Patriot political group, that is, the critics of George III and not what we mean today by patriotism—was "the last refuge of a scoundrel.") Burke was the friend of Dr. Johnson, but he was the friend and political ally of the reformers—of Sir Philip Francis (the probable author of the Junius letters), of Sheridan, of Charles James

Fox. Jeremy Bentham read with approval and copiously annotated his reformist speeches, and Burke was admired from afar by Tom Paine. If we could transport the pre-French Revolutionary Burke to our own times, we would consider him a moderate and a reformer, humanitarian in his sympathies; he was, notwithstanding his politics, half in love with philosophy and literature. But the French Revolution did occur, and it changed all this. Burke's principles did not change, but the deep transformation of the world cast him into an entirely different role.

Dramatically, Burke found himself separated from his former allies, who sympathized with the French Revolution—and separated from them not only politically but personally, so far-reaching and decisive did the issues seem to him. In the spring of 1791, during a parliamentary debate on matters unrelated to France, Charles James Fox, well known to be an admirer of the Revolution, interpolated into a speech some comments favorable to it. Burke decided to reply to Fox at the earliest opportunity, and on May 6, during a debate on the Canada Bill, Burke rose to speak on the Revolution. As he spoke, Fox's followers repeatedly interrupted him and created an atmosphere of general disorder in the House. Irritated, Burke commented angrily on Fox's eulogies of the Revolution and finally spoke these irrevocable words: "It is indiscreet at any period, but especially at my time of life, to provoke enemies or give friends occasion to desert me. Yet firm and steady adherence to the British Constitution places me in such a dilemma; I am ready to risk it, and with my last words to exclaim, 'Fly from the French Constitution.' " Charles James Fox eagerly called to him that there need not be any loss of friends. "Yes, yes," replied Burke, "there is a loss of friends. I have done my duty at the price of my friend. Our friendship is at an end." Aghast at these proceedings, the members watched Burke stalk from the chamber. This event was unexpected and dramatic but by no means fortuitous: only a few months before, after a sharp argument over the *Reflections on the Revolution in France,* Burke's long friendship with Sir Philip Frances had come permanently to an end.

No doubt Fox and Francis, worthy enough men but certainly not thinkers of the first order, were perplexed by Burke's behavior. They were men of generous spirit; they wished the people of France well. Fox in particular was a sympathetic and colorful character. He was fat; he gambled for enormous sums in the front window of Brooks';

he stabled a string of racehorses; he kept a mistress; and after relentlessly attacking Lord North for years, he reversed himself, in the
genial manner of the time, and formed a coalition with him. But
men of this sort, good men though they were—possessed, we might
say, of all the Dickensian virtues—the very creatures, indeed, of the
old order—were not equipped either imaginatively or intellectually
to understand the implications of the revolutionary threat to the
European order or of the doctrine underlying that threat.

Burke was. The focus of the *Reflections* is, finally, on political
things. We do not go to it for a definitive account of the economic
conditions of France in 1789 or for a character sketch of Marie
Antoinette or for an apt account of the members of the Assembly.
We do go to it for Burke's insight into the intellectual and spiritual
issues, for the French Revolution seemed momentous to Burke. It
was important not because of its violence or because it threatened
the peace of Europe—these things were derivative. Instead, Burke
was, as he says, "alarmed into reflection" by what he considered a
"revolution of doctrine and theoretic dogma," evoking emotions
that, it seemed to him, would render impossible any stable and
settled condition of society and that would result, indeed, in *permanent* revolution. As he says near the beginning of the *Reflections,* in
a sentence that reverberates in the mind like the opening bars of a
great and dark symphony, this was "a great crisis, not of the affairs
of France alone, but of all Europe, perhaps of more than Europe."

iii

Perhaps the best way of stating Burke's fundamental objection to
the Revolution would be to say that it turned on a definition of
"freedom," and that for Burke, freedom was a concrete and historical
thing, the actual freedoms enjoyed by actual Englishmen: they enjoyed the historic rights of *Englishmen.* What revolutionary theory
proposed, he thought, was a freedom that was abstract and unhistorical, not the rights of Englishmen but the Rights of Man. For Burke
there was no such thing as an abstract man, and to evoke one, as
Rousseau had done in the famous first sentence of *The Social Contract,* was to construct a battering ram against all normal social
relationships. "Man is born free," said Rousseau, "but everywhere
he is in chains."

I do not mean to suggest, idiotically, in the remarks that follow
that Rousseau caused the French Revolution. Such is not the role of

ideas in relation to historical events. In addition, I know very well that there is a good deal of discussion among Rousseau scholars today regarding the precise intention behind that sentence. Nevertheless, I think it remains true that in the *rhetoric* of the sentence we can find articulated the longings that were at the heart of the revolutionary ethos and continue today to inform the modern revolutionary spirit.

In what sense was man "born free?" we might well ask with Burke. The infant does not look free; he seems completely dependent. And the violence of the statement is suspicious: *everywhere* in chains? *Everywhere?* And it is significant that the chains—man's social circumstances "everywhere"—are concretely imagined in Rousseau's metaphor, but that the "freedom"—man is "born free"—remains hypothetical, abstract, a mere proposition, whatever its rhetorical authority as the opening statement of the sentence. Just what is this freedom? It evidently is not the concrete, historical *freedoms* that Burke has in mind, but rather the hypothetical—indeed, mythical—freedom of a presocial self. It is the freedom of man as an essence, not as an existence. Traditional thought—and this is the real reason why religion is necessary to any viable conservative politics—envisioned man as achieving essential being (that is, a being as an essence) only outside of time, in eternity. Obviously, this view is logically consistent and intellectually respectable. But revolutionary theory sought—and this goal was the source, is the source, of its deep appeal in the West—the experience of *essential freedom,* the freedom of man as an essence *within* time. Any concrete circumstance standing in the way of *that* freedom—and any concrete circumstance would have to stand in the way of that freedom—is at best regarded as a bothersome and interim thing and at worst as contemptible and intolerable, something to be spat upon and smashed.

The theoreticians of the French Revolution proposed, as Taine put it, to strip from man his artificial garments, all those fictitious qualities that made him "ecclesiastic or layman, noble or plebeian, sovereign or subject, proprietor or proletarian." Only when these supposed fictions were stripped away could "natural man," man *qua* man, make his appearance in history—man liberated from false appearance and thus spontaneous, innocent, and free. The actual results of the French Revolution did not diminish the vitality of this hope, nor have the results of subsequent revolutions done so. There is, indeed, a sense in which the revolutionary hope cannot *be* defeated historically, since it is fundamentally unhistorical. By the time Shelley wrote *Prometheus Unbound,* the French Revolution was part of history, and it had not transformed human nature. Yet the revolutionary vision retained all its original vitality, and Shelley longed for another revolution, a final and successful one, that would liberate man at last from the "masks" of actual social existence:

> The loathesome mask has fallen, the man remains
> Scepterless, free, uncircumscribed, but man
> Equal, unclassed, tribeless, and nationless,
> Exempt from awe, worship, degree, the king
> Over himself; just, gentle, wise; but man
> Passionless? no, yet free from guilt or pain.

But if Shelley is a poet of the revolutionary vision, Burke is a poet of the vision of man as a social being, man as we have actually known him *in* history. He identified the revolutionary vision with great precision and in the *Reflections* launched a powerful attack upon it. In a passage reminiscent of *Lear,* and employing the traditional metaphor of clothes to signify—as in Shakespeare or Swift—man's social aspect, Burke describes the informing impulse of the French Revolution:

All the decent drapery of life is to be rudely torn off. All the superadded ideas, furnished from the wardrobe of a moral imagination, which the heart owns and the understanding ratifies as necessary to cover the defects of our naked, shivering nature, and to raise it to dignity in our estimation, are to be exploded.

In Burke's metaphor, clothes, what he calls "the decent drapery of life," correspond to Shelley's "loathesome mask" and to Rousseau's "chains"—that is, they are our actual social roles. When they are stripped away, there remains "our naked shivering nature"—or in Shelley's terms, "man ... scepterless, free," or in Rousseau's terms, man "free" as he supposedly was when he was born.

At the center of the *Reflections,* then, is this issue: if, indeed, that "self" does exist, can it really be divested of its "artificial" attributes, and if it can be, will its nakedness be productive of joy? Burke was one of the first to understand that the spirit of the French Revolution—and, as I wish to insist, the spirit of revolutionary modernity (which is not here a merely chronological concept)—was at its roots characterized by a hatred of the very idea of *society.*

He knew that a defense of what the *philosophes* called "appearances" or "masks" is a defense of society itself, that the reality of society consists of appearances, of "roles." The natural man of revolutionary theory is only a myth, though a powerful one as well as a destructive one. The critique of roles, of forms, the assault upon Rousseau's "chains" (an element of his sentence that I will explicate shortly) has brought about, precisely because natural man is a fiction, not a more intense experience of selfhood but an experience of emptiness, disgust, and alienation, a deep hatred of the actual circumstances of social life, a deep hatred, indeed, for historical existence itself—that is to say, it has resulted in the special anger of the revolutionary spirit that we daily feel all around us.

This spirit, as Christopher Dawson has remarked, is characterized by a disgust with the concreteness of man's being. Jean Paul Sartre, a very great man in my view, conceives of himself, quite correctly, as a continuator of the revolutionary tradition, as the heir of the *philosophes,* and he has made immense contributions by way of deepening and expanding that tradition intellectually. He is certainly a much more formidable figure than Camus, whose sensibility, much more traditional in character, surely strikes many as more attractive. Now, it is characteristic of the Sartrean hero as we meet him in, say, Roquentin of *Nausea,* that he feels a deep revulsion in the presence of what he regards as "absurd" limitations on his freedom. "I see," says Roquentin in a moment of illumination, "I recall better what I felt the other day at the seashore when I held the pebble. It was a sort of sweetish sickness. How unpleasant it was! It came from the stone. I'm sure of it. It passed from the stone to my hand. Yes, that's it, that's just it—a sort of nausea in the hands!" Mere things seem to Roquentin simply to be there, without reason or purpose, devoid of consciousness. "The world of *Nausea,*" as Francis Jeanson has said, "is the world as it threatens to appear to us when we look at it passively, when we refuse to project a future for it. It becomes a petrified consciousness." The man of Sartrean sensibility, as he moves away from consciousness toward the unconscious, experiences increasing "viscosity"—we hear of "the stickiness," "the rising triumph of the solid over the liquid," "thoughts made sticky by their own objects," as well as, even more frequently, of "bloatedness," "insipid flesh," "pink flesh," "clammy flesh," and so on. Consciousness for Sartre is freedom, experienced as complete lucidity, while unconsciousness is a prison of "facticity." And the emotion includes his own body: "a dull and inescapable nausea perpetually reveals my body to myself."

This polarity between freedom and imprisonment is the reality of human experience for Sartre, but against it men of bad faith, whom Sartre calls "salauds" (stinkers) and who are principally to be identified with the middle class, erect the barriers of habit, conventional assumption, and social role. All these constitute refusals of consciousness and freedom. Thus, in a characteristic gesture, the Sartrean hero (Roquentin, Mathieu, Goetz) asserts his freedom from facticity by actually stabbing himself: "My saliva is sweetish, my body lukewarm; I feel insipid. My penknife is on the table. I open it. Why not? In any case it would change things a bit. I place my left hand on the writing pad and dispatch a good knifethrust into the palm." It is by asserting himself against all forms of facticity and unconsciousness that the Sartrean hero becomes a free and spontaneous individual. "Sartre's essential philosophical trend," observes Wilfrid Desan, "is one of *negation,* a negation of all limitations to freedom, all hampering of man's free movement." Surely Desan is correct here, for the attitude in question pervades Sartre's philosophical writings, his drama and his fiction, and even his criticism, which is savagely moral rather than aesthetic: Genet is a "saint" because of his negation of conventional morality; Giacometti is a great sculptor, for his wiry, fragile figures show man stripped of all "artificial" attributes.

This radical dualism between consciousness and object, lucidity and density, or, in Sartre's terminology, the *Pour-soi* and the *En-soi,* moves, by implication, toward a rejection of the social possibility, as Merleau-Ponty pointed out in his famous critique of Sartre, *Les Adventures de la dialectique.* In accepting only *man* and *things,* Sartre overlooks the *entremonde,* the both-and, that in-between-world of symbolism, value, and history—all that "man" finds and has found to be true. It is as if the individual consciousness alone counts, and both history and the social order are something extraneous. Of course, this sensibility looks at the individual consciousness as something that, "naturally," does not incorporate history (its memory) or the social order (its roles) into itself. That is to say, any memory and any social role is unnatural. Sartre defines integrity as *permanently* revolutionary, revolutionary against any of its conceivable concrete circumstances. That is why he is the greatest and deepest of the *philosophes,* and probably the last.

This hatred of the physical and of limits, of the concrete and irreducible, represents at its deepest reaches (to shift into another idiom) a rejection of the doctrine of the Incarnation, which in one of its meanings expresses the possibility that the concrete and the limiting—the flesh—can enter into union with spirit. To enter into the world at all, the spirit must become flesh—concrete and embodied. We know no naked essences. This union constitutes, in Donne's phrase, "that subtle knot" that makes us man. The Incarnation is the epitome of the very both-and that Sartre intends to split apart. But it is Sartre's power, even perhaps his greatness, that he can move us with his dream of radical freedom and make us, for a moment, desire to untie that knot.

No one can doubt in reflecting upon Burke's penetration of these matters that he illuminated the heart of portentous issues, that he played, indeed, a prophetic role. If his revolutionary opponents conceived of the self as an entity separate from, and hidden behind, false appearances, their modern intellectual descendants have professed what, to coin a phrase, we might call a conspiracy theory of reality. Not the appearances of society, they have maintained, but the secret and hypothetical economic or sexual basis is the "reality." Our naive experience of the world, we hear, is deceptive; the truth lies behind the appearances, waiting to emerge under the proper auspices when the proper key is turned. Marx, for example, conceives of society as a constricting thing, inimical to spontaneity and freedom—the derivation of these terms in Marxist thought should now be familiar—and he argues that all historical societies at best have helped to move toward, at worst have culpably blocked, the emergence of the ultimate "freedom." This freedom we are to enjoy in the future. Marx' "natural man" is the worker; not, of course, actual workers as they are known to us—*they* often have to be dealt with very severely—but a kind of ideal worker. The artificial thing he is to be liberated from is called "capitalism." And its overthrow will bring about a classless and stateless condition (no "roles") in which we will all be "free"—that is to say, liberated from the false appearances that now imprison us. In Marx and Sartre, however, much as in Rousseau, the negation is considerably more vivid than the affirmation. The "chains" are concrete, but the "freedom" is abstract and vague. These writers are much more successful in telling us what we must not be than what we ought to be. The "free" man who is to emerge from all these entangling alienations remains unknown.

Freudian theory also belongs to this tradition, though it has special characteristics of its own and is deeply suspect from the point of view of the Marxist or the Sartrean. (Sartre's position, of course, is philosophically irreconcilable with Marxism, but that is not the point here. More significant from the point of view of this essay are his heroic attempts to reconcile them in the *Critique de la raison dialectique.* Clearly, he recognizes their common tendency.) Freud's system also conceives of society as repressive. Here "natural man" is the infant, and "civilization" painfully confines him; the pain, however, is to be alleviated not by revolution but by psychoanalysis. In matters of detail, some striking analogies appear between the Labor Theory of Value and the psychoanalytical theory that holds culture to be a product of sublimation. Both theories describe the valuable as proceeding from a source customarily rated as "low" (the libido and the worker). Freud, to be sure, defected from the revolutionary tradition in not holding out, actually in explicitly rejecting, the possibility of revolutionary freedom or radical libera-tion. He said in *Civilization and Its Discontents* that we must *endure* our historical pain. (There is an amusing passage somewhere in his correspondence in which he remarks to a friend that he is "half" a Marxist. Asked for an explanation, he replied that Marx said that history would be marked by wars, revolutions, and vast suffering, but that the process at last would bring forth the bliss of the classless society. Freud said he believed only the first part.) From their different points of view, therefore, both Sartre and the Marxists regard Freud's work as a piece of theoretical backsliding and bour-geois bad faith, particularly his positing of an unconscious that cannot be finally transformed and that, even worse, is *inherited.* The unconscious, in Freud, is recalcitrant—it is connected with the past, a *donnee,* a given. It is, in fact, a reactionary idea, and it has, as we will see, some interesting connections with the idea of habit in Burke. Sartre's psychoanalytic theory, in contrast, issues in a theoret-ical denial of the existence of the unconscious.

iv

Earlier in this essay, I quoted Rousseau's famous sentence, "Man is born free, but everywhere he is in chains," and the foregoing remarks have constituted a kind of meditation (perhaps, out of filial piety, we should say a reflection), under the auspices of Burke, on the first four words of that sentence: "Man is born free." I would like to turn now to the second part, "but everywhere he is in chains," because it is precisely those chains, quite differently judged, that Burke's political philosophy tries to protect. There is a much older form, familiar to everyone, that occurs prominently in Shakespeare, Hooker, Milton, and Pope, among many others, and that, like Rousseau's sentence, oddly enough employed the "chain" metaphor. I speak of course of the great hierarchy with God at the top, the angels below him, man in a "middle state," and the lower forms of life below him. Ontologically, man was thus one "link" in the chain. This older thought also conceived of society as a hierarchy in which social roles were links, this time in the "chain" of society. In each order, ontological and social, man's identity depended upon his limitations; he was a man ontologically and not an angel or an ape, and socially his identity was constituted by his roles. He was not "free"; he was a king or a soldier, a merchant or a farmer; he belonged to a neighborhood and perhaps to a guild, and so on. The metaphor recognizes that man is not an abstract essence and, beyond that, connects his "being" with the "chain"—with, in other words, his concrete relations. The metaphor thus *confirms his historical existence:* he is this and not that; he has one identity and not another. Though he certainly enjoys freedoms, constitutional or customary ones, he is not in the radical sense free.

To continue to employ the chain metaphor, we might say that Burke views man as naturally involved with links, and that he believes that as those links dissolve, man's identity does too. One such link in Burke's thought is the link in time. "People will not look forward to posterity," he says in the *Reflections,* "who never look back to their ancestors," and he thinks that men isolated from their past are little better than "flies of a summer." A man's sense of his place in a succession of generations gives him an awareness of being located in a coherent chronology that is not just a sequence of mechanical clock minutes or calendar days. The past is not anonymous, and so neither will the future be. "Respecting your forefathers," he said to the revolutionaries, "you would have been taught to respect yourselves." Clearly his position here is correct. We know from the work of modern sociologists and psychologists the role the father plays in the formation of identity, and Freud has a great deal to say about the father's role with regard to ego and superego formation—that is, with the establishment of identity and of principles. The father's own identity, in turn, is the result of his own ancestry. Groups in which the family structure is weak or the father's sense of identity uncertain—as in the case of the American Negro at the present time—tend to be characterized by identity "crises" and deep uncertainty about goals and values. As Burke argues repeatedly in the *Reflections,* imaginative awareness of the links between himself and his past prevents the individual from feeling that his existence is arbitrary or, in the fashionable term, absurd.

Another link, in Burke's thought, is the link to one's contemporaries: to the family, first of all, but extending beyond that to the neighborhood and the region and thence to the nation and the civilization. Burke characteristically moves outward from the immediate to the more remote, insisting upon the importance of the group closest to the individual: "To be attached to the subdivision, to love the little platoon we belong to in society, is the first principle (the germ, as it were) of public affections. It is the first *link* [my italics] in the series by which we proceed towards a love to our country, and to mankind." In his concern to protect the various groups to which the individual is most immediately linked and that help to constitute his identity, Burke characteristically refuses to begin in the abstract, unhistorical way with Mankind or the Brotherhood of Man. Here again Burke anticipated some of the best in modern social thought and, in particular, what might be said to be derived from Georg Simmel's *The Web of Group Affiliation.* Simmel argues that a person's identity is formed by the "pattern" of his group affiliation, and that individuality is maintained by variety among the patterns. The more distinctive groups there are—clubs, professional associations, church congregations, and so on—and the more independent they are, the more various will be the patterns of affiliation and the wider, therefore, will be the possibilities of individuality. Other social scientists—I particularly have in mind the work of Almond and Verba—have pointed out that independent groups, by fostering commitments on levels below the political and the ideological, help to defanaticize the political order. They produce a kind of tolerance through complexity of commitment.

Still another link for Burke was the link to place. A man's identity is very much involved with his attachment to place, his sense of himself as associated with a geographic locality. The length of time he has lived there has much to do with the strength of such local feeling, as do the distinctive characteristics of the place itself. Burke was attached to the "irregularities" of things and instinctively rejected a uniformitarian idea of "reason." But the link to place also has much to do with ownership; the man who owns his house is likely to have a deeper imaginative involvement with the neighborhood than one who does not. Here we may observe that Burke, drawing upon Locke perhaps but also on his own common sense, put a very high valuation on the protection of property. He did not make that grotesque but familiar distinction between property rights and human rights but viewed property as a human right. It is not, after all, a vegetable or a mineral right.

As such links as these are dissolved, Burke thought, man's identity is proportionately dissolved as well. These links prevent him from floating away psychologically as a kind of angry abstraction or, to put it another way, from resembling psychically those odd modern sculptures composed of coat hangers, tin cans, and stove bolts. We may indeed suppose that much of the distinctive pain of modern existence does proceed from the assault that has been carried forward against such links. They have sometimes been weakened or broken, of course, by historical developments of a nonideological character—by industrialization, urbanization, the widening possibilities of geographical and social mobility. But the point to be made here is that the bad effects of these developments have been intensified rather than moderated by the ideology Burke fought. A moral assault as well has been conducted on these natural links, a moral assault that would seem to have as its intention the isolation of the individual, the reduction of the individual to a "free" self. Think of the deeply antidomestic implications of progressive pressure for sexual freedom, for relaxed divorce laws, and for more abortions. Or the implications of the advocacy, by R. H. Tawney on moral grounds, of a 100 percent death tax.

V

I would like to turn now to a matter that plays a very important role in Burke's political thought. Like the links I have been talking about, it is primarily a psychological point, but, like them, it also raises a political principle. Burke's politics, like any genuinely conservative politics, places a high valuation on *habit.* "Prejudice," he says in the *Reflections,* "renders a man's virtues his habit, and not a series of unconnected acts. Through just prejudice, his duty becomes a part of his nature." This high valuation of habit proceeds from an awareness of the complexity of social life and from the elementary observation—though Burke was the first to make it (in a sense, *he* was the discoverer of the unconscious)—that habit performs complex tasks with greater ease and efficiency than does conscious reason. The daily tasks that we perform most easily (we say, usually, that we perform them "naturally"), from tying our shoes to handling the day's social encounters, we perform habitually. If we were forced to think them through analytically, our activities would come rapidly to a halt. There is a sense, indeed, in which it is really habit, paradoxically enough, that renders one free, since freedom actually is experienced only as a quality of an activity. One is free to do this or that; one is not "free" in an abstract way apart from activity. Castiglione spoke of the courtier's quality of *sprezzatura,* by which he meant his ability to perform his role with ease—through long practice, that is, he could perform it *with ease*—"naturally." In a similar way, Lord Chesterfield advised his son to practice entering a drawing room properly so that he could do it with ease. A skillful musician is "freer" to play his instrument than a novice; and these examples may be taken as synecdochic of our other activities.

It can be seen, therefore, that considerable advantage resides in circumstances that permit social roles themselves to be rooted in habit, though no conceivable circumstance of course could render them entirely habitual. And the sort of society advocated throughout Burke's works operates to strengthen the element of habit in social role. Wealth, property, and power are not to pass with great rapidity from one hand to another. He opposed any mobility rapid enough to endanger social habit. "I do not hesitate to say," he wrote in the *Reflections,* "that the road to eminence and power from obscure condition ought not to be made too easy, nor a thing too much of course. If rare merit be the rarest of all things, it ought to pass through some sort of probation." In the society thus adumbrated, a man might be a soldier, a merchant, a landholder, or a nobleman and expect to remain one. His identity is to a considerable degree "given" rather than willed. In a more fluid society, however, individuals become to a much greater degree free to create themselves, to become, in Don Quixote's marvelous phrase, the children of their deeds rather than the children of their actual parents. To the extent, though, that careers are open to talents—to the extent, that is, that one's social role is the result of one's own talent and will—one's identity must be experienced as *arbitrary.* One might just as well have willed something else. When identity thus partakes of the duality of the willed and the arbitrary, it is experienced as a kind of mask, or even as a lie. One's roles seem absurd, perhaps even hateful. The self comes to stand in an ironic or antagonistic relationship to all its social manifestations. Perhaps this is one reason why the literature of the Enlightenment, responding at once to actual conditions of increasing social mobility but also to the ideological assumption that mobility is simply *good,* has as one of its central themes the critique of roles and appearances. Even such ostensibly conservative writers as Swift and Goldsmith shock conventional views by examining society through the wrong end of a telescope or from the perspective of a Chinaman.

Nevertheless, as Burke saw, there is an intimate connection between habit and ease, and this condition applies as much to society at large as to the individual. The vast majority of its activities, from delivering the mail to running a legislature, go forward smoothly as long as they follow habitual procedures. It is the habits of society—its customs, institutions, and prejudices—that embody the results of its historical experience and enable it to function and preserve its coherence in the present. It was one of Burke's great accomplishments as a political philosopher to show that Hobbes and Locke erred in assigning to reason rather than to habit the function of maintaining the stability of a society. Habit, to be sure, is not an appropriate instrument for dealing with *novel* experience, but on that very account, as Burke saw, a society is better off if it can absorb novelty in small and manageable amounts.

At the very beginning of this essay, I spoke of the moral division of the West. We may observe here that that division is less exacerbated, even though present, in England and America than in France, say, or Italy. A study entitled *The Civil Culture,* by Gabriel Almond and Sidney Verba, makes a Burkean point about this national difference. Ideological division is less comprehensive in the former two countries precisely because they have not had revolutions and have attempted, so to speak, to solve their problems *one at a time.* In consequence, solutions have had less of a tendency to become features of a comprehensive program. Novelty was absorbed gradually. Almond and Verba, moreover, agree with Burke in viewing revolutionary ideology as the mortal enemy of stable, representative government, which depends, they argue, on a number of quite subtle, "informal" factors—a general atmosphere of trust among the citizens, a tradition of political legitimacy, and a tacit agreement to "play by the rules." Paradoxically, they argue, representative

institutions thrive only in an atmosphere of *limited* political commitment on the part of most people. A political commitment cannot
become so powerful that it refuses to subordinate itself to the
assumptions about trust, legitimacy, and playing by the rules. Most
persuasively, Almond and Verba define the attitude appropriate to
the citizen in what they call a "civic culture": he simultaneously
does *not* participate in politics and assumes that *he could if he
wanted to.* The civic culture thus balances activity and passivity by
a norm Almond and Verba call "the potentially active citizen." We
may notice, moreover, the contrast between this attitude and the
one recommended by civics texts and democratic ideologists, who
urge participation and activism.

It is only recently, it seems to me, that scholars and social scientists
have recovered anything like Burke's imagination of the delicacy
and complexity of our social arrangements. I have in mind the works
of Talcott Parsons, Leonard Broom, Robert Merton, and Almond and
Verba, among others, as well as the resurgence of interest in those
aspects of such older writers as Bagehot and Simmel that bear on
the question of social stability.* In society, as Burke put it, "there

---

*Merton and Broom, for example, have provided the theoretical framework for a
sociology of anger that is highly relevant to American society at the present time and
that in a variety of ways confirms Burke's insights. Our commonsense assumption is
that non-neurotic anger proceeds from a "grievance" and would disappear if the
grievance were "corrected." In his classic study *Suicide,* however, Emile Durkheim
showed that feelings of grievance and deprivation are relative to goals—that, paradoxically, such feelings intensify as possibility is enhanced. Robert Merton moved a step
further in the relativization of grievance in his development of "reference group
theory." The individual feels deprived, he shows, relative to those with whom he is
accustomed to compare himself. The feeling of deprivation flows from the comparison—for it is the comparison that gives meaning to the objective circumstance (see
Merton's great essay "Notes Toward a Theory of Reference Group Behavior" in *Social
Theory and Social Structure*). Leonard Broom has added a further dimension to our
understanding of social anger by, in effect, internalizing Merton's conception of
relative deprivation. Broom applies the theory of relative deprivation to the question
of social status. Pointing out that an individual's status is not a monolithic thing
but made up of manifold components—wealth, education, ethnicity, occupation,
neighborhood, and so forth—Broom shows that comparisons can be made between
one component and another. An individual might be "high" in one—say, education—
and "low" in another—perhaps ethnicity. Comparing one with the other, he would
feel *relatively* deprived as regards his low component. Consistency among the
components of an individual's status produces a better social "fit"; conversely, status
inconsistency is generative of social anger. It is worth noticing that rapid mobility—as
on the campus today—almost inevitably generates status inconsistency (see Broom's
"Social Differentiation and Stratification" in *Sociology Today,* edited by Merton,
Broom, and Cottrell).

are often some obscure and almost latent causes, things which appear at first of little moment, on which a very great part of its prosperity or adversity may most essentially depend"; and further, that "it is with infinite caution that any man ought to venture upon pulling down an edifice which has answered in any tolerable degree for ages the common purposes of society."

vi

The emphasis in Burke's writing upon man in his historical existence and his denigration of "abstract" speculation have led many to suppose that his thought is pragmatic in character and informed by no permanent principles. John Morley, for example, who wrote a good short book on Burke during the nineteenth century, was of this opinion. But this view is quite mistaken and ignores the special way in which Burke made use of history.

Burke believed that an "eternal law" is discoverable in history. Men, he says, "attain to the moral reason in their collective experience, they realize and embody it in their stable social relations and organization." For Burke, that is to say, the moral law is eternal and universal, though men cannot, because of their limited reason, apprehend it directly. The moral law does, however, acquire concrete existence and so can be apprehended historically—in man's stable (and that word is crucial) social arrangements. The stability of those arrangements demonstrates that the moral law is being obeyed. Thus there exists for Burke two sources of our knowledge of the "eternal law"—Christian revelation and our historical experience. From this perspective, novel theories of government and human nature, though they may be the product of brilliant thinkers, can scarcely compare in validity either with revelation or with institutions that have been created throughout many generations. Such novel theories are presumptuous in attempting to set themselves up as rivals of "eternal law," and their inadequacy is proved by the catastrophes that result when they are used as principles of government.

When the statesman acts in conformity with the eternal law, Burke thinks, *tranquillity* is fostered in society. Running through his work is a vocabulary indicative of a set of fundamental polarities. On the one hand are the qualities to be desired in society—stability, public tranquillity, peace, quiet, order, harmony, regularity, unity, decorum. Opposed to these are the symptoms of social disease—

discord, contradiction, confusion, violence, excess, the need for coercion. The task of the statesman is to promote "tranquillity."

The attitudes and doctrines that informed the French Revolution, Burke thinks, make tranquillity impossible. Asserting a mythical freedom ("man is born free") against an actual, experienced freedom, the theorists wielded a weapon to which any society would be vulnerable. Against such demands, he said, "No agreement is binding; these admit no temperament and no compromise; anything withheld is so much fraud and injustice." On the other hand, the rights Burke was defending were rights he had known as historical facts. With those rights, he stood in the path of a permanent shattering of tranquillity, a permanent revolution.

Of course, the belief that tranquillity is man's social goal has by no means been a matter of universal agreement. There are those, and Burke knew them well, who delight in agitation; there are literary and intellectual *voyeurs* of revolution; there are temperaments for which, as Burke said, it "is a war or a revolution or it is nothing." There are those who, finally, agree with Goethe that the achievement of tranquillity represents the defeat of the human spirit. Faust, that symbol of the restlessness of the modern temper, is never to say to the moment, "*Verweile doch, du bist so schon*" ("Stay, thou art so fair"). Only a perpetual dissatisfaction, for the Faustian spirit, is truly human. Faust represents the deep anti-ontologicality that is, as we have seen, one feature of the modern mind, its hatred of what *is*, or of the given, its impatience with what it regards as "irrational" differences of nationality, social class, race, or sex (modernity is coeducational, as, indeed, was Faust). Of course, differences are what define particular existence—this and not that. In opposition to this temper, though, there is another and older sense of things, an alternative to the restless spirit of transformation that most certainly is willing to say to the moment, to the world, "Stay, thou art so fair." Do not change: *Be.*

In his splendid brief study of Piero della Francesca, Bernard Berenson speaks of a quality to be found in many of the greatest portraits that date from before the nineteenth century. A kind of silence surrounds those figures, he says; they do not gesture or grimace at us from the canvas. A portrait by Piero or Botticelli, Velasquez or Murillo, Reynolds or Gainsborough seems to say that the existence of its subject in no way appeals to *our* presence before the canvas. Those dukes and cardinals and princesses and statesmen take their existence as a matter of course. They are *there,* self-contained; their being is concrete, actual, accepted. Perhaps it is that sense of being that is in true harmony with the deepest intuitions of the West about the proper mode of the human, for it is that sense that comes to us from the oldest and most continuous of our moral traditions—from Plato and Aristotle, Cicero, Aquinas, Hooker, Elyot, Samuel Johnson, Burke. And so, in politics, it is to Burke that we logically turn as we seek to reconstitute that tradition in the teeth of another revolution.